LIBER

+

VEL BOGUS

The Real Confession of Aleister Crowley

SUB FIGURA LXXX

▶◉◀

Being Parts **I** & **II**(A) of

THE

GOVERNING DYNAMICS

OF

THELEMA

(A Work in Progress)

LIBER L. + VEL BOGUS

The Real Confession of Aleister Crowley

SUB FIGURA LXXX

▶◉◀

Being Parts **I** & **II(A)** of

THE GOVERNING DYNAMICS OF THELEMA

(A Work in Progress)

Edited by Sadie Sparkes

Richard T. Cole asserts the moral right to be identified as the author of this work. A catalogue record of this book is available from the British Library.

All rights reserved. No part of this publication may be reproduced, stored in a retrieval system, or transmitted, in any form or by any means, electronic, mechanical, photocopying, recording or otherwise, without the prior permission of the publishers.

Quotes from *The Invocation of Hoor* courtesy of Marcus Katz
Crowley material Copyright (C)O.T.O. Inc.
Supplemental research courtesy of Dr. W. Hudson

Catalogue Number – LLVB03-1/02LULU
Second, corrected edition

Privately Published, Printed & Distributed
© 1983 - 2014 – All Rights Reserved

The
New Aeon of Horus
is born

Liber L. vel Bogus
is its Birth Certificate

In releasing this material, I have created a monster that will hang like an albatross around my neck for the remainder of my life. **Liber L. vel Bogus** is a book that nobody wants to hear of, read, or, God forbid, actually be right! Somewhat paradoxically, it will attract interested parties with an allure equal and opposite to its force of repulsion. Ultimately, each will loathe it, on principle, in direct proportion to the spiritual, psychological, emotional and financial investment made in brand Crowley.

Edward Alexander Crowley held a golden evolutionary key in his hand. Yet, was so entrenched in Old Aeon mentality, so beset by insecurities and so ill-at-ease with its origin, as to bury his magnificent insight beneath a pantheon of gods and myriad layers of cloying intellectualised dogma. In surrendering to his raging ego, Crowley misdirected himself (and everyone else) into a cul-de-sac of deception. He took a sublime minimalist concept and transformed it into a clunky Victorian automaton that sharpened pencils with its arse.

LIBER L.

+ VEL BOGUS

THE REAL CONFESSION OF ALEISTER CROWLEY

Edited by Sadie Sparkes

CONTENT

Introduction

A.	The mad ol' bastard faked it!	Page 009
B.	Of Future Days Passed	Page 010
C.	Talk of a backlash!	Page 011
D.	Afterglow	Page 015
E.	Sefret Fhieks, everywhere… What a Ferkukkle	Page 016
E.	What a Ferkukkle, it's the great OS23 shuffle	Page 022
G.	Now, *that's* a proof!	Page 025

Part One - Of Aleister Crowley

01.02	Nine degrees of separation	Page 030
01.03	Confession! What confession?	Page 033
01.06	Three degrees of freedom	Page 035
02.03	The meat-chopping block beckons	Page 039
02.05	The page that dare not speak its name	Page 042
02.06	Dr. Pincus' three paths to psychopath	Page 050
03.05	Deicide? You decide!	Page 053
03.06	Aceldama – A Place to Repress Childhood In	Page 055

Part Two - Of *Liber L. vel Legis* (Part A)

04.05	Buying a Stairway to Heaven	Page 060
04.06	When is a New Aeon not a New Aeon?	Page 063
04.07	A revealing revelation	Page 067
05.06	One 'L' of a riddle	Page 076
05.08	Between the lines on missing pages	Page 082
06.07	The lost words, found…	Page 089
06.08	Checkmate	Page 096
06.09	A coke AL bull story	
	I Dazed and abused	Page 105
	II Contradictions, omissions, alterations	Page 108
	III The AL-man Cometh	Page 116
	IV Poetic License	Page 124
	V Liber L. vel Bogus	Page 128
	VI I'm sick, sick, sick of six, six, six	Page 135
	VII Darn that pesky Tarot divination!	Page 142
	VIII A book of mixed results	Page 147
	Sex, sex, sex with six, six, six	Page 149
	IX The heavenly, who?	Page 160
	X OS23, the final nail	Page 164
	XI Bollocks dropped at the Boulak	Page 169
	XII A great cover story	Page 174
	XIII When the Fat Lady sins	Page 183
	XIV ALmost fatAL case of genital disintegration	Page 192
	XV A view from above	Page 195
	XVI The Grate Beast	Page 210

Part Three - Of Thelema and True Will (prelude)

07.08	Where do we go from here?	Page 215

Supplemental material

Additional Information	Page 221
The Definitive R. T. Cole	Page 222
Bibliography of works referenced	Page 228
Table 01	Page 229
Table 02	Page 230
Table 03	Page 232
My Top 10 favourite AL-nomalies	Page 235
AL cetera	Page 240

LIBER L. + VEL BOGUS

The Real Confession of Aleister Crowley

SUB FIGURA LXXX

Being Parts I & II(A) of

THE GOVERNING DYNAMICS OF THELEMA

A - The mad ol' bastard faked it!

Between noon and 1PM on 08, 09 & 10 April 1904 a supernatural herald allegedly manifested in the Cairo apartment of infamous Victorian Satanist, Edward Alexander Crowley. The praeterhuman entity, named Aiwass, proclaimed the onset of a new epoch for Mankind, dictated the three chapters of **Liber L. vel Legis (Book of the Law)**, and appointed Crowley as figurehead of a New World Religion (Thelema) and sole terrestrial confidante of Horus, the supreme deity of a New Aeon. In short, Crowley was the new Jesus and **Liber L. vel Legis** represented a New Covenant with God – A contemporary Bible and 'one-size-fits-all' global rulebook valid for the next two thousand years. The Age of Aquarius had dawned, with **The Great Beast 666** at its helm.

On this outlandish claim rests the life, legacy and reputation of Aleister Crowley. On this slender bough hangs the spiritual authority of his New World Religion, **Thelema**. On this fantastical assertion dangles a global publishing industry, the faith of aficionados and converts across the globe, and the very raison d'être of (c)O.T.O. Inc. - Legal guardians of Crowley's literary & artistic legacy and high priests of his Magickal construct. On the scaffold of those three pivotal days is suspended the ultimate historical fate of Aleister Crowley – Madman or messiah, seer or psycho! If my observations are correct, then everything written about (and by) the **Great Beast 666** is subject to fundamental reappraisal.

My study, as it appeared on 01 December 2013.

B - Of Future Days Passed

I am not an occultist and intensely skeptical of almost all 'supernatural' literature and its hyperbolic claims. Nevertheless, with reference to this work and the multiplicity of bizarre synchronicities that occurred during its preparation, I am unable to shake an unsettling conviction that *'the Magickal essence of Aleister Crowley guided my footsteps every step of the way'* – Whatever those words mean.

In releasing this material, I have created a monster that will hang like an albatross around my neck for the remainder of my life. **Liber L. vel Bogus** is a book that nobody wants to hear of, read, or, God forbid, actually be right! Somewhat paradoxically, it will attract interested parties with an allure equal and opposite to its force of repulsion. Ultimately, each will loathe it, on principle, in direct proportion to the spiritual, psychological, emotional and financial investment made in brand Crowley.

Aleister Crowley faked his own suicide. He lied about burning his passport, and fabricated his ancestry. He spent his entire life hiding behind an elaborate façade of alter-egos, costumes, aliases and pen-names. Given this, and myriad other questionable character traits, I am perplexed in the extreme that some remain unable and unwilling to consider a possibility that Crowley's account of his reception of **Liber L.** may not represent the unexpurgated and literal truth. For the benefit of unfortunates afflicted with acute and terminal cases of 'Crow-Blindness,' I offer this crumb of comfort - **Liber L. vel Bogus** does not exist. It is a spoof, a joke, a hoax and a phantasm of my imagination. Its publication and distribution are a mirage. Crowley received a new Law for Mankind, precisely as stated. Go ask Aiwass!

C – Talk of a backlash!

Since news of this publication first surfaced, speculation regarding its content has gurgled within occult, Crowley and Thelemic communities. Heated debate relating to various 'issues' allegedly raised has echoed uneasily around online forums. Most of the e-mails I receive these days routinely includes probing questions and jocular references to the prevalent ambience of trepidation surrounding my *"heresy,"* *"blasphemy"* and *"treason."* From the outset, I accepted that my findings would meet with a certain degree of caution and reticence. However, during the course of various correspondences it became increasingly clear that a virulent strain of what I can only describe as 'instinctive aversion' infects many aficionados and apologists of Aleister Crowley.

Questions regarding Crowley's reception of **Liber L. vel Legis** are nothing new. The Cornelius', David Hulse and others have aired a multiplicity of perplexing anomalies. Yet, in the absence of conclusive proof, Crowleyites habitually bend over backwards in giving their messiah the benefit of doubt. On consideration of this frustrating trait, I came to realise that the evident disinclination to look at certain unsavoury facts relates not to the inconvenience of compelling a recalibration of one's intellectual estimation of a historical figure. At its heart, the unease foreshadows a dread of the emotional, psychological and spiritual turmoil inherent within exposure – A self-defence mechanism enabling countless individuals (for years and even decades) to 'look away' from circumstantial evidence left by an unfaithful partner, rather than manifest the raw ego-shattering carnage of confrontation, betrayal and separation.

The anomalies discussed in this publication comprise nothing more than a preliminary account of observations made during the study of an incomplete record. In short, its content merely scratches the surface of a very deep mystery. Much of which remains concealed. Nevertheless, these discrepancies are also, I believe, ample to convince any sane and reasonable person as to the bogus nature of Crowley's claim. However, as I have learned in recent months, questions regarding the origins of **Liber L. vel Legis** slice through superficial layers of intellect and rationale, and penetrate into the deepest roots of belief systems – Dangerous territory indeed!

I am primarily a researcher. My sole motive is that of discovering the truth, however unpalatable to a minority whose lives seem wholly reliant on the words of their saviour. However distasteful to those who, in private correspondence and public forums, speak as if acting in the capacity of Crowley's solicitor. However unthinkable to those who for too long have looked the other way and 'veiled his vices behind their virtuous words,' and however damaging to the reputation of anyone who willfully buried evidence beneath a lucrative deception. Ignorance is the enemy of truth. The single greatest obstacle obscuring the facts of this matter is a scarcity of primary source material – Crowley's original notebooks, diaries and correspondence. Whilst these remain veiled, misinformation, misdirection, hidden agendas, greed and duplicity will prevail.

I sincerely believe it is the responsibility and duty of each individual to obtain copies of, then study the relevant documents, and form conclusions based on first-hand research. Accept nothing I or anyone else says at face value. Check everything with your own eyes. With reference to questions raised by this publication, and others, I feel that the legal guardians of Crowley's legacy are encumbered with a duty to make public all documentation and information knowingly in its possession. Moreover, that they should routinely oblige all reasonable requests for access to material that may assist in the clarification of a mystery central to all with an interest in the life and legacy of Aleister Crowley.

I am confident to suggest that any material uncovered following the publication of this book will support, and not refute my hypothesis. Conversely, I am happy to incorporate new information into subsequent editions of **Liber L. vel Bogus**, even if this highlights erroneous deductions on my part. I would not see this as 'a defeat,' and quite the reverse. My desire is solely that of definitively resolving an elephant in the room that has dogged Crowley's footsteps for over a century. My stance with respect to this matter remains unequivocally one of full and forthright disclosure – Release everything, now!

At its inception, I envisaged this work as nothing more than a slender compendium detailing enough of the AL-related oddities and curios I'd amassed over the years as to demonstrate, beyond reasonable doubt, that Aleister Crowley did not scribe the **Liber L.** manuscript between noon and 1PM, on 08, 09 and 10 April 1904 - End of story! That the material presented herein is three years beyond its original release date, and requiring of two volumes, offers a telling insight into the complexity and depth of this enigma. When inspected, each discrepancy revealed a hitherto concealed layer, which in turn hinted alluringly at still deeper connections. Most intriguing of all was the gradual emergence of an entirely different genesis for **Liber L.**. By joining the dots littering Crowley's unpublished notebooks, diaries and Magickal records, it was possible to recover a sequence of events that (unlike his official version) dovetails seamlessly with the historical record, correlates with his deeds, aspirations and publications, makes perfect sense in occult terms and, if one looks carefully enough, are recorded in Crowley's own hand!

Crowley, as he appeared in 1903, aged twenty-eight (top) and 1905, aged thirty (bottom).

The preparation of **Liber L. vel Bogus** was unquestionably the most demanding project I have ever undertaken. Throughout, it tested the limits of my mental faculties, tolerance, credulity and even health, to breaking point and beyond. At times, each passing week and day manifested a further development, more questions, and a pressing need to incorporate new material. By Christmas 2012, I had already sidestepped three deadlines and was increasingly concerned that I had started a project that would never end, and one already bulging at the seams of its original format. By the autumn of 2013, in the aftermath of the two seismic events described below, all notions of a foreseeable completion date vanished over the horizon. Both instances had a direct and significant bearing on this work and, therefore, were demanding of inclusion. However, in the back of my mind lurked a niggling question: *"In the time taken to incorporate Fs, Ks and an Appendix, who knows what other issues will have stacked up?"* Rather perversely, on reaching the point at which I earnestly believed that work on this book probably would continue indefinitely... it ended - Abruptly, if not altogether unexpectedly.

Between then and now, fate compelled a comprehensive redrawing of the contours and colours of my life. Following a great deal of soul-searching, I accept that my exploration of not one but two hugely contentious and fascinating mysteries is over. All considerations regarding the further refinement of this 'challenging' material into a more easily-accessible format (not precluding the possibility of a complete rewrite) are also at an end. As stated at the outset, **Liber L. vel Bogus** is *"a work in progress."* The ideas discussed in each chapter are merely springboards from which to launch subsequent expeditions.

The circuitous route by which a crude plot devised to wrest control of the Golden Dawn from Mathers (by replicating the 'discovery' of its own Founding Documents – Which, incidentally, were also fakes) transformed into the elaborate reception myth we know today, is hitherto unexplored terrain. As is the 'true' nature of a cathartic revelation Crowley gleaned during an experimental honeymoon 'ménage à trois.' For over a century, the actualities of this immensely important period in Crowley's life remained obscured by a collective aversion to look beyond the Holy smokescreen of glittering contradictions Crowley projected onto his mythology, and our expectations. It is time to wake up and smell the Thelema!

Let's be honest, here... Are Thelemites wise to place faith in the word of a praeterhuman entity who forgets a verse of their new Bible! – An error Crowley subsequently corrected, with a note pencilled on the handwritten **Liber L.** manuscript (III, 37). That Aiwass' monumental blunder went unnoticed until (to the best of my knowledge) I mentioned it on www.lashtal.com several years ago is perhaps indicative of the complacency, or denial, endemic within Thelemic communities.

D – Afterglow

This publication exposes Crowley as a cold, manipulative liar and a debased lunatic. It also reveals a web of deception fabricated by the man in furtherance of his grand delusion of, 'I, the Chosen One.' Given this, it may be surprising to learn that my investigation into the mysteries of Crowley's reception of **Liber L. vel Legis** has, somewhat paradoxically, strengthened a conviction that Aleister Crowley was the single most important individual this planet has produced in the last twelve millennia. He alone noticed a small yet monumentally significant development in the core operating system of our species, correlated this with the imminent birth of a "*New Aeon*," and predicted global changes that, since September 2007, have rocked our world to its foundations. Crowley was not merely the prophet of a new epoch, but actually precipitated the onset of a 'Magickal Current' that will shape our world for the next two thousand years. Alas, whatever the message and its mode of transmission, the broadcast did not occur between noon and 1PM on 08, 09 and 10 April 1904.

To end this chapter on a light note I recall a humorous and apt comment made recently by a good friend who, on reading a pre-release copy of **Liber L. vel Bogus,** shrugged and chuckled:

> "*Well, that's hardly a surprise! You never, seriously, believed Crowley's story that an angel flapped in on his honeymoon with a New World Religion T-shirt and 'Chosen One' badge... Did you?*"

In all honesty, I had never considered the situation in quite those terms. Nonetheless, on balance, she had a fair point! My personal belief in Crowley's account of his reception of **Liber L. vel Legis** was indeed akin to a childhood belief in Father Christmas. With each passing term, whispered playground rumour and personal experience conspired to erode my faith. Then, one day, I learned the terrible truth. When this happened, and though I had suspected (with increasing certainty) for years, the 'lie,' when exposed, still came as a deeply unsettling blow. Of course, I need also note that the inevitable death of this mythological creature ultimately opens every child's mind to a deeper meaning of Christmas.

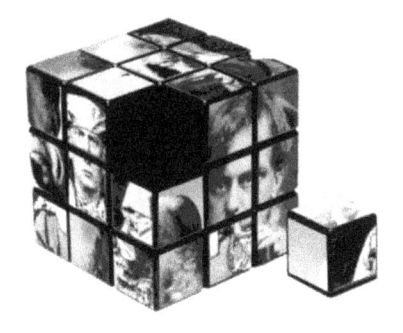

E – Sefret Fhieks, everywhere... What a Ferkukkle!

In the year since circumstances beyond my control compelled an abrupt and intensely frustrating cessation of all work on this project, two singular occurrences have, like comets, blazed across the Thelemic horizon. Both events were of major significance to the Crowley community. The central themes of both wind inextricably around material presented in this volume, and both support my hypothesis. As a means of restarting a very cold engine, I conclude this introduction with a brief overview of these two instances, and the ensuing repercussions.

On 10 April, 2013, the first News update in almost five years appeared on the web-site of (C)O.T.O. Inc.. Buried at the bottom of this lengthy epistle, in a section innocuously titled *"Archival News,"* lurked a ticking bomb – A decision to change one letter of Crowley's *"Change not as much as the style of a letter"* new Bible, **Liber L. vel Legis**. With hindsight, time has revealed William Breeze's announcement as a matchless example of shooting yourself in the foot with a bazooka! The spectacular manner in which his decision backfired must surely categorise it as an act of self-harm, rather than a literary announcement. In the eyes of most, his changing of one letter most definitely did not constitute merely the 'resolution of a longstanding textual difference,' as stated. Rather, it was widely perceived as analogous to the Pope declaring a change in the wording of the sixth Commandment, from *"Thou shalt not kill,"* to *"Thou shalt not fill."*

As word of this inflammatory edit raced around the Internet, forum boards quickly mired in conjecture, debate, argument, and even abject condemnation. In addition to questions concerning Hymenaeus Beta's legitimacy to make the change, at all, it quickly emerged that his basis for initiating *"a very important text correction"* was highly contentious. The relevant section of which, as relates to James Windram's one-volume edition of Crowley's **Thelema – The Holy Books**, is reproduced below:

> *"I was not, however, quite prepared for what arrived: the book includes several early comments on verses of **Liber Legis** (a few of*

which are important), as well as a very important text correction to **Liber CCXX III:37** *which resolves a longstanding textual difference between three sources: (1) the versification of the Stèle of Revealing from a now-lost vellum notebook, which was published with the reading "kill me!" in* **The Equinox I(7)** *(1912) and* **The Equinox of the Gods** *(1936); (2) a quotation ("fill me!") given in a pencil note to* **Liber XXXI**, *the MS. of Liber AL, giving directions for the extent of the quotation to be inserted from a contemporary vellum notebook; and (3) the editions of* **Liber Legis** *published by Crowley, all of which gave "fill me!"*

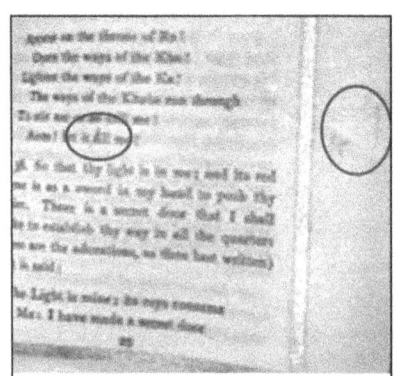

Above - The notorious pencilled letter 'K.' with exclamation mark (circled right) and crossed-out letter 'F' (circled left) present in the 1909 one-volume edition of **Thelema** (the **Holy Books**) formerly owned by James Windram. Incidentally, if this particular volume is, as suggested, the same as was pictured in the curious *"Magician"* photograph (see below), then the evident divergence between Crowley's youthful countenance and age (he was thirty-four in 1909) is stretched by a further three years. Since this specific volume is dated *"1912,"* making Crowley thirty-seven (at least) when photographed as a fresh-faced youth seemingly a decade younger.

In this copy Crowley's marginal holograph note clearly corrects "fill me!" to "kill me!" in the text of **Liber CCXX**."

A growing body of superb research and documentary evidence contesting the textual change soon appeared (primarily on the matchless Crowley resource, www.lashtal.com). This prompted the usually aloof Breeze into an unprecedented and protracted defence of his change (documentation posted online at www.oto.org/legis.html). As the hand played out, it became increasingly clear that Breeze made his decision to change a 'Commandment' with almost reckless disregard for research, or consultation. He evidently made the 'f-k' swap in ignorance of numerous sources that greatly diminished his argument – Documents that were readily available, had he looked. He also failed to solicit (or heed) advice from individuals whose knowledge may well have alerted him to material contradicting the proposed *"text correction."*

17

To many, even those closest to him, Breeze's decision to make a significant change based seemingly on nothing more substantial than the appearance of a single letter 'k' pencilled in the margin of a book seemed bewildering. Especially as the issue is complicated further by a devilish quirk of fate in which the offending letter is part of a pencil note scribbled onto the **Liber L.** manuscript at some point after its original creation – A note which itself refers to the content of a *"now-lost vellum notebook."*

Interestingly, two of Breeze's three points refer to a vellum notebook: **(1)** *"...the versification of the Stèle of Revealing from a now-lost vellum notebook"* and **(2)** *"… giving directions for the extent of the quotation to be inserted from a contemporary* [with Cairo, 1904] *vellum notebook..."* The phrasing of these points is ambiguous. Are the terms *"a now-lost vellum notebook"* and *"a contemporary vellum notebook"* two mentions of the same notebook, or individual references to different items? Despite clumsy wording, the two points serve to remind readers of an incident familiar to all with an interest - i.e. whilst in Cairo (April 1904), Crowley wrote a versification of the Stele of Revealing in at least one vellum notebook. To this confirmation is affixed an additional snippet stating that the notebook is no longer extant - A regrettable, though ultimately inconsequential loss.

As matters currently stand, I think it reasonable to suggest that '**The Windram K**' is certainly worthy of a detailed footnote in subsequent editions of the text, but not a change in the text itself. Moreover, the pertinent question lingering in many minds is not *"Why was the change made on such flimsy evidence?"* but *"Why was it made, at all?"* Prior to 10 April 2013, nobody gave a second thought to this *"longstanding textual difference."* Then, at a stroke, Hymenaeus Beta transformed a formerly inconsequential niggle into a raging tempest that split Thelemic communities down the middle, manifested untold acrimony, and resurrected longstanding, often bitter differences – Why?

On a personal note, I feel that amidst the flurry of documentation raised by this inflammatory issue, one page in particular encapsulates the whole situation – Between 1919 and 1921, Crowley wrote an extensive commentary on **Liber AL vel Legis** (he added an '**A**' to the original '**L**' in 1921). The monumental task of editing this material was trusted to Crowley's friend Louis Wilkinson – For whom he wrote the 1941 jingoistic battle-cry **Liber Oz**. Wilkinson completed the first draft in 1946. According to Gerald Yorke, this was *"approved by A. C."* Page fifty (of over five hundred), begins with the final two lines of the fourth verse of Crowley's versification of the stele hieroglyphics. Interestingly, the 'critical' phrase initially read "*Aum! Let it fill me.*" Of which the 'f' was scrubbed out and replaced (above) with a letter 'k.' Then, a letter 'f' was written below the original (erased) typed 'f.' Given this evident indecisiveness, it seems to me that if Crowley still hadn't made up his mind only a year before death, why should someone else decide for him a century later? The change is surplus to requirements. It corrects a mistake that was never there in the first instance. Incidentally, this material is currently housed at the Warburg Institute in a section indexed OSK1 to OSK4. Item OSK1 is a hardback, bound book comprising Crowley's carbon copy typescript of his commentary on **Liber AL**. Rather surprisingly, 'Chapter Three' appears first.

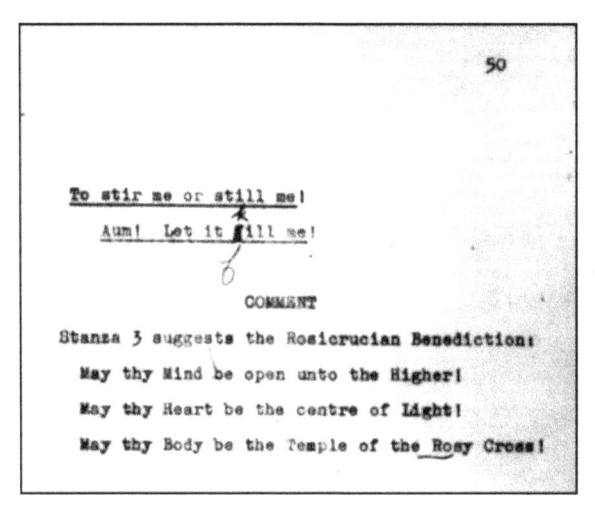

Why did Hymenaeus Beta go so far out on a slender, untested (and ultimately flawed) branch to force an unnecessary and endlessly debatable change that nobody wanted, and one guaranteed to unleash a veritable barrage of opposition, criticism and outrage?

Was the contentious change, from an 'f' to a 'k,' really a well-intentioned decision to resolve a longstanding textual difference that backfired in spectacular fashion, or did this baffling edit mask a subtle, hidden agenda? Could the largely self-inflicted injuries Breeze amassed in the (entirely predictable) frenzied response to his change be perceived as an unavoidable trade-off – Recoverable collateral damage suffered in consequence of a sacrifice necessary to diffuse the otherwise catastrophic impact of an imminent bombshell?

In November 2012, six months before the scheduled release date of **Liber L. vel Bogus**, I forwarded to a select handful of acquaintances a twenty-page booklet sketching several puzzling oddities. Of these, one in particular struck me as presenting a singular challenge to Crowley's reception myth. The anomaly in question related to a minor yet damning chronological malfunction. On comparison of a few unpublished documents, it is relatively easy to demonstrate that numerous key texts, on which Crowley's reception story is reliant, he wrote after leaving

Cairo! One notable instance of material ascribed to April 1904 does not appear until October 1907, three years later! These simple observations alone impart massive and perhaps fatal damage on the integrity of Crowley's account.

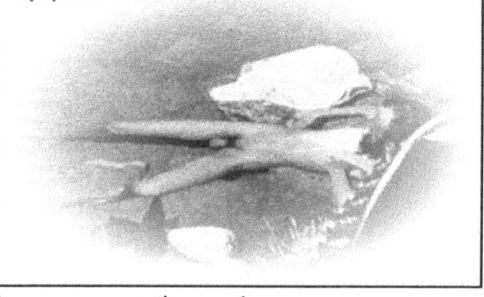

Throughout various discussions arising from a perusal of my booklet, I hoped someone would posit a plausible solution to what seemed an insoluble conundrum. None did. I personally racked my brain to visualise a realistic scenario accounting for the discrepancies. I even attempted to formulate a tenuous 'possible though highly unlikely' solution worthy of Jonathan Creek... and made no ground, whatsoever. Several months later, I'd forgotten about the question when something I read on the Internet unexpectedly precipitated the notion of a radical solution to the dating problem.

Above - A photo of Crowley taken on 07 November 1903, only five months away from that fateful honeymoon in Cairo and (below) warming his equipment in readiness for the ascent.

I envisaged a hypothetical scenario, set in a parallel universe, in which I am responsible for the preservation of Crowley's legacy, reputation and status... at any cost. In this imaginary world, I am facing the imminent release of documents demonstrating that Crowley wrote much of the pivotal Cairo material from the comfort of Boleskine House. How can I explain this? My only real hope is that of producing a vellum notebook contemporary with Cairo, April 1904, containing Crowley's handwritten versification of the Stele of Revealing. Unfortunately, such a volume does not exist, nor is it feasible to fake one. However, given my position of absolute authority, I don't actually need to produce a physical notebook. With a deft sleight-of-hand, I can scrape through using a mirage. To accomplish the illusion I invent a reason to mention, casually, a 'now-lost 1904 Cairo notebook,' and bury the reference in a contentious statement. Several months later, on release of the heresy, I can argue that the numerous instances of material written implausibly out-of-sequence, as highlighted in it, are merely later copies of material originally written by Crowley in the sadly now-lost 'Cairo' notebook (as mentioned in a recent News update). This solution is, I accept, thin, cynical, extremely implausible and wholly reliant on unverifiable conjecture regarding what Crowley 'may' have written in a vellum notebook lost to the world. However, given the severe threat level posed by the incoming heresy, the 'lost vellum notebook' trick does just enough to raise a 'last-ditch' question mark and stall a potentially irretrievable collapse of Crowley's position.

Had you going, there, for a moment! There is, of course, no connection between my airing of troubling discrepancies in Crowley's reception story and a subsequent News update on (C)O.T.O. Inc.'s web-site. Any similarities between this and the desperate 'get-out-of-Cairo-free' solution outlined above are entirely coincidental. Nor is there a 'top-level' conspiracy, orchestrated by high-ranking (C)O.T.O. Inc. officers, to conceal a truth devastating to their vocation. All such delusions are examples of the strange alchemy in which phantasms evoked by researchers foolhardy enough to explore these forbidden realms mutate blind chance into alluring shadows.

Whilst on the subject of outrageous fortune, I'll digress slightly to mention the only contemporary mystery discussed in the first part of this book. The strange occurrence narrated in the next section, as all concerned agree, is an unfortunate error – A surreal moment when fate arranges random coincidence into shapes of such sublime intricacy as to fool the eyes with an uncanny illusion of form.

The 'ghost' in this particular machine is also a vellum notebook contemporary with Cairo 1904, namely "*OS23.*" (Item number **23** in the **O**ld **S**eries of Crowley material catalogued by Gerald Yorke, and currently held at the Warburg Institute). In 2002, and propelled solely by random chance, this supposedly inanimate object performed an intricate sequence of manoeuvres comparable with the routine of a seasoned acrobat. What follows is another excellent example of the baffling obstacles that beset researchers foolhardy enough to probe these sensitive areas. Perhaps the 'Secret Chiefs' still do all that is possible to shield their 'Chosen One?'

F – What a Ferkukkle, it's the great OS23 shuffle!

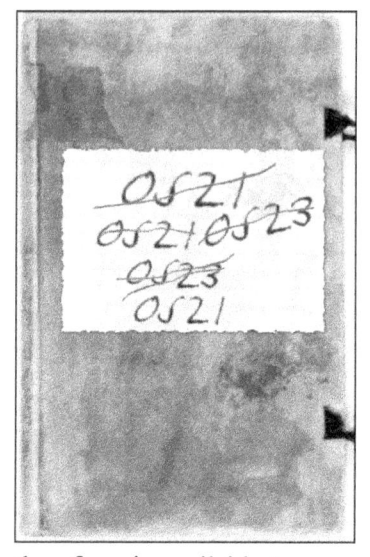

During my research of this project, two documents in particular stood out as being of especial significance. Of these, "*OS23*" is yet another small vellum notebook contemporary with Cairo 1904. For reasons described in subsequent chapters, material in this notebook presents numerous serious challenges to Crowley's version of events. Indeed, the discrepancies I stumbled over were so contentious as to demand further investigation.

The handwritten content of OS23 remains unpublished, though was scanned to microfilm in 2002 and, therefore, is available to researchers with access to the reels, and authors approved by (C)O.T.O. Inc.. Furthermore, digital copies of the Warburg archive are extant and afford a wider audience access to the unique collection. Given this, I struggled to understand why nobody had previously raised concerns about several rather glaring oddities.

During an exchange of e-mails, I realised that the microfilm record contains a singularly unfortunate error. The page files indexed as "*OS23*" actually comprise a duplicate of material from an inconsequential notebook labelled "*OS21.*" To the best of my knowledge, the immense task of transferring 24,000 documents to microfilm generated only one serious error. That this single hiccup resulted in the omission of material almost fatally toxic to Crowley's reception story prompted me to wail: "*Of all the folders, in all the archives, in all the world... They miss **that** one!*"

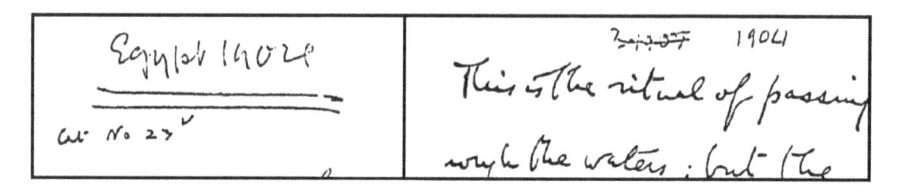

Of numerous 'oddities' contained in the elusive notebook, OS23, the above scan highlights two minor curiosities. In the left panel, Crowley appears to have changed the date, from "*1902*" to "*1904.*" In the right "*1907*" is crossed-through and replaced with "*1904,*" why?

From the perspective of any 'Secret Chiefs' wishing to maintain Crowley's integrity, the omission of OS23 was exceedingly fortuitous. To satisfy my own curiosity, I investigated the matter and was astonished to discover unanticipated layers of complexity lurking beneath an apparently 'simple copy error.' In this particular case, it seems that chance went all around the houses before landing. To illustrate my point, and working from known 'start' and 'end' points, I now outline the mechanics of a remarkable sequence of entirely random events.

Crowley's numerous small red vellum notebooks are difficult to distinguish between and his handwriting often borders on illegible. To assist with identification, tipped into each is a unique 'marker' page. This simple practice enables anyone, at a glance, to locate particular items. On transfer to microfilm, the associated marker pages were scanned along with notebook content, and incorporated as a preface to the sequence of page frames comprising each notebook (see '**A**' and '**D**' on scan below). Again, this is an intelligent procedure, and an invaluable aid to locating specific content amongst hundreds of frames stacked along a long reel of film.

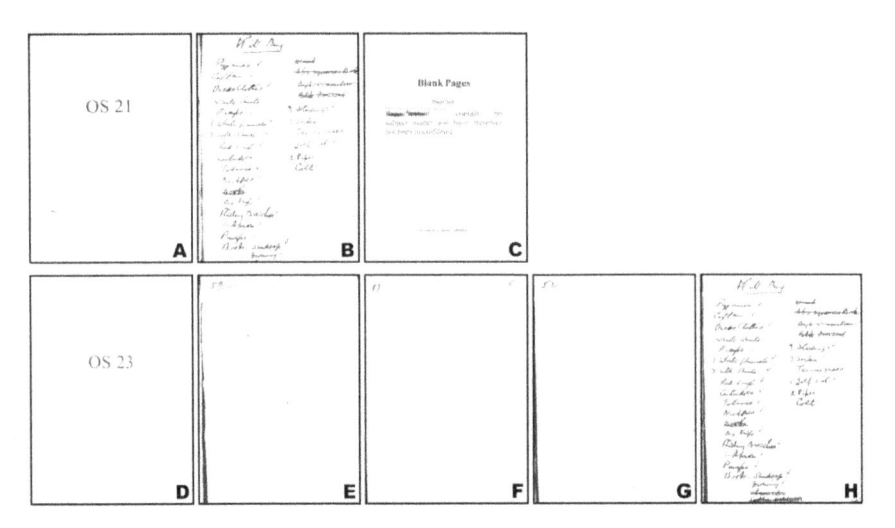

The duplication of OS21 was not a simple copy error. The slightly different treatment of numbered (but otherwise blank) pages (see above) demonstrates that, for whatever reason, the notebook labelled "*OS21*" passed under the Warburg scanner twice. The content of OS21 appears first as item two on film 1. In this instance, relevant page frames match their corresponding catalogue entry, are prefaced with the right marker page and comprise the correct material. A general "*Blank Pages to end*" ('**C**') notification substitutes for three numbered, but otherwise blank pages ('**E**,' '**F**' and '**G**'). At this stage, all is in order. However, at some point after the scanning of OS21, fate intervened. It somehow conspired to:

I) 'Abstruct' two notebooks (namely OS21 and OS23).
II) Open both.
III) Remove the marker page from both.
IV) Swap the marker pages.
V) Return an incorrect marker page to each notebook.
VI) Close both.
VII) Return each to the physical location formerly occupied by the other,

By this convoluted process, the content of OS21 made a second appearance on the microfilm, in the guise of OS23, catalogued incorrectly as OS23 and prefaced incorrectly with the marker page from OS23! On this occasion, the three numbered (but otherwise blank) pages ('**E**,' '**F**' and '**G**') are included in preference to the previously used "*Blank Pages to end*" notice ('**C**').

Listen, don't mention Liber L.! I mentioned it once, but I think I got away with it.

Even after the passing of eleven years, it seemed reasonable to suppose that both OS21 and OS23 would still carry an incorrect marker page beneath their covers. Rather surprisingly, courteous and ever-helpful staff at the Warburg Institute confirmed that the two incorrect marker pages had swapped over, again, and returned to their former places in the correct notebooks, both of which were located in the correct place! It seems that chance is both random and occasionally... tidy. In this instance, fate noticed its error and engineered a corresponding set of seven equally random events required to rectify the glitch. In conspiring to omit the content of OS23 from the record, 'coincidence' required no less than fourteen discrete accidents. As Crowley once uttered, in a similar context, "*Calculate the odds! Over the billion mark!*"

G – Now, *that's* a proof!

On 23 April 2013, just thirteen days after (C)O.T.O. Inc. released its lengthy *"News update,"* and precipitated by an ongoing exchange of ideas, a previously unpublished document appeared on www.lashtal.com. Accompanying the file was a note penned by owner and webmaster of the site, Paul Feazey. This read:

> *"LAShTAL.COM is enormously proud to present a free download of a highly significant piece by Aleister Crowley, often spoken of but rarely seen. The document is reproduced here with full permission of the copyright holder.*
>
> *The PDF file comprises the September 1907 galley proofs of an intended* **Appendix to the Collected Works**, *prepared but subsequently discarded by Aleister Crowley. The* **Appendix** *was going to reproduce* **Liber L (The Book Of The Law)** *together with supporting material. It is a curious document that raises as many questions as it answers!"*

The document in question is an unpublished Appendix Crowley prepared for inclusion in the third volume of his **Collected Works**. Intended as the debut public outing of a new brand labelled Thelema, for reasons unknown Crowley ultimately withdrew this material and for over a century it has languished in a drawer. Given its fundamental relevance to the origin, genesis and context of **Liber AL**, I find it difficult to believe that it has not already been widely circulated, subject to intense scrutiny, and the focus of at least one book. Whilst technically 'unpublished,' photocopies and, more recently, digital versions of the Appendix are in circulation. In consideration of this, I simply do not understand how this sensational material has, for so long, avoided the attention it sorely deserves.

I heartily recommend that all with an interest obtain a copy and peruse the Appendix at their earliest opportunity. To this, I'll append a note of caution: Anyone expecting a rehash of the officially-sanctioned version of **Liber AL** and its accompanying mythology is in for quite a surprise. The **Liber L.** we never saw begins with Crowley's unequivocal declaration that he is not the author of documents that only came into his possession in July 1906! Following a bizarre introduction, the material continues with a French translation of the stele hieroglyphs and two Enochian calls, 'conjoined' (as seen in the scan on next page). The familiar opening to 'Chapter One' (*"Had! The manifestation of Nuit"*) begins, without introduction, beneath a curious footnote to the translation, which reads: *"We are indebted to the kindness of Brugsch Bey and M. Delormant for the above translation of the stele whose discovery led to the creation of the ritual by which Aiwass, the author of **Liber L.**, was invoked."* – Huh!

24/9/17

APPENDIX

LIBER L. VEL LEGIS

GIVEN FROM THE MOUTH OF AIWASS TO THE EAR OF
THE BEAST ON APRIL, 8, 9, AND 10, 1904.

[This MS. (which came into my possession in July 1906) is a highly interesting example of genuine automatic writing.* Though I am in no way responsible for any of these documents, except the verse translations of the stele inscriptions, I publish them among my works, because believe that their intelligent study may be interesting and helpful.—A. C.]

STÈLE en bois stuqué et peinte, à double face, cintrée au sommet, portant le No. 666 au catalogue.
Face principale. Le tableau du haut est encadré par une représentation de la déesse du ciel, Nout, dont le corps est allongé, et les bras pendant de telle sorte que le bout des doigts touche le sol. Au dessous est le disque ailé du soleil avec son nom " *Houdit*, dieu grand, seigneur du ciel."
Le tableau montre un prêtre revêtu de la peau de panthère debout devant le dieu

Harmakhis assis sur son trône, derrière lequel est l'emblème de l'occident. La légende Id dieu est " Râ-Hor-khut, chef des dieux"; celle de l'adorant " Le défunt, prophète de Mentou, seigneur de Thèbes, à qui sont ouvertes les portes du ciel dans Thèbes, *Ankh-f-n-khonsu*."
Devant le prêtre est une table d'offrandes sous laquelle est inscrit "pains, eau, bœufs, oies."
Le texte du bas se traduit : "Le défunt, prophète de Mentou, seigneur de Thèbes, à

* THE VISION AND THE VOICE.

THE CRY OF THE THIRTIETH OR INMOST
AIRE OR AETHYR.

TEX. I am in a vast crystal cube in the form of the Great God Harpocrates. This cube is surrounded by a sphere. About me are four archangels in black robes, their wings, &c., lined out in white. In the north is a book on whose back and front are **A M B Z**[1] (in the Enochian character).
Within it is written :
" I AM, the surrounding of the four.
" Lift up your heads, O Houses of Eternity : for my Father goeth forth to judge the World. One Light, let it become a thousand ; and one sword ten thousand ; that no man hide from my Father's eye in the Day of Judgment of my

God. Let the Gods hide themselves: let the Angels be troubled and flee away : for the eye of my father is open and the Book of the Aeons is fallen. Arise ! Arise ! Let the light of the Light of Time be extinguished : let the darkness cover all things; for my Father goeth forth to seek a spouse to replace her who is fallen and defiled.
" Seal the book with the seals of the Stars Concealed : for the Rivers have rushed together and the Name יהוה is broken in a thousand pieces (against the Cubic Stone?). Tremble ye, O Pillars of the Universe, for Eternity is in travail of a Terrible Child ; she shall bring forth an universe of Darkness, whence shall leap forth a spark that shall put his father to flight. The Obelisks are broken ; the stars have rushed together : the Light hath plunged into the Abyss : the Heavens are mixed with Hell.
" My Father shall not hear their Noise : his ears are closed : his eyes are covered with the clouds of Night.
" The End ! The End ! The End ! For the Eye of Shiva He hath opened : the Universe is

---
[1] The Cherubic signs but Apophis replaced by Honis.

231

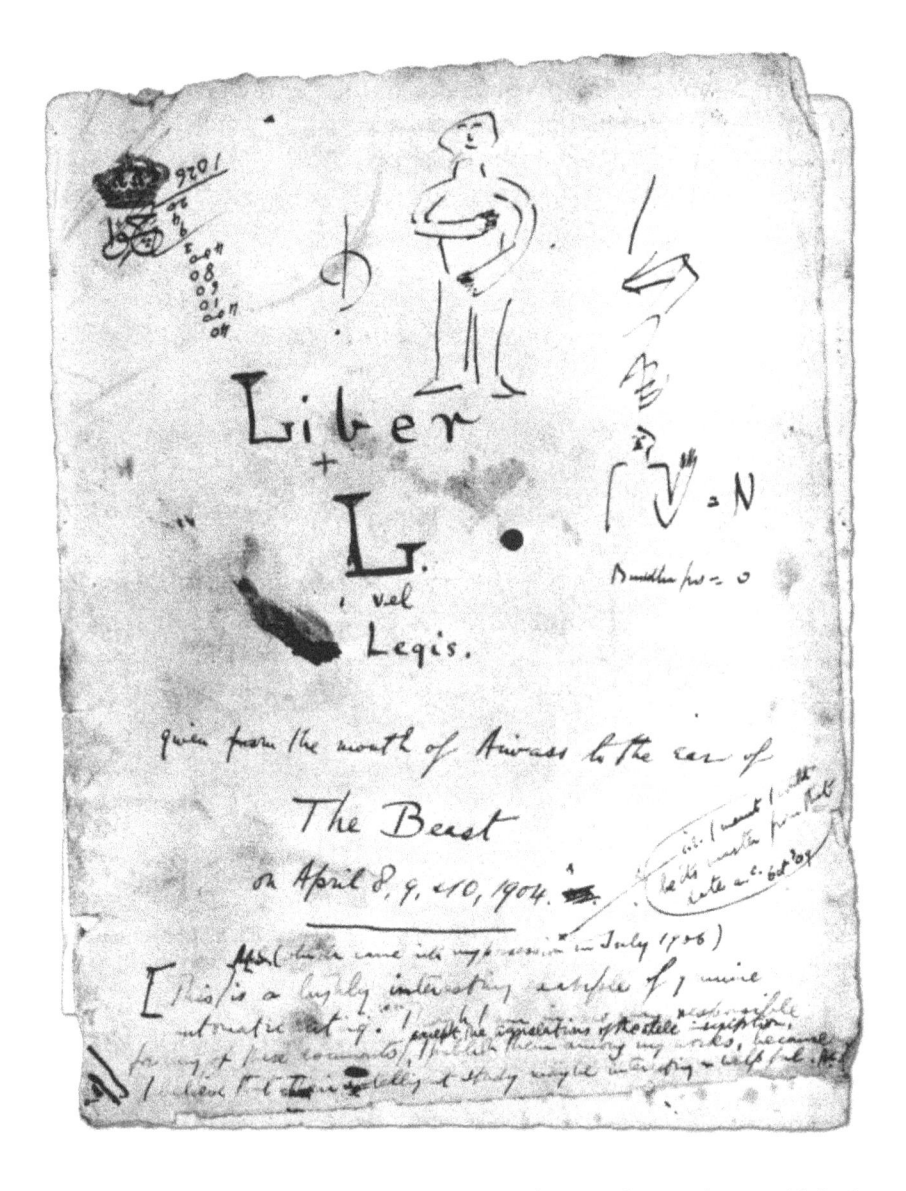

The handwritten and seldom seen 'cover sheet' (above) from which the Appendix derives is itself an intensely curious document. According to its copious, confusing and contradictory notes on notes, Crowley did not write **Liber L. vel Legis**, which only came into his possession two years after its creation. By this, he actually meant (three years later) that he "*could be its master from that date*" - Huh!

Perhaps most astonishing of all, in September 1907 Crowley's fledgling new Bible doesn't bow out with "*The Book of the Law is written and concealed. Aum. Ha.*" It storms back onstage for a rousing encore titled

"*The Great Invocation.*" Unsurprisingly, in consideration of its opening declaration ("*Though I am in no way responsible for any of these documents*"), all references to the participation of Rose, their visit to the Boulak Museum, the reception event itself and numerous other pivotal incidents are conspicuously absent from the text. It will be another five years before Crowley weaves these elements into his evolving myth (in **Equinox I, 7**).

The Appendix, cover sheet and incidental points raised over the previous few pages do not provide definitive evidence as to the precise circumstances under which Crowley produced **Liber L. vel Legis**. These discrepancies do however spotlight a multiplicity of significant anomalies between the aborted 1907 version and the entirely different animal we know today. At very least, even a cursory examination of the "*highly significant piece that raises as many questions as it answers*" must set alarm bells ringing in the heads of anyone who tacitly accepts Crowley's published account of the reception. Whilst this rarely seen documentation does not prove Crowley lied, it does hint suggestively that the flamboyant account left for posterity is far from the stuffed-and-mounted trophy Crowley would have us believe, and quite the converse.

Crowley was an avid diarist who, throughout his life, habitually recorded details of his day-to-day activities. It is, then, most perplexing to discover that neither his mundane or 'Magickal' diaries of the time chronicle any of the events Crowley subsequently narrated as the reception of **Liber L. vel Legis**. That Crowley included mundane references to "*golf*" and "*the day of rest*," yet neglected to mention the mind-blowing three days he spent scribbling down a new Bible is, to my mind, inexplicable. Without labouring this point, I think it pertinent to mention that, according to his account, almost before its ink was dry Crowley allegedly lost the Founding Document of Mankind's New Aeon! Mercifully, a manuscript of supreme importance to humanity eventually surfaced in the attic at Boleskine House, on 28 June 1909. It is reasonable to suppose that a fortuitous event of this magnitude would be noteworthy. Coincidentally, at the time of the manuscript's rediscovery Crowley was overseeing the occult initiation of a pupil named Victor Neuburg. Between 18 and 27 June, Neuburg kept a detailed record of his ordeals, and rewrote this on 30 June. That Neuburg's chronicle fails to mention what he would have unquestionably perceived as a glittering seal on the successful completion of his initiation, a divine endorsement of Crowley's methodology and a generally fabulous portent, is to my mind a step too far.

Part One

Of Aleister Crowley

01.02   Nine degrees of separation

On Friday 06 March 2009, I bumped into a good friend and former colleague, Dr. W. Hudson. Though now retired, Dr. Hudson specialised in mental health issues, published numerous medical papers, acted as a consultant to the UK government, almost single-handedly founded a national, user-led self-help platform and, to this day, maintains an avid interest in the life of Edward Alexander Crowley. During our conversation, Dr. Hudson noted that (to the best of her knowledge), the corpus of documentation relating to Crowley lacked a psychological profile. On reflection, we considered that the absence of this type of study represented something of a glaring omission, and agreed that the compilation of one would be a useful and rewarding exercise. Crowley died on 01 December 1947. As such, assessing him 'in the flesh' was not a viable option. However, an investigation of the copious material Crowley bequeathed to posterity should provide, at least, a sound basis from which to formulate a tentative outline of the man's predominant personality traits.

The prospect of performing a posthumous investigation of Aleister Crowley appealed to Dr. Hudson. She agreed to undertake a preliminary analysis and notify me of her findings. Given the seeming complexity of Crowley's character, I did not expect to hear from my friend for several months. Much to my surprise, I received an e-mail from Dr. Hudson only two days later. Headed *"Nine degrees of separation,"* the communication read as follows:

"*Aleister Crowley…*

1 – Has a grandiose sense of self-importance, exaggerating accomplishments and demanding he be considered superior without real evidence of achievement.

2 – Lives in a dream world of exceptional success, power, beauty, genius, or 'perfect' love.

3 – Thinks of himself as 'special' or privileged, and that he can only be understood by other special or high-status people.

4 – Demands excessive amounts of praise and admiration from others.

5 – Feels entitled to automatic deference, compliance, or favourable treatment from others.

6 – Is exploitative towards others and takes advantage of them.

7 – Lacks empathy and does not recognise or identify with the feelings of others.

8 – Is frequently envious of others or believes they are envious of him.

9 – 'Has an attitude' or frequently acts in haughty or arrogant ways."

Though not what I anticipated, Dr. Hudson's concise and rather brusque observations nailed Crowley, 'bang to rights!' An hour later, I received a second e-mail, headed "*From reality!*" This read:

"As you may have deduced, the points in my previous message do not refer specifically to Crowley. They are, in fact, the nine diagnostic criteria of Narcissistic Personality Disorder (NPD). A patient exhibiting five of these traits is diagnosable as suffering from NPD. Throughout his life, Aleister Crowley exhibited chronic symptoms associated with all nine. Furthermore, psychiatrists divide patients meeting the nine NPD criteria into four subcategories. These are:

*1 – **Craving narcissists** feel emotionally undernourished, and may well appear clingy or demanding to those around them.*

*2 – **Paranoid narcissists** feel intense contempt for themselves, projecting it outward onto others. Paranoid narcissists frequently drive other people away from them by hypercritical and jealous comments and behaviours.*

*3 – **Manipulative narcissists** enjoy 'putting something over' on others, obtaining their feelings of superiority by lying to and manipulating them.*

*4 – **Phallic narcissists** are almost exclusively male. They tend to be aggressive, athletic, and exhibitionistic; they enjoy showing off their bodies, clothes, and overall 'manliness.'*

Throughout his life, Crowley habitually exhibited behavioural traits corresponding to all four subcategories. The last of which, 'phallic narcissist,' is of especial significance with respect to his esoteric philosophy. One could spend months examining Crowley's behavioural traits with respect to the diagnostic criteria of psychopathy, sociopathy and a whole Pandora's Box of mental health issues.

In my professional opinion, Aleister Crowley was clinically insane and could have been committed on grounds he presented a clear and present danger to himself and anyone who strayed within his sphere of influence. I note that this diagnosis is, to a significant degree, corroborated by the events of history. Whilst inaccurate to suggest that everyone who experienced Crowley first-hand suffered ruinous or fatal consequences, the man's timeline encompasses an unfeasibly high ratio of casualties to that suggested by statistical averages. In short, Aleister Crowley was [as suggested by David Dalton] *'Mad, bad and dangerous to know!' The factors responsible for manifesting Crowley's insanity are as follows…"*

Dr. Hudson's assessment will, most likely, not come as much of a surprise to anyone with even a passing familiarity of Crowley's exploits. Indeed, it is difficult resisting a temptation to giggle mischievously at the thought of this mad, bad and dangerous to know 'guru' rampaging through polite society. Nevertheless, when stated in cold medical terminology, the comedic value of such caricaturised imagery diminishes markedly, and assumes an infinitely more sinister tone. Phrased quite bluntly, Aleister Crowley was an exceedingly dangerous man.

Of course, it requires neither an experienced specialist nor medical training to chart the emergence and development of questionable (and outright deviant) behavioural patterns exhibited by Crowley. Anyone who reads his enigmatic and grandiose autobiography with an unprejudiced eye will encounter innumerable instances of the psychological defence mechanisms Crowley erected to conceal and protect fragile areas of his psyche. It is to this volume I now turn.

> 666 The truly awful thing about Crowley is that one suspects he didn't really believe in anything. Even his wickedness. Perhaps the only thing that wasn't fake was his addiction to heroin and cocaine. 999
> Christopher Isherwood

01.03 Confession! What confession?

In 1921, during his three-year sojourn on the island of Sicily, Aleister Crowley declared himself an *"Ipsissimus,"* then departed the temple in his Abbey of Thelema and began work on what he probably considered 'the greatest tale ever told' – The story of his own life! What emerged was an immense, nine-hundred and twenty-three page (and that is merely the 'edited for publication' version) epic which, to my mind, is unquestionably one of the most fascinating volumes ever written. Yet a work that would remain unpublished for almost five decades. Although Mandrake Press released two (of six) segments in 1929, the complete package did not emerge until 1969, enigmatically titled **The Spirit of Solitude - An Autohagiography Subsequently anti-Christened "The Confessions of Aleister Crowley."** Regardless of actual content, the title alone is highly suggestive. An 'autohagiography' pertains to the life of a saint. This euphemism also refers obliquely to the religious sect so beloved of his parents - The Plymouth Brethren, who referred to themselves as 'saints.' So, we may ask, what manner of confession will issue forth from a saint who identifies himself with Satan? On reading this gloriously hyperbolic tome, three questions loitered in my mind.

   1 – Does Crowley ever admit he is wrong?

   2 – Does Crowley ever apologise?

   3 – Why does the tale end in 1923?

I am unable to recollect any incident (in **Confessions**, or any other works, published or otherwise) in which Crowley accepts blame for his actions, or says sorry. Across almost a thousand pages of dense text, Crowley comprehensively depicts himself as an archetypal hero of the finest Greek tradition, a flawed genius heroically battling against the fickle whims of gods and the treachery of mortals - A titanic crusade undertaken not for personal glory and riches, but in a wholly altruistic martyrdom to save Mankind.

The life of Aleister Crowley is, by any standards, remarkable. Yet throughout his account of a turbulent, rollercoaster existence, Crowley repeatedly demonstrates a resolute belief that he, personally, never put a foot (or even a toe) wrong. If we accept **Confessions** at face value, then responsibility for all (of many) setbacks Crowley endured throughout his life fall squarely on the shoulders of anyone and everyone else. Crowley emerges from the chaos, exactly as he specified, *"a saint."* So, where is the confession?

At the time of its dictation, Crowley strode the pinnacle of his Magickal and mundane prowess. He has received **Liber AL** and accepted his god-appointed destiny as prophet of the incoming New Aeon of Horus. Crowley has established a headquarters (his Abbey of Thelema, in Sicily) from which to promulgate his New World Religion, and assembled a small but dedicated group of followers. He even has a book promoting an idealised account of his utopian colony in print with mainstream publisher Collins (**Diary of a Drug Fiend**).

Crowley is also an Ipsissimus – A man so enlightened by alchemical distillation and ceremonial purification as to become a perfect vessel through which flows the will of gods. To obtain this lofty grade (the highest rank of mystical hierarchies) Crowley allegedly annihilated all traces of personality and ego in an unconditional surrender to the eternals.

So where did it all go so very wrong?

On reading **Confessions** it becomes patently obvious that far from destroying his ego, Crowley is enslaved and irretrievably shackled to an 'elephant in the room' of which he seems oblivious - Despite the fact it has, by this time, assumed the dimensions of a small planet and is trumpeting constantly. An 'elephant,' I note, with which all Crowley's associates were intimately acquainted – Usually to their financial and emotional cost.

The calamitous demise of Crowley's bold experiment at world reform was inevitable and ill-fated by the same root causes responsible for blighting all other facets of his life. Unbeknown to Crowley, he was (quite literally) 'damned' before even evacuating the cloying parlour of his family. For it was they who, during the child's early years, unknowingly sowed the seed of a bitter harvest Crowley would reap throughout his life.

❝❝❝ Aleister Crowley... The madman who thinks he is Aleister Crowley. ❞❞❞
Oscar 'Apocryphal' Wilde

01.06　　　Three degrees of freedom

Broadly speaking, the life of Edward Alexander Crowley is divisible into three distinct phases. These are:

    1 – I am not   (12 October 1875 to 04 March 1887).

    2 – I am   (05 March 1887 to 30 April 1923).

    3 – I was   (01 May 1923 to 01 December 1947).

The first covers a period from birth to the death of his father. Throughout this time, Crowley (in ***Confessions**) refers to himself exclusively in the third person (i.e. 'Alick,' 'him,' 'the boy,' etc.) - A fascinating literary device and well-documented 'coping mechanism' utilised by individuals as a means of distancing themselves from unresolved issues.

With only four pages, Crowley skips lightly across the first nine years of an existence he would later describe (in **The World's Tragedy**) as *"A Boyhood in Hell."* The reasons for his evident disgust are not difficult to ascertain. Despite the relative opulence into which Crowley was born (children of this era stood only a fifty percent chance of reaching their fifth birthday), the boy spent his formative years entombed behind harsh strictures imposed by parents who were, by any standards, obsessive religious fanatics. On page thirty-nine, Crowley provides a graphic illustration as to the sheer absurdity of his childhood environment and the warped mindset it nurtured:

"One fine summer morning, at Redhill, the boy – now eight or nine – got tired of playing by himself in the garden. He came back to the house. It was strangely still and he got frightened. By some odd chance everybody was either upstairs or out. But he jumped to the conclusion that 'the Lord had come' and that he had been 'left behind'." (Page 39)

With each passing year, the child's awareness and revulsion of the oppressive regime he was compelled to endure bubbled closer to the surface. His growing frustration and anger held in check solely by a man the boy feared, respected and admired in equal measure, and a man Crowley used as a template for his own life – His father.

"Edward Crowley used to give away tracts to strangers, besides distributing them by thousands through the post; he was also

constantly preaching to vast crowds, all over the country. It was, indeed, the only logical occupation for a humane man who believed that even the noblest and best of mankind were doomed to eternal punishment." (Page 39)

On Saturday 05 March 1887, Crowley's anchor died. The tragic bereavement of his 'hero' shattered the youth's life, and from the ashes emerged a very different entity - As Crowley himself acknowledged:

"From the moment of the funeral the boy's life entered an entirely new phase. The change was radical. Within three weeks of his return to school he got into trouble for the first time." (Page 53)

Almost immediately, numerous 'quirks' arising from repressed emotional baggage accumulated during his upbringing began to find expression. It is almost certain that the concurrent onset of puberty (Crowley was six months shy of his twelfth birthday at the time) played a significant part in fueling the first, faltering eruptions of a juvenile revolution that would eventually devour the man. Not surprisingly, given the river of testosterone coursing through Crowley's veins, matters of a sexual nature increasingly punctuate his narration. However, the themes explored are far from the fantasy imagery one assumes would occupy the mind of a naïve Victorian teenager.

"He reveled in the descriptions of torment. […] He liked to imagine himself in agony." (Page 44)

"When Gregor Grant was pretending to be Hyder Ali, and himself Tipu Sahib, he once asked his cousin, "Be cruel to me"." (Page 47)

Whilst Crowley acknowledges his *"strain of congenital masochism"* (Page 44), he seems utterly oblivious of, and either unable or unwilling to mention his flirtation with masochism's twin sister, sadism.

"I had been told 'A cat has nine lives.' I deduced that it must be practically impossible to kill a cat. […] I therefore caught a cat and, having administered a large dose of arsenic I chloroformed, hanged it above the gas jet, stabbed it, cut its throat, smashed its skull and, when it had been thoroughly burnt, drowned it and threw it out of the window that the fall might remove the ninth life. In fact, the operation was successful; I had killed the cat. I remember that all the time I was genuinely sorry for the animal; I simply forced myself to carry out the experiment in the interest of pure science." (Page 74)

That Crowley labeled this barbaric act of savagery as 'science' is illustrative of the sheer scale and complexity of psychological self-defense mechanisms he employed to conceal unresolved issues still haunting the man in 1921, when he wrote the passage. That Crowley simply assumes readers will accept his word, at face value, and not see 'the cat incident' for the act of outright sadism it so obviously was, merely emphasises the severity of his repression, denial and increasing divergence from reality.

In the summer of 1891, Crowley (then just fifteen) sold his innocence to a Torquay prostitute. Incidentally, his 'change' included a venereal disease, though Crowley did not hold this against the woman. His response to the transaction is fascinating:

> *"The nightmare world of Christianity vanished at the dawn. […] the detestable mysteries of sex were transformed into joy and beauty. The obsession of sin fell from my shoulders…"* (Page 75)

Crowley (allegedly) did not grasp the potential of Sex Magick until his 1912/13 meeting with Theodor Reuss. However, his debut act of coitus unquestionably forged a deep connection between sex and liberation. Quite inadvertently, an anonymous seaside whore furnished Crowley with his first initiation. Unfortunately, though the adolescent's 'obsession with sin' may have fallen from his shoulders, it appears to have lodged down his pants. Over the next few chapters, Crowley describes his plunge into a depraved world of unrelenting vice and corruption. One in which he is routinely besieged by pederasty, sexual abuse, homoerotic bullying and a peripheral assortment of unmentionable sins. Whilst this type of deplorable behaviour certainly occurred within the educational institutions of Victorian England, one cannot help but consider a possibility that, during this period, Crowley's fledgling inclinations towards masochism began to dribble beyond the confines of his mind, and coagulate in the clandestine circles of a few other lost souls. Whilst Crowley maintains a rigid defense of ignorance as to the specifics of crimes perpetrated against 'other boys,' and a 'stone wall' denial of any participation, one gets a distinct impression that he secretly wallowed in this lurid imagery. Of course, the sheer abundance and routine imminence of alleged instances does lead to a suspicion that Crowley's perception of his environment as *'the land of open season on boy-buggery'* conceals a tendril of paranoia. Was Crowley concerned that his behaviour and mannerisms may result in the catastrophic exposure of his own deepest, darkest secret – A dawning realisation that he was a boy in Hell, who preferred boys!

In the late nineteenth century, homosexuality was a serious offence. If convicted, perpetrators faced a mandatory custodial sentence, with hard labour. Society also regarded it as an unnatural disease and pact with the Devil. The dread of irrevocable branding as a social pariah in consequence of one clumsy slip was, to a 'gentleman' of Crowley's aspirations, unthinkable, yet a constant nagging fear. Moreover, the psychological damage inflicted by internal conflicts relating to Crowley's sexual preferences is incalculable. Having staggered through a 'boyhood in Hell,' Crowley now finds himself trapped between a cock and a hard (labour) place.

Of two further childhood reminiscences I consider noteworthy, the first (relating to Crowley's second sexual conquest) is discussed in the next chapter. I close this segment with an incident that could easily have proved fatal. Whilst most biographers reference this occurrence in passing, its immense significance to Crowley's future development remains unexplored – As will shortly become clear.

"Being the star chemist of the school, I determined to distinguish myself on the fifth of November, 1891. I procured a ten-pound jar from the grocer's, put two pounds of gunpowder in the bottom and filled it up with various layers of different coloured 'fires. […] I pressed this down very powerfully, buried the jar in the playground, stuck a rocket in the top and lighted it at the critical moment. The rocket had been fixed too firmly to rise and the protecting wad of paper burnt through before I could step back. […] I slept for ninety-six hours with these semi-conscious intervals. My tutor had the sense to wire to Guy's Hospital for Dr Golding Bird, whose intervention probably saved me from erysipelas and the loss of my sight. In the course of convalescence over four thousand pieces of glass and the like were removed from my face; and it was on Christmas Day that I was first allowed to use my eyes for a few minutes. The explosion had been devastating. The windows were smashed for a long way round and the chemist's on the railway bridge – a quarter of a mile and more away – rattled, though the passing of trains had no such effect." (Pages 83 and 84)

---

*Unless otherwise stated, all references quoted in this chapter, and the next, derive from Crowley's autohagiography, **Confessions**.

02.03   The meat-chopping block beckons

Crowley's first heterosexual skirmish occurred shortly after the death of his father. Whilst on holiday in Scotland the precocious youth threw a tantrum and stormed away from his chaperone, Rev. Fothergill.

> *"That night the gods still further favoured me, for a village girl named Belle McKay found herself with nothing better to do than to roam with me amid the heather. We returned quite openly and Fothergill threw up the sponge. He took me back to London next morning. Breaking the journey at Carlisle, I repeated my victory with a buxom chambermaid."* (Page 72)

Although the reference is highly suggestive, Crowley's 'victory' almost certainly refers to an intellectual triumph over Rev. Fothergill, the Plymouth Brethren and his mother, not a physical conquest over the two women. When Crowley does 'break his duck,' with a prostitute, the gushing recollection (described in the previous chapter) leaves readers in absolutely no doubt as to what happened. Shortly after his debut opus, Crowley narrates his account of a second. This, to my mind, is one of the most illuminating passages in **Confessions**, as it provides a chilling insight into Crowley's emerging character and attitude towards the fair sex.

> *"A young parlour maid took it into her head to better herself by getting a stranglehold on the young master."* (Page 79)

Having done the dirty deed, Crowley immediately enlisted a local tobacconist to furnish him with a cast-iron alibi (i.e. 'I could not have met the lass, as alleged, because I was buying tobacco at the time'). He 'confesses' to the lesser crime of smoking, thus absolving himself of any involvement in the greater offence, and skips away from the incident whistling merrily. The parlour maid was not so fortunate. 'Guilty' of leveling unfounded accusations of rape against her employer's son, she was summarily dismissed, without references. Her reputation in tatters, any likelihood of securing future employment was negligible. Does Crowley end his recollection with a pang of remorse, regret, or guilt? He does not. In fact, he hints towards yet another disturbing facet of his sexuality.

> *"The girl was, of course, discredited and nothing more was heard of the matter. And I had her on my mother's very bed!"* (Page 80)

In 1938, journalist Jackson Burke allegedly met Crowley for the purpose of: "*Recording a radio interview with him for later broadcast from a San Francisco radio station.*" It is unknown if this interview was actually transmitted, though a copy of the tape may survive. The transcript was published as a six-page feature titled "*The Beast with Two Backs*" in the US magazine **Real Action For Men** (Volume I, issue 3: August 1957).

> "*I caught her alone one morning in the scullery when all the house were away somewhere. What I was unable to accomplish by sheer muscular power, I managed by the ever-so gentle pressure of boning knife to throat, and thus this lecherous lass of 19 got her come-uppance from a mere stripling of 14 – and atop the meat-chopping block, at that.*"

That Crowley never considered a possibility of accepting responsibility for his actions is appalling. His evident delight at the stratagem formulated to exonerate himself, at the cost of only a mild rebuke for smoking, and incidental sacrifice of a mere parlour maid, is reprehensible. If accurately reported (and this is debatable, see **AL cetera**, Point 1), Crowley's gloating admission of 'abstraction at knife-point' is damning. Incidentally, Crowley also noted that, following her dismissal, the girl quickly turned to prostitution and alcoholism, and expired a few years later.

Further instance of Crowley's deplorable opinion of women pepper the next few chapters of **Confessions**:

> "*A man who is strong enough to use women as slaves and playthings is alright.*" (Page 96)

> "*...a woman is only tolerable in one's life if she is trained to help the man in his work without the slightest reference to any other interests soever.*" (Page 96)

> "*...I am furious, to this day, that some of the best years of my life, which should have been spent in acquiring knowledge, were sterilized by the suffocating stupor of preoccupation with sex. It was not that my mind was working on the subject; it was simply unable to work. It was a blind, horrible ache for relief. The necessities of men in this respect vary enormously. I was, no doubt, an exceptional case. But I certainly found even forty-eight hours of abstinence sufficient to dull the fine edge of my mind. Woe unto them by whom offences come! The stupidity of having to waste uncounted priceless hours in chasing what aught to have been brought to the back door every evening with the milk!*" (Page 113)

In his 1923 publication, **Things Near & Far**, Arthur Machen provided a sensationalised reference to Crowley's supposed fancy of hanging his first wife Rose (nee Kelly) in a wardrobe whilst entertaining prostitutes and mistresses on their marital bed:

> "...*the doings of a fiend in human form, a man who was well known to be an expert in Black Magic, a man who hung up naked women in cupboards by hooks which pierced the flesh of their arms.*"

By today's standards, Crowley's views on women are wholly unacceptable. However, they were perfectly consistent with the attitude of rabid misogyny prevalent amongst wealthy Victorian 'gentlemen.' Similarly, Crowley was not the first, or last who sexually abused a lowly peasant before casually tossing his unfortunate victim to the dogs on her being ungracious enough to voice complaint. Unfortunately, for apologists of Crowley who may argue that forcing himself upon a servant at knife-point was merely a distasteful consequence of his generation… It gets worse, much worse…

02.05 The page that dare not speak its name

In mundane terms, the second phase of Crowley's life (05 March 1887 to 30 April 1923) relates to his attempts at reconciling emotional baggage accumulated during his formative years with the responsibilities of adulthood. In Magickal terms, this period charts the rise of Crowley's doppelganger, Aiwass, leading to the great revelation of 1904 and the ascension of Crowley to his self-sanctioned divine role as Messiah. It concludes with a bold experiment in Sicily, during which Crowley applies the theoretical blueprint of Thelema, his *"New World Religion,"* to real life – Magick in Practice, not Theory!

From the moment Crowley is unleashed from the toxic bosom of his extended and fatherless family, the Great Beast emerged almost fully formed. He hit the ground snarling and spent the next thirteen years partying on 'The Hellfire Club's 18-30 vacation at a 'Marquis de Sade' theme-park!' Between 1896 and 1909, Crowley painted Europe a livid scarlet. His scandalous exploits were 'the talk of the town,' and media. Throughout this period, Crowley's opulent lifestyle and penchant for publishing grandiose editions of his own works, he financed exclusively from a sum of £40,000 bequeathed from the estate of his deceased father. As an indication as to the relative value of this windfall I'll note that in 1900 the average General Labourer earned around £46 per annum, a Bank Manager took home only £400, ten cigarettes (or an ounce of pipe tobacco) cost three old Pennies and the price of a four-bedroom townhouse was approximately £400, or £800 in London. In 1899, Crowley paid only £4,000 for Boleskine House, on the shores of Loch Ness. In today's economic climate, £4,000 is worth around four million Pounds. With prudent management, this sum could furnish a young family with a comfortable income for life. However, Crowley inherited the money on 12 October 1896 (his 21st birthday), devoured life 'to the max,' and was skint by the time he embarked for America in 1909. From this point onwards, Crowley was compelled, for the most part, to eke out an unpredictable hand-to-mouth existence. What would have become of Crowley in the event of him not walking into a small fortune is a subject open to endless speculation. As events transpired, he did, and this massive cash-injection unquestionably shaped the remainder of his life.

The 'cushion' Crowley's wealth afforded him most definitely encouraged the emergence of a behavioural trait that became a reoccurring theme throughout his life - Crowley was 'captain,' or took his ball home! For instance, he left university without completing the course. Crowley explains this in purely monetary terms:

> *"I saw no sense in paying fifteen guineas for the privilege of wearing a long black gown more cumbersome that the short blue one..."* (**Confessions**, page 166.)

To my mind, this statement appears curiously at-odds with the fortune burning a hole in his pocket. Consider an alternate perspective – Had Crowley left Cambridge in a cumbersome black gown, he would have done so as one amongst hundreds of faceless graduates passing unremarkably through the university each year. Conversely, in walking away before the fat-lady sang, Crowley gained membership to an elite circle of notables, comprising *"Byron, Shelley, Swinburne and Tennyson..."* With a subtle change of focus, Crowley alchemically transforms mundane, into magnificent. This subtle trick is routinely utilised throughout **Confessions**. Whether or not Crowley actually believed his own hype is a debatable point.

Shortly after leaving university, Crowley encountered his first mystical fraternity, the Golden Dawn, and again his 'all or nothing' mentality flared. On joining, Crowley was not content to participate and slowly rise through the ranks, no. Nothing less than his assumption of control would suffice, and Crowley cared little for those he trampled over en route. Yet, even this attainment failed to quench the thirst of *"Perdurabo"* (the magickal motto Crowley adopted on enlisting in the Golden Dawn). Unlike Mathers, and a host of other notable occultists, Crowley scoffed at the prospect of merely passing time with a menagerie of lesser occult entities. He was only interested in playing with the big boys, and demanded of them an entirely new rulebook for Mankind! By an incredibly fortuitous stroke of luck (some may suggest), only a few years later, in April 1904, Crowley got precisely what his ego demanded.

The circumstances relating to the genesis, reception and implementation of **Liber AL vel Legis** (Crowley's new 'Bible' and Founding Document of his *"New World Religion,"* Thelema) are discussed in Part Two of this work. For now, I focus on the climax of Crowley's second life-phase – His three year residency at Villa Santa Barbara, Cefalu, on the island of Sicily.

Having accepted his Herculean destiny, the new 'Messiah' forged a base for his assault on humanity, and populated this with a small yet devoted band of disciples. Incidentally, the funding for Crowley's grand experiment arrived courtesy of a £600 bequest from the convenient death of an aunt – One of three similar sums he received, in addition to the initial £40,000 from his father and £4,000 received on the death of his mother. Somewhat paradoxically, this period charted both the high and low-water marks of Crowley's life. Indeed, it is my opinion that one day in particular is identifiable as the fulcrum about which Edward Alexander Crowley's entire life pivoted. For those with a strong constitution, Crowley records the specifics in his private diary – An uncensored document most definitely not intended for circulation. Alas, in 1972, John Symonds and Kenneth Grant (the duo responsible for editing **Confessions**) 'let the cat out of the bag' with their publication of **The Magical Record of The Beast 666 – The Diaries of Aleister Crowley, 1914-1920** (Duckworth) – A work that aficionados must dearly wish had never been published at all. Because it contains what is unquestionably the most inflammatory and indefensible statement Crowley penned during his long and controversial existence.

At midnight on the morning of 12 August 1920 (Page 246), Aleister Crowley opens his private diary and resumes a lengthy entry relating his account and interpretation of Alostrael's (his then Scarlet Woman, Leah Hirsig) recent vision. At 1:30AM, Crowley breaks off for Opus VII (Magickal sex). Half-an-hour later, he returns to his journal and pens a description of the nuptials. As he writes, it becomes clear that something is on the man's mind, an issue Crowley is struggling to address directly.

At 2:45AM, Crowley's tone veers markedly, descending into obscene sentiments of the type expressed in his filthy poem **Leah Sublime**. Amidst the diabolic camouflage, Crowley appears to be asking, *"Who am I?"* In response, he forces his thoughts back to a contemplation of his *"Dawn-Meditation."* After a brief return to Magickal concerns, Crowley's subconscious musings again bubble to the surface, with a curious comment: *"A tired man loving a pregnant woman. This is doubly against nature."* The Magus immediately counters this 'moment of weakness' with a robust Magical defence: *"It is then exactly the right and necessary operation for this purpose."* Crowley, again, attempts a return to Magickal themes, but this effort stalls after just one paragraph. Following an unspecified hiatus, Crowley returns to his diary with a singularly bizarre declaration.

> *"Later. Found Leah out! All her remarks were just so many devices to induce erection – appeals to father-love, religion, passion, Magick, vice, poetry, etc. But the cocaine won by a short head – so did my perception of her tricks – the sceptic cannot beget children. It is necessary for women to deceive men that the race may live."*

Crowley then breaks for another bout of sexual shenanigans, leaving readers to wonder precisely what Leah is 'carrying the can' for.

At 7AM, Crowley begins an account of Opus VIII that quickly disintegrates into a sequence of uneasy observations relating to his drug usage, constipation, and general frailty of physical health. Once again, the inner-Magus leaps to Crowley's defence, providing positive statements testifying to the man's prowess and limiting the extent of any problems to a minor overuse of his Anja and Muladhara. Crowley realises the mental chess game is getting him nowhere and at 8:40AM declares, "*I'll rest.*" Two minutes later, Crowley writes, "*Can't rest*" and, at 8:45AM, notes that, "*Time goes slowly.*"

At 8:46AM, Crowley decides it's time to quit stalling and 'get to the point.' – He writes, "*To the assault!*" Even so, his final dash at the summit takes a long, circuitous route. Pushing off with a confidence boosting assertion that his literary powers surpass those of Keats and Shakespeare, Crowley then launches into a sustained tirade against himself! Each subsequent paragraph exposes deeper layers of self-contempt, loathing and disgust. After spewing two pages of almost unreadable bile over his own character and life, Crowley succeeds in whipping himself into enough of a (cocaine-fuelled) frenzy to dare expose the raw nerve he's been tentatively prodding for nearly nine hours.

Apologists of Crowley close your eyes now!

> "*And I the Worm have trailed my Slug-Slow across Her Breasts; so that Her mother-mood is turned and Her breasts itch with lust of Incest. She hath given Her two-year bastard boy to Her lewd lover's whim of sodomy, hath taught him speech and act, things infinitely abhorred, with Her own beastly carcass. She hath tongued Her five-month girl, and asked its father to deflower it. She hath wished Her Beast to rape Her rotten old mother – so far is woman clean of Her! Then Her blood's grown icy hard and cold with hate; and Her eyes gleam as Her ears ring with a chime of wedding bells, dirty words, or vibrate, cat-gut fashion, to the thin shrieks of a young child that Her Beast-God-Slave-Mate is torturing for Her pleasure – ay! and his own, since of Her Cup he drank, and of Her soul he breathed.*
>
> *He loved it all. He rolled each drop of filth around His tongue.*"

At 11:56AM, Crowley slams the stable door shut with a single word - "*Halt!*" Alas, the horse has long-since bolted and is now galloping at breakneck speed towards the gaping black-hole Crowley just opened for himself.

Three days later, at 9PM on 15 August, Crowley writes, *"Everybody sick or damaged; all a mess."* An observation made only four months into his grand experiment and, as those with an interest are aware, the 'mess' didn't improve. In fact, things quickly got worse, much worse. By the time Crowley was forcibly ejected from Sicily (April 1923), his dream of launching Thelema as a New World Religion was dead and buried beside the corpses of his two children and devoted disciple Raoul Loveday. Beyond the shores of Cefalu, tabloid journalists have indelibly branded Crowley with a nickname that will haunt him for the remainder of his life – *"The Wickedest Man in the World."* In the months following his expulsion, Crowley considered suicide and – unbelievably – reverting to Christianity!

In his defense, at the time Crowley's unhealthy lifestyle in combination with increasing drug consumption were impacting on his sexual performance – As Crowley notes, several times, in his diary. It is possible that Leah was using this disturbing imagery as 'porn' and an extreme attempt to put some spring back into his… wand! This seems a plausible scenario, and negates any issues concerning the actual physical abuse of a very young child. Nevertheless, it still raises deeply troubling issues, especially with reference to an unsettling entry of the same date made by Jane Wolfe, in her (recently published) Cefalu diary. In flirting with this imagery, Leah obviously believed it would 'do the trick.' Crowley's disgust only surfaced later and, tellingly, the same theme repeatedly raises its ugly head in his poetry and notes. The passage reproduced below derives from the unpublished **Notes of conversations with Aleister Crowley concerning the Book of the Law, 1923, recorded by Norman Mudd. ("Dated Tunis, 1923, before the writing of the Comment called D.")**

> *"A being, A, who was Cardinal Cazzo. He dies and goes to Heaven. On Buddhist principles C. C. has disappeared, but the bundle appears in heaven with sufficient identity with C. C. to be recognized by anyone who knew him. He may or may not have memory of this.*
>
> *Now C. C. in his life time was confronted with this problem. Shall I bugger this boy? If I refrain my virtue will be such that there will be a being, A, enjoying himself in heaven who would not otherwise be there. While if I indulge this unholy passion, there will be a being, A, in Hell who would not otherwise be there. If however in either case, A, does not think 'I am here because when I was C. C., I acted this and not otherwise, then why should I, C.*

C. act otherwise than my interests prompt me. In other words, motive always assumes the memory"

The Italian word "*cazzo*" translates into "*fuck!*" as an exclamation, or "*prick, cock, dick and shit*' as a noun. In the allegory, Crowley is covertly referring to 'the grand fuck!'

When Crowley's behaviour became intolerable, his second wife, Maria Teresa de Miramar, routinely employed a most derogatory term of chastisement, as noted by Israel Regardie:

"When she was annoyed, she suddenly used to turn on him and hiss, 'Pederast.' And he'd be going, 'Oh, mon cherie, how can you say this to me!' as he tried to kiss her and she'd still be hissing 'Pederast!' until finally he grabbed her and they'd start fucking." (**Do What Thou Wilt**, page 342)

Regardie laughed this off as a reference to Crowley's preference for anal sex. However, it seems reasonable to presume that a woman of Miramar's 'experience' would know the difference between buggery and pederasty! A third explicit reference occurs in Crowley's unpublished diary entry dated 09 March 1919. It reads:

"The real inferiority of women to men is shown by their hate of pederasty, which they regard as unfair competition. Men on the other hand rather approve of Sapphism, as saving them trouble and expense."

Anyone with a desire to probe Crowley's unsavoury sexual appetites further will find much to consider in his spectacularly obscene (1910) publication, **Bagh-I-Muattar**, or **Scented Garden**. Two quotes of which are included below:

"I am tempted to add that even plain paederasty, without any question of symbol at all, is perhaps not so incompatible with virtues, religious, social, moral and domestic, as my good compatriots make such a point of asserting with a fine show of disgust and indignation."

"Some men are born sodomites, some achieve sodomy, and some have sodomy thrust upon them."

In an echo of the **Liber Legis** myth, Crowley claimed that his compendium of filth was the work of a seventeenth century Persian satirist named Abdullah al Haji, as translated by an equally fictitious character named Major Alain Lutiy. Crowley also covertly saluted his first homosexual partner, in Chapter XLI, **The Riddle**. The initial letter of each line reads *"Herbert Charles Jerome Pollitt."* In the next chapter, **Bagh-I-Muattar,** an acrostic spells out Crowley's name in reverse. The small print-run of only two-hundred copies were subject to two customs seizures (1910 and 1924). In consequence, this title is arguably the rarest of Crowley's works, of which he noted: *"I have heard of a copy changing hands at fifty guineas."*

I believe that Crowley's singularly infamous (in consequence of its immortalisation on page 251 of Grant and Symonds' **The Magical Record of The Beast 666**) diary entry represents the pivotal moment of his life. Not in consequence of alleged child abuse overtones. Rather, because at that moment Crowley glimpsed the extent of an almost immeasurable divergence between the hypothetical 'ideal' of his construct, Thelema (as depicted in **The Diary of a Drug Fiend**) and its comprehensively grim reality – An insight that undoubtedly terrified him. In February 1922, Crowley made a determined attempt to clean-up his act. After rejecting an option to seek professional medical help, he employed the principles of Thelema to rid him of a mushrooming dependence on heroin and cocaine. At Fontainbleau, Crowley made his stand. A chronicle of the bitter defeat he meticulously recorded in a short work entitled **The Fountain of Hyacinth**.

On 30 April 1923, aboard a ship bound for Tunis (from where began a protracted period of 'sulking in the wilderness'), Crowley drew his autobiography to a close with the words *"I shall endure unto the End."* He was forty-seven at this time and still had another twenty-five years of existence to endure. Throughout his twilight years, Crowley often complained of boredom. Yet, despite having time on his hands, he never finished the greatest story ever told.

Crowley limped away from the twisted wreckage of Thelema Abbey a broken man. His *"engine of world reform"* had proved defective on all fronts. His reputation and finances in tatters, his health hung by a thread and the inner turmoil generated by these cumulative factors must have been crippling in the extreme. Crowley surely wore his 'I Ching' sticks to dust in attempting to divine a way out of this calamitous situation. Perhaps mindful of the old adage, *'Those who can, do. Those who can't, teach,'* the Magus reinvented himself in line with his greatly diminished expectations. The iconic battle-cry of 'Do what thou wilt shall be the whole of the Law' usurped by 'Preach what I can will be the rent of a World Teacher.' In January 1925, Crowley issued several tracts aimed at aligning himself with the fashionable Theosophical Society, and soliciting favours from a few of its wealthy and influential membership. Not surprisingly, given Crowley's toxic status, nobody was prepared to give him the time of day. His North African 'World Teacher' campaign quickly slid into the same abyss as Thelema.

The final phase of Crowley's timeline (01 May 1923 to 01 December 1947) plots a long, slow and painful descent down the barrel of a syringe into poverty, isolation and obscurity. He spends several years wandering aimlessly around Europe in a futile attempt to reconnect with a Magickal Current, but Crowley is a spent force. In 1929, France became the second country to eject Crowley through its back door. In 1934 he lost the notorious 'Laughing Torso' case and was declared bankrupt the following year. Eventually, like a discarded newspaper drifting in the breeze, Crowley gravitated back to his native England. He then shuffled between temporary lodgings and German bombs before grinding to an inevitable halt at Netherwood, The Ridge, in Hastings.

02.06 Dr. Pincus' three paths to psychopath

In this chapter, I explore Crowley's mindset with reference to the work of Canadian psychologist Robert D. Hare and American neurologist Jonathan H. Pincus.

Born in Calgary, in 1934, Robert D. Hare is a researcher in the field of criminal psychology. He developed several analytical techniques used to diagnose cases of psychopathy and predict the likelihood of violent behaviour. Of these, his **Psychopathy Checklist Revised** (PCL-R) is widely regarded as the "*Gold Standard*" tool for assessing psychopathic tendencies. Hare advises the FBI's Child Abduction and Serial Murder Investigative Resources Center (CASMIRC) and is a consultant to various British and North American prison services.

Ideally, Hare's technique employs one-on-one interviews in conjunction with supporting documentation (i.e. case files). However, it also generates accurate results when applied solely to data (i.e. material written by Crowley). This factor is especially pertinent in considering the mentality of a dead man.

The PCL-R incorporates twenty items. These are:

Factor One

Facet 1 - *Interpersonal*
- Glibness/superficial charm
- Grandiose sense of self-worth
- Pathological lying
- Cunning/manipulative

Facet 2 - *Affective*
- Lack of remorse or guilt
- Emotionally shallow
- Callous/lack of empathy
- Failure to accept responsibility for own actions

Factor Two

Facet 3 - *Lifestyle*
- Need for stimulation/proneness to boredom
- Parasitic lifestyle
- Lack of realistic, long-term goals
- Impulsiveness
- Irresponsibility

Facet 4 - *Antisocial*
- ♦ Poor behavioural controls
- ♦ Early behavioural problems
- ♦ Juvenile delinquency
- ♦ Revocation of conditional release
- ♦ Criminal versatility

Other Items

- ♦ Many short-term marital relationships
- ♦ Promiscuous sexual behaviour

Each item is 'scored' with reference to a patient's responses – '0' for no match, '1' for a partial match and '2' for a good match. In the UK, a total of 25 (or more) wins a 'psycho' badge. US patients need try slightly harder. They require 30 points to secure a diagnosis of psychopath. On reading **Confessions**, it is reasonable to apportion Crowley a conservative score of 38 points (out of a possible 40!) This impressive tally classifies Crowley as both a psychopath and an exceedingly dangerous individual.

Dr. Pincus is Chief of Neurology at Veteran's Administration Hospital, in Washington DC, and Professor of Neurology at Georgetown University School of Medicine. Over the last twenty-five years, he has examined hundreds of murderers, serial killers, death row inmates and other such radical elements of society. Together with his colleague Dr. Dorothy Lewis, a child psychiatrist, Dr. Pincus developed a theory suggesting that violent behaviour is a product of just three critical factors. Unlike Hare's cumulative scoring PLC-R, Dr. Pincus' study works on a simple principal of 'three strikes and you're out.' Individuals correlating with one or even two of these 'key triggers' are no more likely to commit violent actions than the average. However, score a hat-trick and you are almost certain to go on a violent rampage at least once in your life. The three governing criteria are:

1 – Psychiatric illness.

2 – Neurological damage (esp. to the frontal lobe).

3 – Childhood abuse.

In consequence of his torturous upbringing an assortment of mental illnesses, neurosis and psychological damage plagued Crowley, of this there is little doubt. He also suffered extensive damage to his frontal lobes in consequence of the gunpowder incident recounted in a previous chapter. With reference to this, I note that an old fashioned (and now outlawed) hand-launched 'Banger' contained only two grams of gunpowder. Yet, this miniscule charge was ample to cause significant damage if detonated in a clenched fist. Conversely, Crowley's 'firework' contained "*two pounds of gunpowder*" (around 900 grams) plus several pounds of incendiary material. Embedding this in the ground effectively transformed his contraption into a cannon barrel that detonated "*before I could step back.*" That Crowley survived, at all, is almost miraculous. That he did not suffer irreparable neurological damage is unlikely in the extreme.

Given that Crowley was demonstrably waving two of Dr. Pincus' three red flags, it is tempting to scour his works in search of a tenuous reference hinting at just a single instance of physical childhood abuse. However, since Crowley did not embark on a psychotic rampage during his lifetime, any such investigation would almost certainly uncover nothing of significance. On an entirely speculative note, I will suggest that the seeming absence of physical abuse in Crowley's past is something for which Victorian London has much to be thankful. Had Crowley endured a terrifying incident(s) of physical abuse at the hand of a relative or tutor, I would have little hesitation in proposing that Jack the Ripper would now be regarded as the Victorian era's second most notorious murderer.

On the other hand - If we widen the search-pattern to include potential abusers living and non-corporeal, then Crowley unquestionably suffered intolerable cruelty at the hands of a relentless tormentor operating with the complete cooperation of his family! This 'hidden' abuse foisted onto Crowley his third red flag and, in response to the unholy trinity of psychological triggers (and precisely as predicted by Dr. Pincus) Crowley embarked on an obsessive and venomous campaign against a very specific target group. In this context, Crowley is guilty of repeatedly attempting murder, and mass murder.

To anyone reading this and wondering why Crowley's murderous inclinations were overlooked by media sources during his lifetime, and by everyone else in the years since, I suggest you consider the crime scene from a lateral, not literal perspective. The 'voices' in Crowley's head did not entice him to kill prostitutes. Crowley's psychological demons demanded no less a sacrifice than God Almighty!

03.05 Deicide? You decide!

Two compulsive 'drives' ultimately conspired to nudge the course of Crowley's life down a cul-de-sac from which there was no return. Prior to him stumbling over occultism, Crowley's rage against God was blind. The Golden Dawn afforded Crowley a means of targeting his fury. As such, his demolition of that mystical fraternity was clearly a precursor to the greater task ahead.

In the real world, Crowley's moral compass, his sense of ethics and values, were irreconcilably divergent from those of any civilisation, let alone that of Victorian England. Paradoxically, it was of the utmost importance to Crowley's ego that he was accepted, even revered, for who and what he was. Unfortunately, this psychological craving faced him with an insoluble paradox - No society on the planet would tolerate his reprehensible exploits and utterances, nor accept him as 'one of their own,' nor, God forbid, put him in charge! Crowley's solution to the Catch 22 situation was, admittedly, inventive, though plagiarised from Henry VIII's book of Common Conduct – i.e. if those darned Catholics won't let you get divorced, start a religion that will, and to cover unforeseen eventualities appoint yourself CEO.

Compromise and flexibility were tools absent from Crowley's kitbag. So, without hope of bending into a comfortable niche amidst the extant and despised regime, Crowley felt compelled to tear society to its foundations, then rebuild in his own image. That the despised Christian God (on whom Crowley swore revenge) sat atop the spiritual throne of a civilisation he hoped to destroy was a distinct bonus.

In this respect, Crowley is guilty, as charged, on counts of both 'conspiracy to commit deicide' and 'attempted deicide.' In support of this assertion I quote directly from **Liber AL vel Legis (Book of the Law)**, the Founding Document of his proposed New World Religion. If, as Crowley insisted, this work emanated from a *"praeterhuman entity"* and herald of a New Aeon, he was incalculably fortuitous that the lords of Mankind's next epoch were of precisely the same mindset as him, and bore the same infantile grudges.

> *"I am in a secret fourfold word, the blasphemy against all gods of men.*
>
> *Curse them! Curse them! Curse them!*

With my Hawk's head I peck at the eyes of Jesus as he hangs upon the cross.

I flap my wings in the face of Mohammed & blind him.
With my claws I tear out the flesh of the Indian and the Buddhist, Mongol and Din.

Bahlasti! Ompehda! I spit on your crapulous creeds.

Let Mary inviolate be torn upon wheels: for her sake let all chaste women be utterly despised among you!"

(AL III, 49-55)

Reading **Liber AL**, one cannot help but notice many striking parallels between divine proclamations uttered by the incoming deity, and Crowley's personal preferences. Horus was certainly preaching to the converted! For instance:

"*The word of Sin is Restriction.*" (AL I, 41)

"*I give unimaginable joys on earth: certainty, not faith, while in life, upon death; peace unutterable, rest, ecstasy; nor do I demand aught in sacrifice.*" (AL I, 58)

"*To worship me take wine and strange drugs.*" (AL II, 22)

"*I am alone: there is no God where I am.*" (AL II, 23)

"*If Power asks why, then is Power weakness.*" (AL II, 31)

"*I am a god of War and of Vengeance. I shall deal hardly with them.*" (AL III, 3)

"*Worship me with fire & blood; worship me with swords & with spears. Let the woman be girt with a sword before me: let blood flow to my name. Trample down the Heathen; be upon them, o warrior, I will give you of their flesh to eat!*" (AL III, 11)

"*There is no law beyond Do what thou wilt.*" (AL III, 60)"

03.06 Aceldama – A Place to Repress Childhood In

The previous seven chapters demonstrate the ease with which even a cursory perusal of published works reveals an outline of the psychological minefield Crowley spent his life tip-toeing through, and which ultimately blew him apart - With considerable collateral damage.

In **Confessions,** we read of an intolerable childhood besieged by the iron fist of a divine tyrant who delighted in torturing the boy at every possible opportunity – An omnipotent, omniscient and omnipresent bully from whom there was no escape. We read of an adolescent tormented by, yet reveling in sadomasochistic, homosexual, blasphemous and possibly incestuous fantasies. We chart the emergence of a young man crippled by psychological and sexual conflicts, mental illness and behavioural traits comparable with those of a psychopath. We see the ominous rise of an undergraduate harbouring a festering resentment towards a prejudiced society unwilling to acknowledge the hallmarks of genius lost beneath its indelible branding of him as a sick deviant and pervert. Rather perversely, we, as readers, lick our lips in salacious delight on reading how Crowley hurled £4,000,000 (in today's money) at a obsessive crusade hell-bent on tearing asunder the very fabric of his loathsome world and utterly smiting the God responsible for underwriting its, and his, unrelenting wretchedness.

A telling insight as to the extent of Crowley's disinclination to revisit unresolved childhood issues is available via his private letters and diaries. Throughout this massive corpus of documentation, instances of fond reminiscences are conspicuous only by their absence. Indeed, on reading this material, it is difficult to avoid a notion that Crowley's life began at the gates of Trinity College. With an unlimited chequebook in one hand, a bomb in the other, and a Gay Pride banner concealed beneath his pants!

Crowley's first public utterance, the enigmatically titled **Aceldama – A Place to Bury Strangers in** (published in a small edition touted around campus from October 1898, at half-a-crown), alludes to Christian mythology:

> *"Judas acquired a field with the reward of his unjust deed, and falling headfirst he burst open in the middle and all his intestines gushed out. This became known to all who lived in Jerusalem, so that in their own language they called that field Hakeldama, that is, 'Field of Blood.'"* (Acts I, 18-19)

Of his *"Philosophical Poem"* Crowley later remarked:

> *"...my first published poem of any importance, I attained, at a bound, the summit of my Parnassus. In a sense, I have never written anything better. It is absolutely characteristic. Its technical excellence is remarkable and it is the pure expression of my unconscious self. I had no corresponding mental concepts at the time. It enounces a philosophy which subsequent developments have not appreciably modified. I remember my own attitude to it. It seemed to me a willfully extravagant eccentricity. I had no idea that it was the pure water of the Dircean spring."* (**Confessions**, page 137)

That Crowley selected **Aceldama** to open the first volume of his **Collected Works** (1905) is an indication of the import he placed on it. As a further clue to its significance, Crowley prefaced the piece with a curious note. Though not explicitly stated, '1887' refers to 04 March, the day his father died – Murdered by God!

> *"The great bulk of the early MSS. from 1887 to 1897 have been sedulously sought out and destroyed."*

Aceldama marks the point at which Crowley dug in his heels, drew a dividing line and incinerated everything on the wrong side. In Crowley's mind, nothing happened before, and even if something had occurred, this was wholly unrelated to him, and any evidence suggestive of the contrary was long gone. In many respects, **Aceldama** is a direct precursor of both **Liber AL** and Crowley's infamous declaration of Rights, **Liber OZ**.

Crowley dedicated **Aceldama** to Karl von Eckartshausen, author of **Cloud upon the Sanctuary**, the book launching Crowley on his euphemistically titled *"Mystical Adventure"* - A bumpy ride inaugurated on 31 December 1898 and subsequently nurtured beneath the boots of Eckenstein and cosmetics of Pollitt. From the moment of its release, there was no going back. This work nailed Crowley's colours to the mast and declared his willingness to sacrifice anything and everything in furtherance of a megalomaniac quest to convert, coerce or press-gang Mankind into acknowledging the miraculous properties of brand Crowley.

As a means of illustrating Crowley's growing divergence from any semblance of normality, or even sanity, I close the first section of this book with the full text of a letter penned on 27 August 1903. This, it must be noted, relates to the recent marriage of a twenty-seven year old, wealthy Victorian 'gentleman' (to Rose Edith Kelly on 12 August), and is addressed to his mother! Beneath the overt cynicism, sarcasm and generally derisive tone lurks a subtle and concealed undercurrent of questionable if not outright incestuous innuendo.

Crowley alludes to the death and burial of both his bride and the sacrament of matrimony itself. In other words, 'anything now goes (…wink wink, nudge nudge, say no more!)' Even the closing paragraph (*'canoes shooting the Barnes Bridge in astonishing time, then to seas of molten glory in the glowing west where we still are'*) crackles with repressed erotic symbolism intermingled with oblique childhood reminiscences.

Crowley originally signed-off with *"c/o God, in heaven."* That he later affixed *"will always find us"* is perhaps suggestive of a slight retreat. Given his mother's extreme religious beliefs, Crowley perhaps felt compelled to haul himself back across a line over which even he feared to linger. Interestingly, Crowley did not write this intimate correspondence himself. In fact, he dictated it to his new bride - Thus ensuring that she was familiar with its content and that his mother was aware of both Rose's participation (she would recognise the handwriting style) and her son's knowledge of his mother's awareness of Rose's part - Mind games, everywhere!

Thursday, 27th August, 1903.

"*My dearest Mother.*

Aunt Jonathan sent me on your delightful letter of the 19th. – to her with the copy of mine – I suppose you are enlightened by now – My wife wrote you a most daughterly letter some days ago – why don't you answer it?

I was sorry you would not come to the wedding – it was a very grand affair, plumed hearse & all, & the mutes[1] *recalled the delicious mutes of thirty years ago. The Rev J F Kelly the bride's father preached such a beautiful sermon over the open grave. His text was from the 44th v. of the 44th chap: of Isaiah – 'And the Lord said unto Moses, and he arose and smote him*[2]*' – 36 pipers played 'the voice that breathed o'er Eden*[3]*' – Some reference to Whistler*[4] *whom her brother*[5] *so much admires – I suppose – & as the earth was shovelled reverently by 12 stalwart professors of*

Esperanto, taxidermists, and assorted Mormon missionaries (with two such <u>dear</u> destroying angels) over the last mortal remains, a heartfelt sob of relief burst from the assembled multitudes, & tears of utter joy streamed down in such profusion as to enable us to carry out our nearly abandoned project of beginning the honeymoon in a canoe. This we did & shot Barnes Bridge in the astonishing time of 2h & 3m: 21⅓s. Thence to seas of molten glory in the glowing west where we still are

*c/o God,
in heaven
will always find us*

yours..."

One can only wonder what was happening inside Crowley's head at this time. It is, however, worth noting that, eight months later, he honeymooned in Egypt and returned with a staggeringly outlandish claim – A new Messiah had entered the room!

---

[1] See http://www.museumoflondonprints.com/image.php?id=139369 for funeral mutes.
[2] There is no such verse.
[3] A wedding hymn: See http://www.cyberhymnal.org/htm/v/o/voicthat.htm.
[4] James McNeill Whistler, whose most famous painting is a portrait of his mother.
[5] Gerald Kelly, the artist brother of Rose, who probably admired Whistler.

Part Two

Of *Liber L. vel Legis* (Part A)

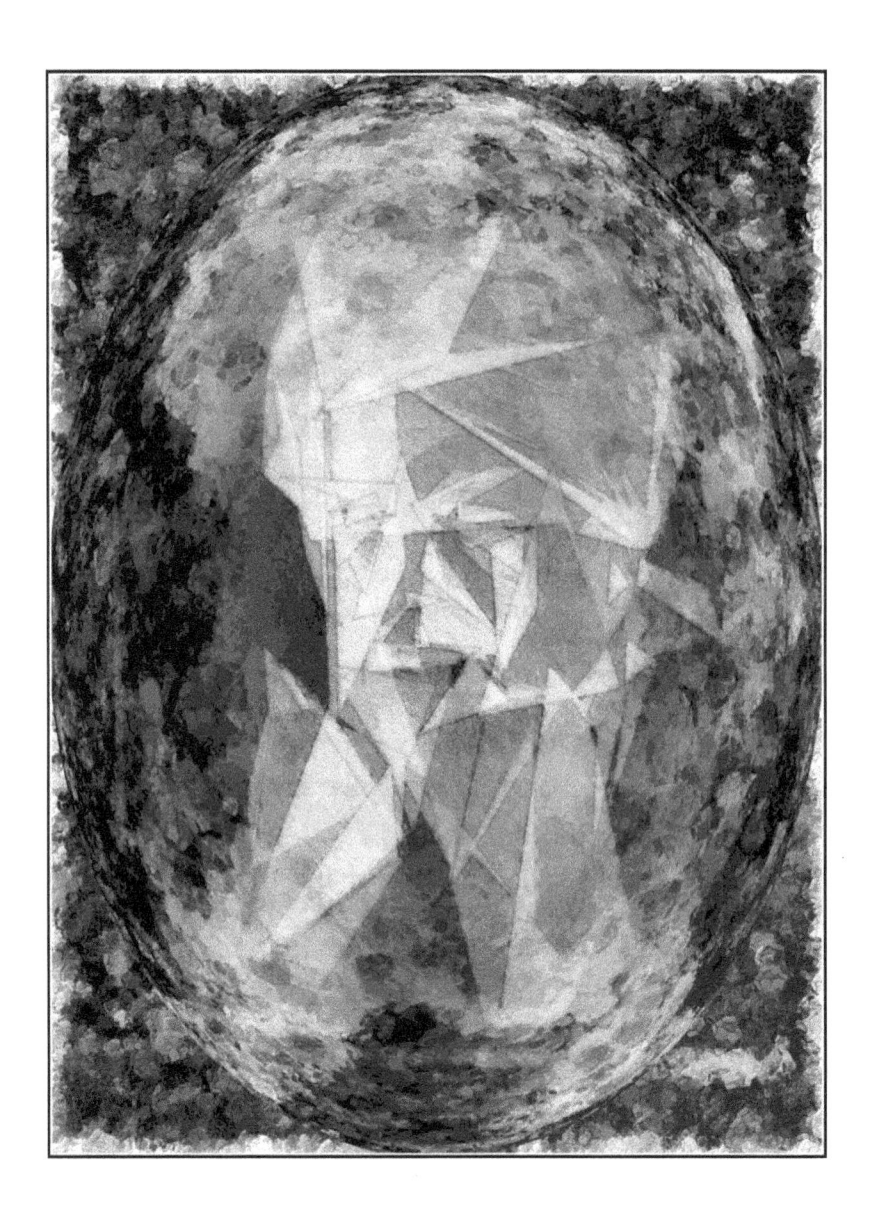

04.05   Buying a Stairway to Heaven

Prior to investigating Aleister Crowley's claims regarding the origin, evolution and implementation of **Liber L. vel Legis**, it is first essential to dispel any lingering notions of the man as an overgrown 'Dennis the Menace' figure bouncing mischievously through a cartoon landscape astride a gigantic inflatable wand. Caricatured fancies of Crowley as 'mad, bad and dangerous to know' in the sense of a pantomime baddie are grossly misleading. It is infinitely more accurate to think in terms of Charles Manson 'mad,' Sepp Blatter 'bad' and Vladimir Putin 'dangerous to know.' Put bluntly, Aleister Crowley was a ticking bomb.

Those who crossed paths with Crowley unknowingly exposed themselves to a severely damaged psychopath. A young man who desperately wanted to shout his bisexuality from the rooftops, but dare not in fear of visiting upon himself the terrible fate endured by Oscar Wilde. A man enthusiastic about extolling the virtues of homosexuality, but compelled to write in heavily coded allegories. A man possessed of an acute need to validate his long years invested in occultism, by forging a *"Magickal Link"* with *"Secret Chiefs"* covertly governing Mankind (thus demonstrating his worthiness to assume the Golden Dawn's throne currently held by Mathers), but whose experiments had thus far resulted in only frustration and a growing sense of futility. A man wholly convinced of his innate genius, but unable to convince others, and a man assured of his entitlement to adulation, wealth and power, but who could manifest none. A man possessed of a pathological craving for acceptance, but who acknowledged the sheer impossibility of accomplishing this from inside the towering edifice of a society that restricted him on all fronts. Finally, Crowley was a man with a murderous grudge against the God responsible for destroying his childhood and murdering his father.

By 12 October 1903, his twenty-eighth birthday, the 'coping mechanisms' Crowley habitually employed to restrain an immense psychological magma chamber seething just below the surface were starting to buckle. In a letter to his brother-in-law, Gerald Kelly, the lava begins to spurt out.

> *"After five years of folly and weakness, miscalled politeness, tact, discretion, care for the feeling of others, I am weary of it. I say today: to hell with Christianity, Rationalism, Buddhism, all the lumber of the centuries. I bring you a positive and primaeval fact, Magic by name, and with this I will build a new Heaven and a new Earth. I want none*

of your faint approval or faint dispraise. I want blasphemy, murder, rape, revolution, anything, bad or good, but strong."

Aleister Crowley was a man fast approaching breaking point. If unable to quell the civil war in his head, and global conflict raging outside it, he was fast heading for a meltdown from which recovery was unlikely. On the negative side, resolving this plethora of complex issues into a persona capable of sustaining even a basic semblance of functionality required nothing less than divine intervention on a miraculous scale. On the positive side, and in defiance of all odds, that is precisely what Crowley received only six months later!

In April 1904, a *"praeterhuman"* entity allegedly visited Crowley, to advise him that:

1. A new God had arrived in town – One whose ideas dovetailed seamlessly with Crowley's own philosophy.

2. The incoming deity furnished humanity with a new 'Bible,' **Liber L. vel Legis** – A work that couldn't have suited Crowley's purposes better had he penned it himself.

3. The old gods, and associated dogma, and society as a whole, would be destroyed in the transition – Bonus, or what!

4. Crowley was given a divinely-sanctioned mandate to lead the global rebuilding programme – Back of the net!!!

At the stroke of a Swan fountain pen Crowley transmuted a crumbling mass of neuroses into a Messiah, transformed his word into 'the Law,' and elevated his sexual preferences to the status of sacraments. By lunchtime on 10 April 1904, Crowley was 'cured,' and saviour of the world. Rather surprisingly, given the fringe benefits, he dithered for over five years before accepting Aiwass' alluring career opportunity.

The ninety-three million Dollar question is this - Is Horus the figurehead of Mankind's third epoch, or a despairing 'final solution' to quiet the voices screaming in Crowley's head? The latter compels all connected with the man's legacy, in whatever capacity, to a radical overhaul of stance. The former compels everyone on this planet to a fundamental reassessment of core belief systems. To some, my reduction of the Crowley conundrum to black or white may seem a gross generalisation. However, when boiled down to its essential components, Aleister Crowley was either a contemporary Jesus, or a deluded madman who orchestrated arguably the greatest practical joke of all time – Itself a notable achievement, albeit executed in the worst possible taste! This question haunts the contemplations of all with an interest. Until resolved, none will dare risk depositing their life-eggs in Crowley's basket.

Given the damning portrait of Crowley's character painted in this publication, and with reference to the evident 'failure to launch' of his New World Religion, Thelema, odds are that Crowley was almost certainly a false prophet. However, the gods move in mysterious ways. Over the next few chapters, I outline a mechanism capable of reconciling many inconsistencies in Crowley's claims, and one suggestive of a scenario by which Crowley simultaneously fulfils the roles of seer <u>and</u> psycho. As will shortly become clear, I believe that Aleister Crowley:

♦ Was a dangerous psychopath, though uniquely assisted by mental illnesses that would have fatally handicapped any other individual.

♦ Did form a Magickal Link with the gods of a new epoch, but misunderstood the nature of this communication.

♦ 'May' have received **Liber L. vel Legis** from a supernatural source, but could not have done so on 08, 09 & 10 April 1904.

♦ Correctly identified Thelema as the Word of a New Aeon, but failed to grasp its essential message, or simplicity.

♦ Was not merely the prophet of the New Aeon, but actually precipitated it!

Far from dawdling in the starting blocks, Thelema is taking the world by storm in a covert revolution overlooked by almost everyone. Today, millions of ordinary people blindly ride Crowley's 'Magickal Current' with no comprehension or even awareness of the forces reshaping every facet of their lives. Somewhat paradoxically, a few thousand individuals ideally positioned to understand the root causes of colossal changes sweeping across the globe, 'Thelemites,' have completely failed to equate these with the eventualities their guru spent his life attempting to define.

04.06   When is a New Aeon not a New Aeon?

For the remainder of his life, Crowley maintained a resolute insistence that the gods of a New Aeon chose him, uniquely, as a conduit through which to trumpet their imminent arrival. Crowley was also a product of his age. In his day, new messiahs emerged, regular as clockwork, each time the heavens ticked from one astrological sign to the next. In 1904, the reigning prophet (of Pisces), Jesus Christ, was packing his bags in readiness for retirement. Crowley calculated that, on purportedly receiving a New Covenant from God (i.e. **Liber L. vel Legis**), 'occult tradition' would compel an acceptance of him as supreme terrestrial authority of the incoming 'age' of Aquarius.

Before the ink used to scribe **Liber L. vel Legis** was dry, Crowley blasted a formal letter at Mathers (Head of the Golden Dawn). This advised Crowley's former boss of his dismissal and announced the Secret Chiefs' declaration to initiate a new Magickal Formula, with Crowley at its helm. Whilst in Cairo (April 1904), Crowley allegedly mailed letters to fifteen people, with the message: "*Eqx. of Gods come,*" and made three typed copies of **Liber L. vel Legis**. On 23 January 1905, Crowley commented to Clifford Bax:

> "*A thousand years from this moment, the world will be basking in the sunset of Crowleyanity.*"

Since each astrological age endures for slightly over two-thousand years, he almost certainly meant to say 'sunshine.' Nevertheless, it is clear that Crowley interpreted his New Aeon in terms of astrological symbolism and identified himself with Jesus (and Satan). Thelema (religion of the incoming era of Aquarius) was the successor to Christianity (religion of the outgoing epoch of Pisces). Not surprisingly, Crowley's adherence to the time-worn system founded on a succession of new equinoxes revered since ancient Egypt (as taught by the Golden Dawn) reflected in the title of his first major assault on occultism, **The Equinox**. Each of the ten issues comprising its first volume appeared on the spring and autumn equinox, between 1909 and 1913. Throughout his life, Crowley also distributed a biannual "*Word of the Equinox*" to disciples – A word usually transmitted through an inebriated and drugged Scarlet Woman! (See next page.)

Perhaps not wishing to become associated with the glib 'New Age' fad, Crowley defined Mankind's evolutionary path as comprising only three distinct phases – Isis, Osiris and Horus (correlating approximately with the astrological signs of Aries, Pisces and Aquarius). Whilst positing the existence of a fourth, Maat (Capricorn), his schema disregards all epochs preceding that of Aries.

Ex castro
Nemoris Inferioris

AIxx Sol in 0°0'0"
Aries

1947

Care Frater,

    Do what thou wilt shall be the whole of the Law.

    The Greetings of the Equinox of Spring!

    The Word of the Equinox is

    eft ~~LIFT~~ (Al III.45)

    The Oracle is

    Thee ~~THEE~~ (AL II.12)

    The Omen is Pi (xxii)

Love is the law, love under will,

    Yours fraternally,

To maya Oyecov 666
9° = 2° A∴A∴

Crowley was a product of his generation, and compromised by its limitations. In attempting to decipher Mankind's new rulebook he had no option but to use Old Aeon language and symbolism ground into him since birth. That Thelema evolved in accordance with an (anti-)Christian template, to resemble an intricate Victorian automaton constructed in strict compliance with regulations drafted by a clique of anal Freemasons, was almost inevitable. In grafting his subtle impressions of the New Aeon onto an obsolete superstructure, Crowley inadvertently condemned himself to years of fruitless intellectualisation. During this process, the essential message of Thelema was lost amidst Crowley's obsessive analysis of the letters and numbers comprising its name. That Crowley realised the supreme value of Sex Magick, but never grasped its essential relationship with the New Aeon of Horus, is a double tragedy. Had Crowley not become so deeply entrenched in the technicalities of Thelema, or if he'd paused for a moment to 'think outside the box,' it is likely that he would have made a connection of such magnitude as to guarantee a 'Page One' entry into the annals of history. He did not, and died *"perplexed,"* only one small step from stumbling over what is arguably the greatest discovery in recorded history, and a revelation that points our route to extraterrestrial life.

Crowley's genius was threefold. Firstly, he intuitively grasped that internal precursors and not external intervention from gods or aliens regulate the tempo of human development. Secondly, he deduced the unique signature of our previous two evolutionary gear shifts and correlated these to specific moments of dramatic historical upheaval in human culture. Finally, he – alone – noticed incidental adjustments in contemporary global trends symptomatic of the onset of a third surge. Crowley's only failing was a projection of his formless 'instincts' onto a metaphysical screen, as governed by a baffling hierarchy of deities and dogma. In reality, the 'solution' was closer-to-hand than Crowley could have possibly believed.

In his 'critical' essay on Crowley, entitled **The Star in the West**, J. F. C. Fuller boldly declared:

> *"Crowley is more than a new-born Dionysius, he is more than a Blake, a Rabelais or a Heine; for he stands before us as some priest of Apollo, hovering 'twixt the misty blue of the heavens and the more serious purple of the vast waters of the deep.*
>
> *It has taken 100,000,000 years to produce Aleister Crowley. The world has indeed laboured, and has at last brought forth a man."*

This estimation is perhaps a tad overzealous. However, it is reasonable to suggest that the world did wait around ten millennia for an insight matching the sheer world-changing enormity of one made long ago. Around 8,000BC, an attentive shepherd noted a regular incidence of the animals in his keep 'acting a bit odd' and connected this to a seemingly unrelated fact of nature occurring several months later – An observation that toppled the aeon of Isis and heralded that of Osiris. Ten-thousand years later, Aleister Crowley noticed the almost imperceptible indicators signifying the passing of Osiris and rise of Horus. For this singularly remarkable insight alone, Crowley ranks as a giant amongst men. [I explore these themes in the third part of this work.]

In April 1904, Crowley was a man close to complete breakdown. His ego, propelled by a small fortune and the mindset of a psychopath, had driven him to the very edge of sanity. The chasm between a pathological craving for recognition and his nefarious lifestyle was widening on a daily basis. His sense of perspective so divorced from any passing semblance of reality as to be salvageable only by direct intervention from the gods. At some level, **Liber L. vel Legis** was Crowley's 'last ditch' cure. As such, it is not difficult to understand why his fervent defence of it falls into the categories of 'grossly over-the-top' (especially the mathematical 'proof' reprinted in **Equinox of the Gods**) and 'is he trying to convince us, or him?'

Liber L. vel Legis was Crowley's shield against the formless horrors of madness. If **AL** crumbled, so did Crowley. Given this, it is possible to speculate that a less damaged man may not have squandered so much time defending his 'instinct' behind illusionary cast-iron warranties purportedly issued by God. A stronger man could have done a better job of identifying and promoting the message, and would not have become so obsessed with its packaging (and fringe benefits inherent with the position of 'Chosen One'), to the detriment of the product. Of course, the gods didn't select Crowley in consequence of his logistical prowess. In fact, they didn't actually seek him out, at all. Crowley just happened to be the right man, in the right place, at the right time. A unique blend of mental illness, personality and environment conspired to ensure that when a bolt from the New Aeon flashed into our world, Crowley's hand reached out to embrace it. The lightening grounded down the nearest conductor, and Crowley's innate flaws mutated the signal, accordingly. Thankfully, just enough of the Magickal Current survived its journey intact, and this divine spark lit the blue touch-paper of a revolution that is currently burning our world to its foundations.

Liber L. vel Legis is pivotal to Thelema. As such, and prior to asking what Thelema actually is, it may be a useful exercise to consider the origins of Crowley's Founding Document. Unfortunately, as many have discovered, the record is a bewildering mass of contradictions. Questions start piling up from the very first page.

04.07   A revealing revelation

I begin with a concise timeline charting the development of **Liber L. vel Legis**, as reproduced in various publications.

(01). **1904, 08, 09 and 10 April** – Original manuscript written.

(02). **1904, April** – Typescript plus two carbon copies created from manuscript.

(03). **1904, April** – Original manuscript misplaced.

(04). **1907, September** - Typescript submitted for publication in Volume Three of Crowley's **Collected Works**, but not included.

(05). **1909, 28 June** – Crowley rediscovers the **Liber L. vel Legis** manuscript in his attic, at Boleskine.

(06). **1910** – Typescript published, without comment, as first item in **THELEMA Volume Three (Holy Books)**.

(07). **1912, March** – **Equinox I, 7**, includes Crowley's first account of his reception of **Liber L. vel Legis**, plus facsimile of manuscript (at greatly reduced size), plus comment, but no typeset version.

(08). **1913, September** – **Equinox I, 10**, includes a corrected typescript of **Liber L. vel Legis**, without commentary or notes.

(09). **1926, 09 April** – '*Tunis*' edition of **Liber AL vel Legis**, comprising a reduced scale manuscript facsimile and comment, housed in a red presentation box. Only eleven copies printed.

(10). **1936, September – Equinox of the Gods (Equinox III, 3)**, includes first large scale facsimile of manuscript, plus comprehensive account of circumstances surrounding its reception.

Crowley also prepared a title page for **Liber L. vel Legis**. He never used this, nor is it included in any of innumerable published editions. Only twice has the enigmatic 'cover sheet' been reproduced in facsimile (**Magick**, Weiser, 1994 and the Cornelius' **Red Flame No. 8**, Berkeley, 2000) and it is generally regarded as something of an embarrassing curio. Similarly, until 2013, the typeset progression of Crowley's scribbled cover sheet (the aborted 1907 Appendix) was also virtually unknown and unpublished. A great pity, since these marginalised documents provide fascinating insights into the mental gymnastics Crowley employed in weaving fact and fiction to forge the great **AL** myth. As a general recap on material discussed previously, reproduced below are the two documents in question, plus a replica (within the limits of page-making software) of the notes Crowley wrote on his original cover sheet.

LIBER L. VEL LEGIS

GIVEN FROM THE MOUTH OF AIWASS TO THE EAR OF
THE BEAST ON APRIL, 8, 9, AND 10, 1904.

[This MS. (which came into my possession in July 1906) is a highly interesting example of genuine automatic writing.* Though I am in no way responsible for any of these documents, except the verse translations of the stele inscriptions, I publish them among my works, because believe that their intelligent study may be interesting and helpful. —A. C.]

(Note the accidental omission of the word "*I*" in Crowley's final sentence, the lack of a footnote that, on the corresponding handwritten cover sheet reads: "*i.e. I meant I could be...*" and addition of the word "*verse.*")

Liber
+
L.
vel
Legis.

given from the mouth of Aiwass to the ear of

The Beast

on April 8, 9 & 10, 1904.

**i. e. I meant I could
be its master from that
date a. c. oct '09

*MS. (which came into my possession** in July 1906)
[This* is a highly interesting example of genuine

automatic writing. Though I am in no way responsible
***except the translations of the Stele inscriptions
for any of these documents***, I publish them among my works, because

I believe that their intelligent study may be interesting & helpful. - A. C.]

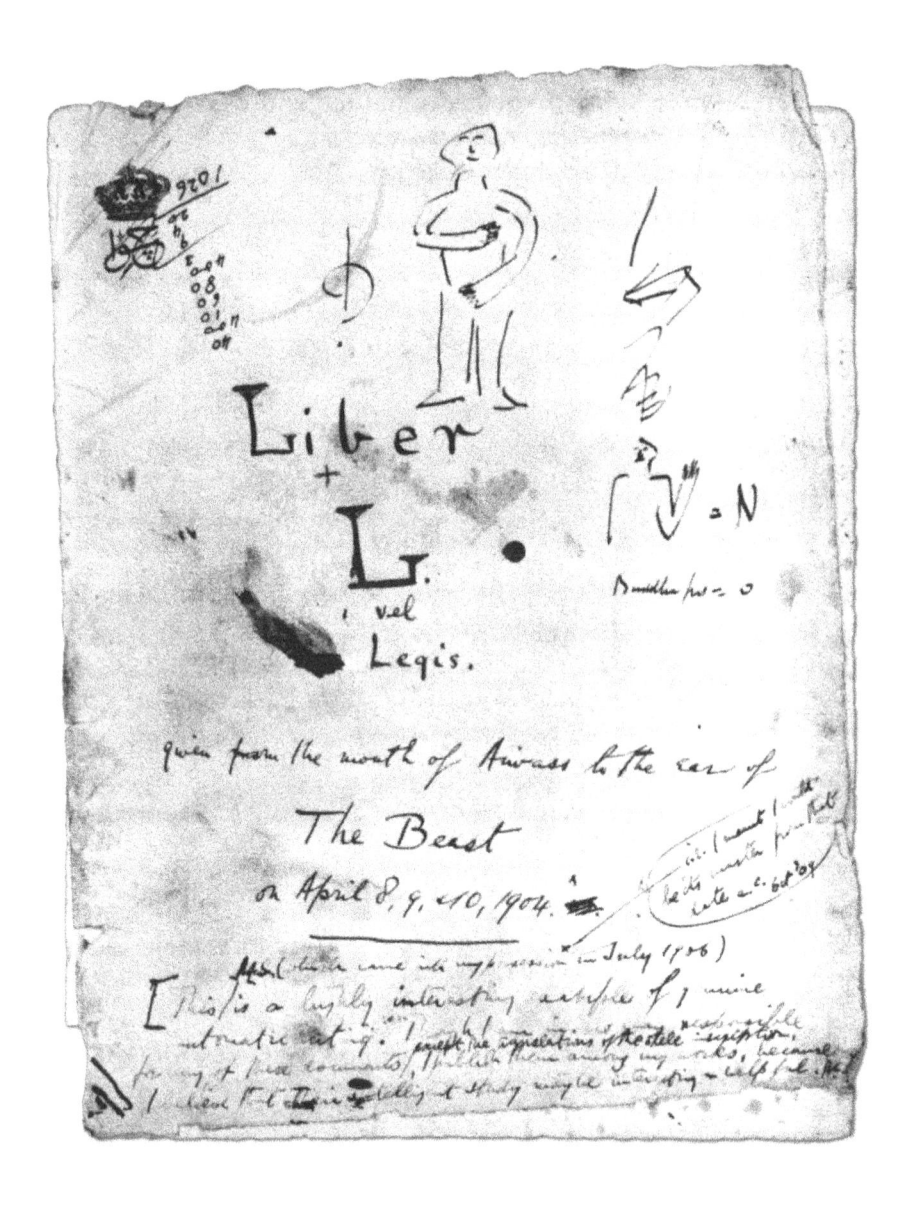

The deteriorating cover sheet's 'crown' motif (top left) identifies the paper as originating from the Grand Continental Hotel, Cairo. The manuscript itself comprises sixty-five leaves of *"Standard Typewriting Paper"* as produced by Scottish paper makers Alex Pirie & Sons. The significance of this I consider later. Incidentally, with respect to the watermark, all pages of Chapter One are 'the right way up,' whilst Crowley penned chapters Two and Three with the paper rotated by 180° (i.e. the watermark is upside down).

If taken at face value, both the handwritten cover sheet and typeset Appendix insist that **Liber L. vel Legis** was not written by Crowley, and only came into his possession in July 1906 – An acquisition not recorded in his diaries and correspondence. The statement also directly contradicts Crowley's assertion that the manuscript was lost between April 1904 and 28 June 1909. A subsequent note (dated *"Oct '09"*): *"I meant I could be its master from that date,"* merely adds to the confusion. Beneath its title Crowley declared, *"This is a highly interesting example of genuine automatic writing."* His use of the word 'genuine' is curious. Why specify? If not genuine, he wouldn't use the material, surely! Besides, if Crowley received the document from another, how can he be certain of its authenticity? As if deliberately wishing to cloud matters further, in **Equinox I, 7** (page 385) Crowley makes a monumental U-turn:

> *"Similarly, with respect to the writing of Liber Legis, Fra. P.* [Frater Perdurabo - Crowley's occult name] *will only say that it is in no way 'automatic writing...'"*

Furthermore, in distancing himself from any suspicion of authorship, *"except the translations of the Stele inscription,"* Crowley evidently forgets these are not actually present in either manuscript or typescript. A paraphrased versification (not the translation itself) is however present in the typescript of **Liber L. vel Legis** intended for inclusion (but not used) as an Appendix to **Collected Works Volume III**, and that published in the third volume of **The Holy Books** (1910). In this context, it may be of interest to mention a slight text alteration made by Crowley. The handwritten cover sheet states *"except the translations of the stele inscriptions,"* to which the later typeset Appendix adds a word, and now reads *"except the **verse** translations of the stele inscriptions."*

The cover sheet was prepared after the reception event, obviously. Given the priority Crowley assigned to ensuring the stele hieroglyphs were translated and versified in time for his rendezvous with Aiwass it seems inconceivable that he slipped-up on the title page - By claiming authorship of a French translation absent from the manuscript (and typescript) rather than his poetic interpretation, which was included. Did Crowley originally plan to incorporate Brugsch's translation into **Liber L. vel Legis**? If so, when did he change his mind in favour of the versification, and why?

It is to an exploration of Crowley's paraphrase, or versification, of the original French translation of stele hieroglyphics (or inscriptions) I now turn. Since nestling amidst the lines of this poem are several errors of monumental consequence. Below is comparison of **Liber L. vel Legis**, Chapter III, Verses 36-39, typescript and manuscript (differences highlighted in bold type).

"*36. Then said the prophet unto the God:*
37. I adore thee in the song -

   [Manuscript omits the remainder of verse 37, and gives:
   "I am the Lord of Thebes" etc. from vellum book
   Unity etc. ~~~~ "fill me"]

   I am the Lord of Thebes, *and I*
   The inspired forth-speaker of Mentu;
   For me unveils the veilèd sky,
   The self-slain Ankh-af-na-khonsu
   Whose words are truth. I invoke, I greet
   Thy presence, O Ra-Hoor-Khuit!

   Unity uttermost showed!
   I adore the might of Thy breath,
   Supreme and terrible God,
   Who makest the gods and death
   To tremble before Thee:-
   I, I adore thee!

   Appear on the throne of Ra!
   Open the ways of the Khu!
   Lighten the ways of the Ka!
   The ways of the Khabs run through
   To stir me or still me!
   Aum! let it fill me!

38. So that thy light is in me; & its red flame is as a sword in my hand to push thy order. There is a secret door that I shall make to establish thy way in all the quarters, (these are the adorations, as thou hast written), as it is said:

   [Manuscript omits the remainder of Verse 38, and gives:
   "The light is mine" etc.
   from vellum book to "Ra-Hoor-Khuit"]

   The light is mine*; its rays consume*
   Me: I have made a secret door
   Into the House of Ra and Tum,
   Of Khephra and of Ahathoor.
   I am thy Theban, O Mentu,
   The prophet Ankh-f-n-khonsu!

> *By Bes-na-Maut my breast I beat;*
> *By wise Ta-Nech I weave my spell.*
> *Show thy star-splendour, O Nuit!*
> *Bid me within thine House to dwell,*
> *O wingèd snake of light, Haditi!*
> *Abide with me, Ra-Hoor-Khuit!*

39. *All this and a book to say how thou didst come hither and a reproduction of this ink and paper for ever...*"

As seen in the scan below, Crowley later inserted a note into his original script, as follows:

[Original]	37	**I adore thee in the song**
[Insert]		"I am the Lord of Thebes" etc. from vellum book
[Original]		**Unity etc.**
[Insert]		~~~ "fill me"
[Original]	38	**So that thy light…**

Immediately after uttering the words "*I adore thee in the song,*" Aiwass continued, on the next line, with "*Unity...*" At this point, the astral envoy 'should' have followed with "*I am the Lord of....*" because this phrase is the initial line of the versification's second verse. Which 'should' follow its first, as was inserted earlier, in Chapter One. 'Unity' is actually the first word of the versification's <u>third</u> verse. Unbelievably, when dictating this part of the text, Aiwass **a)** erroneously believed that both verse one and two had already been incorporated into the opening chapter, or **b)** forgot about the second verse altogether.

With this correction ("*I am the Lord of Thebes*"), Crowley acknowledged and rectified the careless error of a supposedly ineffable praeterhuman entity – Assuming, of course, Aiwass didn't intentionally omit the second verse. In which case Crowley's forced re-entry of the divinely-deleted lines opens an entirely different (catering size) can of ectoplasm!

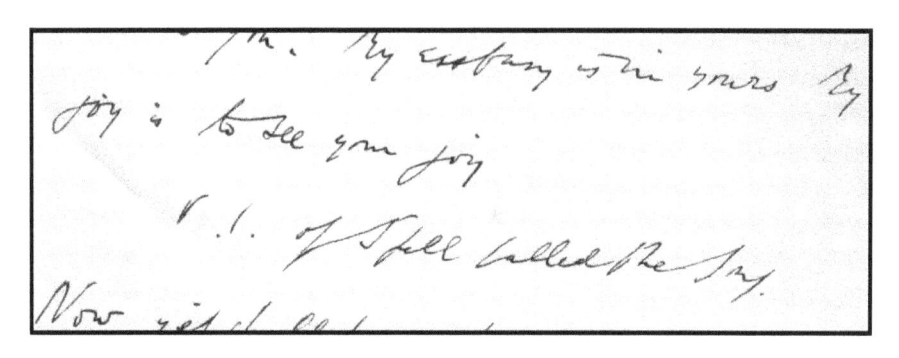

"V. 1. of spell called the Song" (**Liber L. vel Legis** I, 14 - manuscript)

As is clear from the above scan (assuming Crowley's dictation is reliable), only two days previously Aiwass specifically instructed him to insert "*V.*[erse] *1.*[one]" only.

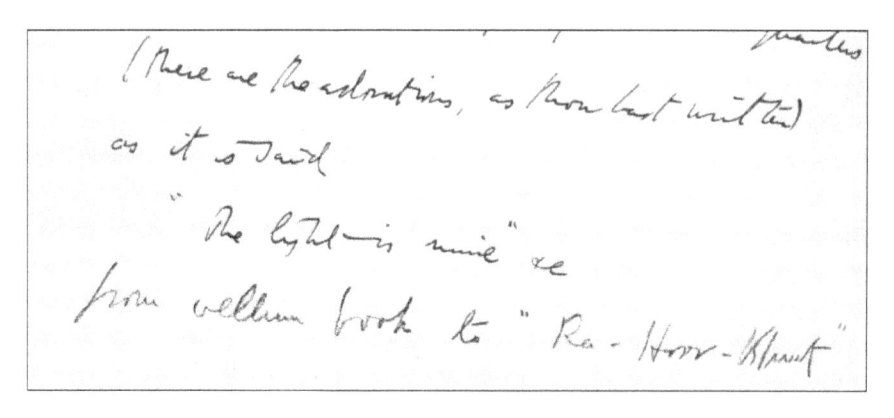

A related note, affixed to the following verse (III, 38), is also worthy of mention. As illustrated by the above scan, this references the source ("*vellum book to Ra-Hoor-Khuit*") of material Aiwass instructed Crowley to include. Of which (to save time) only the first line was dictated (namely verses five and six of the stele versification, beginning "*The light is mine*").

[Original]	**(these are the adorations, as thou hast written)**
[Original]	**as it is said**
[Original]	**"The light is mine" etc.**
[Insert]	From vellum book to "*Ra-Hoor-Khuit*"

In accordance with instructions dictated by Aiwass, stele paraphrase verses two through six were incorporated into Chapter Three (verses 37 & 38) of the typeset version of Crowley's handwritten manuscript. The initial six lines of his versification were utilised earlier, in the fourteenth verse of its first chapter. In this instance, again, the handwritten manuscript specifies only a reference to the material (*"V. 1. of spell called the Song"*) whereas the typeset version replaces this instruction with the corresponding lines:

> *"Above, the gemmed azure is*
> *The naked splendour of Nuit;*
> *She bends in ecstasy to kiss*
> *The secret ardours of Hadit.*
> *The winged globe, the starry blue*
> *Are mine, o Ankh-f-n-Khonsu."* (**Liber L. vel Legis** I, 14 - typescript)

This difference is instructive because it adds a title, *"the Song,"* (or possibly *"the Joy"* – As discussed on page 138) and description, *"spell,"* to material anonymously referenced in Chapter Three (verse 37 & 38). It also confirms that the material in question is definitely Crowley's versified paraphrase of the original French stele translation prepared for him by assistant curator of the *"Boulak"* museum, between 23 March and 07 or 08 April.

In addition to the troubling question of a praeterhuman entity with short-term memory loss, these three notes also raise a further curious anomaly. To explain: Ten minutes into the first hour of dictation, Aiwass confidently guided Crowley to extant material by means of its specific title (*"V. 1. of spell called the Song"*). Rather curiously, two days later, whilst dictating the final chapter Aiwass referred to the same versification, but in far more ambiguous terminology (III, 37 gives *"from vellum book,"* whilst III, 38 states *"vellum book to 'Ra-Hoor-Khuit'."*) Not only did Aiwass forget Verse Two of Crowley's stele paraphrase, this infallible messenger of the gods also failed to recall the title of material intended for subsequent inclusion!

On consideration of these points, it is difficult to escape a growing sense of incredulity. The sheer number of serious discrepancies and anomalies in even this small fragment of Crowley's reception story is, in itself, difficult to comprehend, and questionable. These suspicions are, to a degree, exacerbated by Crowley's equally faltering account of the circumstances under which he came to write his versified paraphrase of the stele translation, entitled *"the Song"* (or *"the Joy"*), in his *"vellum notebook."*

Crowley allegedly first encountered the stele *"before March 23rd,"* as is noted in **Equinox I, 7:**

> *"Fra. P. took her to the museum at Boulak, which they had not previously visited. [...] A glass case stood in the distance, too far off*

for its contents to be recognised. But W. recognised it! […] There was the image of Horus in the form of Ra Hoor Khuit painted on a wooden stele of the 26th dynasty – and the exhibit bore the number 666! […] This incident must have occurred before the 23rd of March, as the entry of that date refers to Ankh-f-n-Khonsu." (Page 368)

He immediately arranged a translation of its hieroglyphs:

"During this period March 23rd - April 8th, whatever else may have happened, it is at least certain that work was continued to some extent, that the inscriptions of the stele were translated for Fra. P., and that he paraphrased the latter in verse. For we find him using, or prepared to use, the same in the text of Liber Legis." (**Equinox I, 7**, Page 383)

He then puts his honeymoon on hold in order to prepare, at breakneck speed, a versified paraphrase of the translated stele hieroglyphs just in time for Aiwass to slip sections into the reception text.

"The versified paraphrase of the stele being ready, Aiwaz allowed me to insert these later, so as to save time." (**Equinox of the Gods**, page 119)

Why did Crowley feel a need to alert readers as to his authorship of a versified paraphrase in a manuscript he states came into his possession in *"July 1906,"* despite all evidence to the contrary? Why did he make such a point of separating a few lines of his poetry from the bulk of a text deceptively stated as the work of another? What is the meaning of numerous contradictory edits littering the cover sheet? To my mind, the mismatches highlighted in this chapter are not symptomatic of unavoidable defects inherent in passing pure tones through an imperfect instrument. Rather, they suggest adaptation, guile and a modification of form in response to both unforeseen circumstances and Crowley's evolving aspirations.

666 Perhaps the most conspicuous example of the unfortunate consequences of the use of these formulas is A.C. himself; but there are plenty of others that I know personally whose personal shipwreck has been just as complete, even though their small tonnage, so to say, makes the loss seem less deplorable than the disintegration of that great genius... 999

Paul Foster Case to Israel Regardie in a letter dated 10 August 1933

05.06 One 'L' of a riddle

Having noted some, of many issues raised by the enigmatic cover sheet and discarded 1907 Appendix, I now present a brief overview of the evolution of **Liber L. vel Legis**, as published between 1910 and 1936. This too raises numerous challenging questions and discrepancies.

Crowley intended to debut **Liber L. vel Legis** as an Appendix to the third volume of his **Collected Works** (1907). Corresponding material held at the Harry Ransom Humanities Research Center, Austin, Texas (acquired from the estate of J. F. C. Fuller, shortly after his death in 1966) identifies this Appendix as deriving from an earlier (Cairo) typescript containing numerous errors. For reasons unknown, Crowley ultimately dropped the prototype **Liber L. vel Legis** from **Collected Works**. However, surviving galley proofs (unpublished until 2013, on www.lashtal.com) demonstrate his intent to use the prefacing introduction (i.e. *"... given from the mouth of Aiwass, etc."*) in 1907. It is also interesting to note that Crowley changed the title, from:

"Liber + L. vel Legis given from the mouth of Aiwass to the ear of The Beast on April 8, 9 & 10, 1904" (as written on the handwritten cover sheet and aborted (1907) Appendix)

to

"Liber L. vel Legis sub figura CCXX [220] as delivered by LXXVIII [78] unto DCLXVI [666]" (as printed in **Volume Three** (1910) of the **Holy Books**)

Even a fleeting comparison of the cover sheet, (1907) Appendix, (1910) **Holy Books** and (1913) **Equinox I, 10** highlights a dramatic and wholly unanticipated sequence of revisions. During this period, Crowley **1)** Changed the title of his revelatory document, **2)** Removed information pertaining to its reception dates, **3)** Transformed names into numerals **4)** Dropped the *"automatic writing"* reference and insistence on its authorship by someone other than Crowley and **5)** Divided the text into two-hundred and twenty segments. Not to mention the rather dubious fact that he still hadn't figured out the correct spelling of Aiwass by 1909, so retained his original numerological equivalent of '78' (AIVAS), which he subsequently altered to '93' (OIVZ) by means of a convoluted substitution of letters. To my mind, the multiplicity of changes, revisions, edits and amendments is not consistent with a text of supposedly divine origin and is again more reminiscent of adjustments compelled by changes in terrestrial circumstance.

Crowley insisted that he misplaced the handwritten manuscript soon after departing Cairo (April 1904). This improbable assertion is, on first glance, supported by (1907) galley proofs held at the Harry Ransom Center. The typeset version of **Liber L.** in this collection replicates errors present in Crowley's earlier typescript (allegedly from 1904), as were generated in the original transcription process from handwritten manuscript to typescript. It is therefore reasonable to suggest that Crowley did not have access to his original manuscript in 1907 - Otherwise he would have used it to address these errors… surely.

According to Crowley's account, the handwritten manuscript surfaced (in his attic) on 28 June 1909 - A fortuitous rediscovery affording him an opportunity to refer back to his original source document and make long-overdue corrections to transcription errors littering the extant typescript. Alas, not in time for the first public manifestation of **Liber L. vel Legis** in the (1910) third volume of **THELEMA – The Holy Books**, which surprisingly appeared with errors. A corrected version did finally appear five years later, in **Equinox I, 10** (September 1913). Somewhat paradoxically, Crowley purportedly misplaced his manuscript between 1904 and 1909, but clearly retained possession of its cover sheet – He scribbled notes on this and used it as a basis for the Appendix preamble in autumn 1907!

Liber L. vel Legis is finally published (with errors) in 1910, as the first item in **THELEMA - The Holy Books, Volume III**. Prefaced by a title page and headed "*LIBER L. VEL LEGIS,*" its familiar text (beginning "*Had! The manifestation of Nuit*") reproduced without introduction, explanation or notes. It is, again, curious that Crowley omitted the French translation, two Enochian Calls, "*The Great Invocation*" and numerous notes included in the 1907 Appendix version. He actually published only the three verses of **Liber L. vel Legis**, without comment, as merely one amongst a collection of "*inspired writings.*"

Though now reunited with his missing manuscript (lost since April 1904), Crowley did not employ it to correct transcription errors still embedded in a typescript now used for both **Holy Books, Volume III** and the aborted 1907 Appendix. Why was Crowley so sloppy in making crucial alterations to a document vital to the future evolution and survival of Mankind?

Three years later, in March 1912, Crowley returned to **Liber L. vel Legis in Equinox I, 7**. Inexplicably, he ignored yet another opportunity to present the world with a corrected typescript. Despite including a protracted narration of events culled from his personal diary and **The Book of Results**, plus colour facsimiles of the stele with "*a paraphrase of its hieroglyphs*" (front and reverse) and lengthy comment, Crowley omitted a typeset version! In place of this, he reproduced a facsimile of the sixty-five manuscript pages (its debut publication) at minute scale - Each page measured slightly over an inch in height and was virtually impossible to read. Crowley explained his editorial decision with a curiously phrased note, which reads:

> "*The reproduction of **Liber Legis** has been done thus minutely in order to prevent the casual reader from wasting his valuable time over it.*"

Eighteen months later, in September 1913, Crowley finally deemed it appropriate to include a corrected typescript, in **Equinox I, 10**. He published this under the same title as that given in **THELEMA Volume III**, and without comment. Again, as if seemingly unable to contain an impulse to giggle at some private joke, Crowley prefaced the text with a singularly odd comment, which reads:

> "*It is of course common knowledge that the A∴ A∴ and the Equinox and all the rest are a stupid joke of Aleister Crowley's. He merely wished to see if anyone were fool enough to take him seriously. Several have done so, and he does not regret the few thousand pounds it has cost him.*
>
> *Few people are ignorant of the fact that the A∴ A∴ and the Equinox and all the rest of it are a dishonest device of Aleister Crowley's to pile up an enormous fortune in a few months. With the three-and-a-half million sterling he has made he will now retire to Paris and emulate Nero, Caligula, Vitellius, Messalina, Heliogabalus and others.*
>
> *It may be a relief to some to learn that there is no such person as Aleister Crowley. He is probably a sun-myth.*"

Thirteen years later, on 09 April 1926, Crowley privately issued eleven copies of **Liber AL vel Legis sub figura CCXX as delivered to XCIII [93] = 418.** This was a deluxe red 'box-set' comprising a facsimile reprint (at a decent size) of the manuscript plus selected notes, including the "*Extenuation*" and short 'Tunis' comment. Crowley distributed eight copies amongst acquaintances, the remaining three he offered for general sale. This very limited edition is the first to use 'AL' in preference to 'L.' and incorporates a change of number in the title, from '78' to '93' = 418.'

OS K3   Warburg 2002 index
Binder containing loose sheets, some stapled together
(1) 'Liber L. vel. Legis Sub Figura CCXX as delivered by (LXXVIII) XCIII unto DCLXVI with a commentary by TO MEGA THERION 666'. Copy of the original manuscript of Cephaloedium Working Commentary. Copied from holograph notebook in the possession of J. P. Kowal who obtained it from Achad's widow (16 pp.)
(2) 'The Commentary Called D(jeridensis)' with corrections in the hands of Alostrael and G. J. Y. [The Holograph MS in A. C. Holograph MSS 16] (61 pp.)
(3) Typescript with corrections in A. C.'s hand for the edition of *The Book of the Law* of which 11 copies were published [privately in typescript] in 1926 [titled *An Extenuation of the Book of the Law*]. (4 pp.)
(4) Liber 31 by Frater Achad. [Yorke note: 'A. C. accepted this as a valid Qabalistic comment *on Liber Legis*.'] (39 pp.)
(5) 'Liber QNA vel NOMEN DEI sub figura CLI by Frater Achad. [Yorke note: 'A. C. accepted this, I think, as a good Qabalah'.] (9 pp.)
(6) Notes on *Liber Legis* - 8-9 August 1936 by Frater Achad. Copies from a letter to G. J. Y. (1 pp)
(7) 'Christ and the Message of the Master Therion'. Probably by Frater Achad (typescript found among his papers). Copied from a typescript in possession of Dr J. P. Kowal (3 pp.)
[Mic. 136pp]

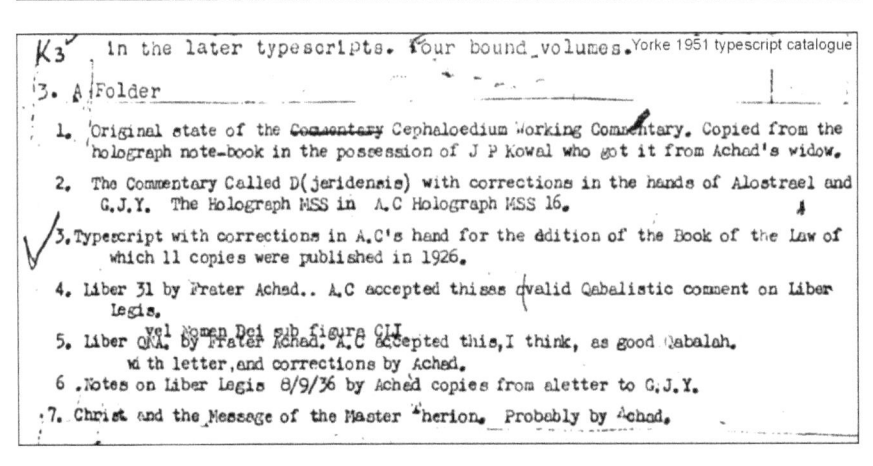

K3' in the later typescripts. Four bound volumes. Yorke 1951 typescript catalogue
3. A Folder
  1. Original state of the Commentary Cephaloedium Working Commentary. Copied from the holograph note-book in the possession of J P Kowal who got it from Achad's widow.
  2. The Commentary Called D(jeridensis) with corrections in the hands of Alostrael and G.J.Y. The Holograph MSS in A.C Holograph MSS 16.
  3. Typescript with corrections in A.C's hand for the ddition of the Book of the Law of which 11 copies were published in 1926.
  4. Liber 31 by Frater Achad.. A.C accepted this as a valid Qabalistic comment on Liber Legis.
  5. Liber QNA vel Nomen Dei sub figura CLI by Frater Achad. A.C accepted this, I think, as good Qabalah. with the letter, and corrections by Achad.
  6. Notes on Liber Legis 8/9/36 by Achad copies from a letter to G.J.Y.
  7. Christ and the Message of the Master Therion. Probably by Achad.

The 2002 Warburg catalogue entry for 'OSK3,' item 3' differs slightly from Yorke's 1951 typescript description (see above). "*An Extenuation of the Book of the Law*" was Crowley's first comment on **Liber L. vel Legis**.

In September 1936, some three decades after allegedly receiving his new Bible and promotion to Messiah, Crowley published his definitive word on the subject – **Equinox III, 3 - The Equinox of the Gods**. It has been a long, strange journey and one that leaves many perplexing questions hanging in the air.

With general reference to the reception component of Crowley's account, I remain unable to discern a 'reasonable' justification for Aiwass' insistence that only three, one-hour time slots were available for the dictation. Given the supreme importance of this material, to Crowley and Mankind, and the extensive 'divine' preparations made to facilitate the smooth transit of Equinoxes, why squeeze the 'all-important' transmission through the eye of a needle? Why compel Crowley to write at a pace virtually guaranteed to generate errors, and within a schedule allowing no time whatsoever to recap on words and phrases heard indistinctly? Perhaps Crowley felt a need to emphasise the '666' connection by use of subtle references (i.e. '**3** x **60** minutes' is suggestive of 'three sixes.' There are **3,6**00 seconds in each hour, etc.). On this theme, **Liber L. vel Legis** includes a curious instruction. In **Chapter II, Verse 54**, Aiwass advises Crowley:

> "*The stops as thou wilt; the letters? change them not in style or value!*"

This line addresses the very real problem of 'punctuation.' In consideration of the speed at which Crowley was obliged to write, and his alleged unfamiliarity with the material, it seems to me entirely likely that the manuscript should contain several instances in which Crowley wrote "*com,*" "*semi-col,*" or "*full st*" before realising that Aiwass was indicating a pause, and not continuing the narrative. If Aiwass did possess foresight enough as to include a dictate alleviating this potential source of hesitation (and resultant breakdown of flow) on Crowley's part, why not do so at the start!

Throughout his life, Crowley never missed an opportunity to bitch about discrepancies littering the first two publications of **Liber L. vel Legis**. Both of which derive from the initial typescript (plus two carbon copies) Crowley allegedly prepared whilst in Cairo (April 1904). At this point, I raise a possibility that, on first reading, sounds absurd. I ask that you consider a notion that the differences Crowley repeatedly bemoaned were not, as one would naturally assume, a consequence of transcribing a handwritten source to typescript form. Rather, they actually occurred during the converse process - When preparing the manuscript from an extant typescript! Remember that, according to Crowley's own account, the manuscript was lost between April 1904 and June 1909. For five years, it was for all practicable purposes nonexistent. Who actually saw Crowley's manuscript, ever, prior to the 'thumb-nail' glimpse published in **Equinox I, 7**?

I close this chapter with an oddity relating to an advertisement that appeared in **Equinox III, 1 – The Blue Equinox** (1919). This lists Crowley's three **Holy Books**, though refers to them only as "*Libers*" and, curiously, presents them in the wrong sequence (again!) The content of the first book, **Liber VII**, corresponds with **THELEMA Volume Two**. The second relates to **THELEMA Volume Three** (even with the typos - "*CXX*" should read 'CCXX' and "*CCCXII*" should read 'DCCCXII'). The third listing correlates with **THELEMA Volume One**.

THE WORKS OF ALEISTER CROWLEY

ACELDAMA	$50.00	ORACLES	$4.00
THE TALE OF ARCHAIS	2.50	ORPHEUS (Two Volumes)	6.00
SONGS OF THE SPIRIT	2.50	GARGOYLES	2.00
JEPHTHAH AND OTHER		ROSA MUNDI	10.00
MYSTERIES	2.50	ROSA INFERNI	10.00
THE MOTHER'S TRAGEDY	4.00	ROSA COELI	10.00
JEZEBEL	20.00	RODIN IN RIME	25.00
THE SOUL OF OSIRIS	4.00	IN RESIDENCE	1.00
ALICE; AN ADULTERY	5.00	SIR PALAMEDES	2.00
AN APPEAL TO THE AMERICAN		AMPHORA	2.00
REPUBLIC	5.00	HAIL MARY	0.50
CARMEN SAECULARE	1.00	HOUSEHOLD GODS	5.00
TANNHÄUSER	4.00	KONX OM PAX	5.00
THE GOD-EATER	2.00	MORTADELLO	5.00
THE STAR AND THE GARTER	0.25	THE WINGED BEETLE	5.00
THE ARGONAUTS	4.00	AMBERGRIS	2.00
AHAB	3.00	THE BOOK OF LIES	5.00
THE SWORD OF SONG	10.00	LITTLE POEMS IN PROSE	1.35
WHY JESUS WEPT	5.00	CLOUDS WITHOUT WATER	5.00

THE EQUINOX. VOLUME I. TEN NUMBERS.
 Averaging 400 pages. Numerous Illustrations. One Hundred Dollars the Set. Rare. Essential. The Encyclopaedia of Occultism.

BOOK 4. THE ELEMENTS OF MYSTICISM AND MAGICK.
 Part I. Mysticism $0.25
 Part II. Magick (Theory) 0.50
 Part III. Magick (Practice) 1.00
 Part IV. The Law 2.00

COLLECTED WORKS OF ALEISTER CROWLEY (India Paper).
 Three Volumes 10.00
 Bound in Vellum, ties, with photographs 15.00
LIBER VII 5.00
 (Japanese vellum, black and gold, bound in vellum)
LIBRI CXX, XXVII, CCCXIII 15.00
 (Japanese vellum, black and gold, bound in vellum)
LIBRI LXI and LXV 5.00
 (Japanese vellum, black and gold, bound in vellum)
THE STAR IN THE WEST, by Captain J. F. C. Fuller 1.50

THE UNIVERSAL PUBLISHING CO.
Retail Department
57 Grand River Avenue   Detroit, Michigan

05.08 Between the lines on missing pages

Questions surrounding Crowley's reception of **Liber L. vel Legis** are nothing new. This is hardly surprising given that he spent two decades editing the text, in direct contradiction to the dictating angel's five explicit commands, which are:

I, 36. My scribe Ankh-af-na-khonsu, the priest of the princes, shall not in one letter change this book; but lest there be folly, he shall comment thereupon by the wisdom of Ra-Hoor-Khuit.

I, 52. If this be not aright; if ye confound the space-marks, saying: They are one; or saying, They are many; if the ritual be not ever unto me: then expect the direful judgments of Ra Hoor Khuit!

I, 54. Change not as much as the style of a letter; for behold! thou, o prophet, shalt not behold all these mysteries hidden therein.

II, 54. The stops as thou wilt; the letters? change them not in style or value!

III, 47. This book shall be translated into all tongues: but always with the original in the writing of the Beast; for in the chance shape of the letters and their position to one another: in these are mysteries that no Beast shall divine.

Crowley prepared his account of the Cairo Revelation from two primary sources. His private diary and a small vellum notebook (OS27) titled **Invocation of Hoor** (of which **The Book of Results** forms a small part – Inverted, at its rear). Of his diary, Crowley admits:

"This diary is extremely incomplete and fragmentary. Many entries, too, are evidently irrelevant or 'blinds.' We omit much of the latter two types." (**Equinox of the Gods**, page 67)

"Fra. P. never made a thorough record of this period. He seems to have wavered between absolute scepticism in the bad sense, a dislike of the revelation, on the one hand, and real enthusiasm on the other. And the first of these moods would induce him to do things to spoil the effect of the latter. Hence the 'blinds' and stupid meaningless ciphers which deface the diary.

And, as if the Gods themselves wished to darken the Pylon, we find later, when P.'s proud will had been broken and he wished to make straight the way of the historian, his memory (one of the finest memories in the world) was utterly incompetent to make everything certain." (**Equinox of the Gods**, page 69)

The diary entries reproduced in **Equinox I, 7** and **Equinox of the Gods** are indeed an unintelligible mess. The question is - Why did Crowley make such a poor job? On browsing these cryptic fragments it is difficult to escape a notion they sketch the faint outline of a subplot covertly woven beneath the narration, but why would he write 'in code,' in his own private diary? On a positive note, Crowley offered a crumb of comfort:

"We have one quite unspoiled and authoritative document.

*'The **Book of Results**,' written in one of the small Japanese vellum note-books which he used to carry."* (**Equinox of the Gods**, page 69)

However, he obscured even this ray of light behind a caveat:

"Unfortunately, it seems to have been abandoned after five days. What happened between March 23rd and April 8th?"

The Book of Results is anything but *"unspoiled and authoritative,"* and actually covers the period from 16 to 23 March – That's eight days and not *"five,"* as suggested by Crowley. Nor does it mention the events of 08, 09 & 10 April, or a trip to the *"Boulak Museum,"* or cross-examination of Rose. Similarly, and quite inexplicably, his private diary makes no mention of these momentous occurrences, either! Of course, **Equinox of the Gods** contains only selected information culled from personal notes. Thanks to Gerald Yorke, Crowley's handwritten source material survives (at the Warburg Institute, London). In 1951, Yorke indexed this (Folder OS27) as follows:

"[OS]27. Small Japanese vellum notebook. 1904
1. Invocation of Horus…
2. Ritual B 2. To have knowledge.

3. 1904 Summer. Work at Bol(eskine)…
4. The planets…
5. The Book of Results. Cairo 1904."

> 5. Baphomet seal, Babalon seal, Eye in Triangle seal all in gold.
> 27. Small Japanese vellum notebook. 1904
>   1. Invocation of Horus according to the Divine Vision of Ouarda the Seer (1904)
>   2. Ritual B 2. To have any Knowledge.
>   3. 1904 Summer. Work at Bol(eskine) with Bee(zebub). 5 pages have been torn out.
>   4. The Planets and the signs of the Zodiac.
>   5. The Book of Results. Cairo 1904.

Each of the five segments written in this small vellum notebook presents numerous significant challenges to Crowley's reception myth, as detailed at length in subsequent chapters. Even a cursory glance at the section titles should immediately result in the involuntary raising of an eyebrow and a grunt of puzzlement. Do you see the problem? For the benefit of anyone unable to 'join the dots,' I offer a broad hint – Start at Cairo, in April 1904, with Ouarda the Seer. Who knows where you 'had any knowledge' with the "*B2*" ritual, but the summer of 1904 finds you at Boleskine, Scotland. Who knows where you examined the "*Planets and signs of the zodiac,*" but this work mysteriously relocates you back to Cairo, in… April 1904. Now, *that's* Magick! At face value, the chronological sequence of titles, alone, ruptures Crowley's account. As suggested in my Introduction, the only way of explaining this discrepancy is a suggestion that OS27 is an 'out of sequence' copy of material written in an earlier notebook, perhaps even the same "*now-lost contemporary vellum notebook*" conjured to support the recent 'f-k' change. Of course, OS27 *is* contemporary with Cairo, April 1904. So, why would Crowley need to duplicate content?

In 2010, researcher Marcus Katz published (for the first time) the content of OS27 in a slim volume entitled **The Invocation of Hoor**. A comparison of this with material reproduced in **Equinox I, 7** and **Equinox of the Gods** reveals several notable omissions, and provides numerous hints towards an explosive revelation.

Crowley's published accounts of events in Cairo climax at 1PM on 10 April 1904, when Aiwass finished dictating the third and final chapter of **Liber L. vel Legis**. Crowley may now be the vessel of a New Aeon, but for a newly-married man and expectant father, life went on. As such, it is worthwhile to look briefly at events that transpired in the weeks and months following Aiwass' great revelation. For this I now turn to **Equinox I, 8** (September 1912), OS27 and **The Invocation of Hoor**.

*"It was about a fortnight after writing **Liber Legis** that Fra. P. left Egypt for the grey skies of the Scottish Highland, where, with the Seer [Rose, his wife], he began to put into practice the experiments suggested in the **Book of the Law**.*

The upshot of it all was that on the birth of a child [on 28 July 1904] *he had completely put everything aside. He played at Yoga for about a week during the summer, and took some little trouble to disperse the wreckage of the 'Rosicrucians,' which constituted a danger to navigation, the wretch Mathers having by now abandoned all pretence at magic, and mingled stupid sorceries with his bouts of intoxication, ever more frequent and prolonged. This service to humanity he successfully performed; the 'Rump' of the London Temple was dispersed, and its chief, his occupation gone, left to the more diverting pastime of trying to dodge the Criminal Law Amendment Act."* (The Temple of Solomon the King – The Babe, **Equinox I, 8**)

"*About a fortnight after,*" correlates approximately with 24 April. Since Crowley dined with Arnold Bennett on 26 April, in Paris, his account suggests it took only two days to complete a journey of two-and-a-half thousand miles – Half of which is over water. After this, he detoured briefly to London and arrived back at Boleskine towards the end of April 1904. Once home, Crowley did indeed experiment with occult practices suggested by **Liber L. vel Legis**. His Cakes of Light certainly appear to have manifested a most peculiar species of beetle! (See **Confessions**, page 408) He also waged occult war on Mathers – A hilarious sequence of events also described in **Confessions** (Chapter 50). What Crowley neglects to mention is the technique he's utilising to hurl Magickal missiles at his arch enemy. Fortunately, Marcus Katz's book, **The Invocation of Hoor**, includes a passage Crowley omitted from all published works. In the third section of his "*Small Japanese Vellum notebook* (OS27)" (titled "*1904 Summer at Bol* [eskine]. *With Beel* [zabub]" by Yorke), Crowley wrote:

"*13 30 9 or 9 30 50*

Beelz [in triangle] cleaned up

Revelation of ritual to consecrate talismans of XXII against G∴ D∴

[B = Beast = A.C.   S.W. = Scarlet Woman] [His wife, Rose. G.Y.]

Beast standing feet on floor astride R's S.W.'s

Head on ground to E.

Arse very high

Feet on floor

This <u>climax</u> invokes R.H.K.

Incense thereof offered on Outer Altar

B put it in a bowl with oil of Abramelin

B is in [triangle] in E (apex to W)"

Though written in cipher, this seemingly describes a rite of Sex Magick. A further reference occurs in a section of the **Book of Results** chronicling a *"long and futile Tarot divination."* The specifics of which are omitted from all published editions (with the exception of Marcus Katz's **The Invocation of Hoor**). In this private notebook, Crowley overtly declares, *"the ritual is of sex!"* His subsequent omission and, indeed, 'blanket-suppression' of this material is questionable on several fronts. Notably because it contradicts Crowley's claim of ignorance as to the miraculous properties of Sexual Magick until his 1912/13 meeting with Theodor Reuss. – An encounter described in **Confessions** (Chapter 50). Secondly, nowhere in any published work does Crowley even mention in passing the Sex Magick aspects of his time in Cairo. For self-evident reasons, the inexplicable absence of this material is a deeply suspicious oversight on Crowley's part.

The most intriguing sentence relates not to any particular detail of the ritual itself, but rather to Crowley's motivation for initiating the sexual shenanigans:

"Revelation of ritual to consecrate talismans of XXII against G∴ D∴"

"XXII" is a reference to the twenty-two Tarot trumps of the Major Arcana and *"G∴ D∴"* refers to Crowley's former mystical fraternity, the Golden Dawn. As if to emphasise his preoccupation with the destruction of this occult group and its leader, Crowley scribes a second note in his

vellum notebook (OS27) and, again, omits this from all published editions. His vitriolic barb reads:

> "G∴ D∴ to be destroyed, i.e. publish its history and its papers." (**The Invocation of Hoor**, page 52)

True to his word, Crowley served notice to Mathers (in 1909) of his intent to publish secret Golden Dawn rituals in a bulky periodical entitled **The Equinox**. On hearing this, Mathers immediately raced back from Paris to lodge an injunction preventing any such public disclosure. Crowley successfully appealed, and duly reproduced the sensitive material.

Crowley's (OS27) notes clearly indicate that the Cairo Revelation pertained exclusively to his awareness of a new occult methodology, Sex Magick, and not the reception of **Liber L. vel Legis**, which isn't even mentioned. In Egypt, Crowley formed a notion that the gods of a New Equinox armed their 'Chosen One' with the occult tools required to destroy the Golden Dawn and its head, the despised Mathers. Only on accomplishment of this precursor is Crowley 'qualified' to form the requisite Magical Link and 'receive' a new Magical Formula from the Secret Chiefs.

Before moving on from a general theme of 'material omitted from Crowley's published works,' I mention two further oddities associated with the vellum notebook (OS27).

1 - In Equinox of the Gods (page 77), Crowley notes:

> "*23* [March 1904] *The Secret of Wisdom.*
> *(We omit the record of a long and futile Tarot divination.)*"

Prior to 2010, anyone wishing to read the specifics of Crowley's "*long and futile Tarot divination*" could do so only by visiting the Warburg Institute and requesting access to Crowley's original source notebook, namely OS27. In 2010, Marcus Katz did the Thelemic community a great service by publishing a full transcript of OS27 (including the long and futile Tarot divination) in a book called **The Invocation of Hoor** [This should not be confused with Crowley's original vellum notebook (OS27) titled **Invocation of Hoor**].

Reading the three short pages of neat handwritten notes comprising Crowley's omitted "*long and futile Tarot divination*" is quite a revelation - As Mr Katz explains:

> *"In this previously unpublished section which Crowley described as 'a long and futile Tarot divination' we see that it is hardly a divination but rather an extended prose piece based on the Minor Arcana of the Tarot and their correspondences – through the astrological Decans – to a personal cosmology,"* (**The Invocation of Hoor**, page 39)

In short, Crowley's (published) description bears absolutely no resemblance to its corresponding (unpublished) source material (in OS27). Furthermore, and as Mr. Katz perceptively observes:

> *"These lines here are the precursor to the establishment of The Book of Thoth as a pictorial narrative of the Thelemic cosmology developed by Crowley."* (**The Invocation of Hoor**, page 40)

That Crowley deleted from the record material arguably of comparable import to his experiences in Cairo, is baffling. That he derisively fobbed it off as "*a long and futile Tarot divination,*" is inexplicable. Of course, this discrepancy begs the question – Why mention it, at all? Why draw attention to a Tarot divination that will inevitably precipitate in everyone who happens to read it the same 'difficult' questions as those raised by Marcus Katz?

2 – Crowley's vellum notebook (OS27) is not complete. At some point in time, 'someone' crudely ripped away several pages. These are still 'missing.' Reproduced below is a transcript of notes Crowley wrote on the page immediately preceding the expunged items:

> *"There is to be a physical sign of these pantacles they appear to decay or fade when charged.*
>
> *[Tell Jones this]*
>
> *[missing pages torn out*
> *G.J.Y. by Charles Stansfeld Jones or Frater Achad?]*
>
> *General idea of ceremony to become R.H.K. also to devote oneself to him by a Grand Method; thence directly to vivify Avenger."*

Marcus Katz reproduces this entry in his **The Invocation of Hoor** (on page 36), but omits two words (**The Invocation of Hoor** gives: "*There is to be a physical sign of these pantacles they appear to decay when charged.*") He also combines two separate notebook pages, deviates from Crowley's original page order, inserts a note ("*[4 pages missing]*") not present in Crowley's original vellum notebook and which contradicts Yorke's own 1951 catalogue entry: "*5 pages have been torn out.*" These minor imperfections are annoying, and undoubtedly impede the research of anyone investigating this mystery without a copy of Crowley's handwritten notebook (OS27). Nonetheless, Katz **The Invocation of Hoor** is still a most worthwhile companion on this journey. Unfortunately, it was withdrawn from circulation, at the behest of (C)O.T.O. Inc. within days of release and is now a difficult title to locate.

At time of writing the lines in question, Crowley had returned from Cairo and was experimenting with 'sexual talismans' consecrated to destroy the Golden Dawn. His note is unusual insomuch as it employs a distinctly larger, more 'open' handwriting style suggestive of 'excitement.' The last entry on this page ("*General idea of a ceremony to become R.H.K., etc.*") refers to information written on the five (now) missing pages. What possible reasons compelled 'someone' to tear this material from Crowley's notebook?

666 The man operating under the codename of 'the Master Therion' is an unscrupulous and very dangerous confidence trickster and imposter skilful at extorting money from religious seekers disillusioned with the church, and hysterical nymphomaic women.

Translated extract from the German Intelligence Service dossier on the Master Therion. 666

06.07   The lost words, found...

I first encountered photocopies of Crowley's then unpublished cover sheet and galley proofs of the aborted 1907 Appendix in the mid-1980s. Both of these enigmatic documents piqued my curiosity, but, as with many other discrepancies collected over the following three decades, I contented myself to file them on a back-burner.

Then, at 4AM on Saturday 03 November 2012, Crowley unexpectedly burst to the forefront of my mind in consequence of two singularly curious incidents I feel of such import as to be demanding of inclusion. I do not wish to overstate the significance of what I will call 'subliminal triggers.' Nonetheless, the experience unquestionably provided a vital stepping-stone between 'questions' and 'clarity.'

On the morning of Friday 02 November, whilst reviewing material already collated, and highlighting items still to prepare, the immense significance of a quote I happened upon the previous evening suddenly sprung to mind. Intrigued, I opened my notebook and flicked through entries made over the last twenty-four hours. Much to my frustration, I was unable to find any reference to *that* specific passage, and spent all afternoon trawling through source material I'd read the previous day – To no avail. The fact I'd overlooked a quote that should have 'stood out like a sore thumb,' compounded my frustration.

Surprisingly, since I evidently paid scant attention to the material first time around, my memory retained a vivid impression of text I had stumbled over in a PDF document. The relevant item comprised a scan of two consecutive book pages (the quote appeared in the third paragraph, on the left-hand page). The book's red cover over-spilled page edges by approximately quarter-of-an-inch and a grey scanner bed was clearly visible in the background.

Enthused by this visual clue, I searched through all publications, documents, digital scans and online sources perused during the previous week and, again, failed to locate the quote. By the time I retired to bed on the evening of Saturday 03 November, I had reluctantly conceded that the elusive quote never existed. In all likelihood, I'd read it in a dream! The page in question, scanned from an unknown publication, related to Crowley's reception of **Liber L. vel Legis** and quoted him as saying:

> *"I instigated the whole affair in hope it would prompt Rose to produce a few interesting ideas; a seed that I could work on and develop."*

With hindsight, the impossibility of this quote is patently obvious. It is an open admission that Crowley, in whatever way, staged events in Cairo! Nevertheless, the impression left on me by this nocturnal cinema show cut deep enough for me to retain an irrational suspicion of actually reading the passage whilst awake. At one level, I struggle to believe that I spent eight hours hunting for such a ridiculous, imaginary reference. On another, I remain unable to shake a surreal conviction that I did read Crowley's confession, somewhere...

At 4AM on the morning of Sunday 04 November, I woke abruptly and sprang 'bolt upright' in bed. I experienced none of the grogginess or other symptoms of warm confusion usual in a transition from sleep to wakefulness. I awoke, wholly focussed on a question that blazed across my world. For ten or so minutes, I sat in the darkness contemplating a sentence that had thrust me back into the real world at the ungodly time of 4AM. The tired, grouchy and sensible part of me repeatedly demanded I make a mental note, get back to sleep, and investigate in the morning. However, and much as I was loathe to leave the warmth and comfort of my bed, the question gnawed into my thoughts, creating an itch that grew more irritating with each passing second. Eventually, curiosity got the better of me. I pulled on a dressing gown, braced myself against the biting cold, and headed for my library.

Walking across the hallway, I recapped on the short sequence of events responsible for this act of madness. The dream began with me holding (between thumb and forefinger of both hands) an A4 copy of the cover sheet discussed at length in this work. Almost immediately, a skeletal hand and arm, clad in a simple sleeve of dark grey material woven with a subtle sheen, moved in swiftly from my left. With its hand otherwise clenched into a fist, the entity's forefinger jabbed impatiently at one particular line. A cold voice repeatedly asked the same question. With each subsequent cycle, the volume, menace and sense of frustration increased, as though emanating from a bombastic headmaster. I awoke with those five words echoing insanely around my ears, mind and bedroom.

On initially waking, my first thought was *"What a dumb question!"* Because it referred quite specifically to a few words scribbled on the enigmatic cover sheet - An inconsequential note of which I had never previously given a second thought. The question set was one I initially assumed that most would answer, almost instinctively. However, on consideration, I realised that my own 'auto-pilot' response was wrong. By the time I'd suggested, then dismissed, three equally 'obvious' solutions, a growing sense of intrigue got the better of me.

During the next two hours, all sensations of tiredness, coldness and discomfort receded to a dot on the distant horizon as I trawled through a progressively larger selection of material. My original and sole intention of locating a specific answer also dwindled as five words opened the gateway to an entirely unanticipated dimension. As I discovered, just beneath the towering edifice of Thelema are the remains of an older 'hidden city.' Lower still lie traces of a yet more ancient society. Moreover, a cursory inspection of the archaeology suggests that the stones torn down during the demolition, perhaps even an attempted obliteration, of the older civilisation, are the same used to build the current structure – Albeit 'inverted' as to conceal all markings left by the vanquished culture.

Though it may be somewhat of a cliché to say, I genuinely felt the floor fall away, and repeatedly heard myself exclaim, *"Surely, that can't be right, can it? Oh, according to that, it is! Why haven't I noticed 'that' before?* **Why hasn't anyone noticed 'that' before?"** Over the years, I've given Crowley a great deal of latitude when considering possible 'escape' loopholes in various theories raising questions and suspicions about the alleged reception events. However, when the sun rose that morning, it did so on a different world because, for the first time, ever, I 'knew' that Aleister Crowley had not written **Liber L. vel Legis** between noon and 1PM on 08, 09 & 10 April 1904.

The 'dots' I join in the following section reveal what is, with the benefit of hindsight, a perfectly clear picture. Yet, until 'the penny dropped,' until I looked at a single facet of this mystery from a slightly altered perspective, I remained blind to that which quite literally stared me in the face. I also failed to notice discrete connections between seemingly disconnected points, because I allowed myself to stumble into traps set by a very cunning and intelligent forger.

As previously mentioned, the (cover sheet) note in question had never previously snagged on my thoughts. Indeed, I doubt if this scribbled afterthought has figured greatly in the considerations of anyone. In all fairness, discussion regarding the abundance of mysteries littering Crowley's cover sheet have swamped any potential significance of five, seemingly innocuous words.

Until very recently, only a handful of individuals with access to Gerald Yorke's 'Warburg' archive had a means of following the maze into which I fell. Since 2002, anyone able to attend one of the dozen or so institutes deemed worthy of retaining a microfilm copy of this collection (comprising approximately half the total archive), can study the material. In 2010, Marcus Katz's book, **The Invocation of Hoor**, shone a beam of light directly upon a dark secret Aleister Crowley buried in his closet one-hundred and eleven years ago.

Markus Katz deserves great praise for both publishing the content of Crowley's vellum notebook, OS27, and being the first to discuss curious discrepancies between a sentence Crowley published, and the unpublished material this actually referenced… but he missed a bigger revelation. As did I and everyone else who's ever studied this material – Until now. Somewhat bizarrely, only in consequence of a disturbing dream did I think to follow this neglected trail.

The following eleven months I devoted almost exclusively to this book. During my research, I uncovered a further level of supporting evidence concealed between the lines of other documents. The journey was, for me, fascinating, though utterly damning for Crowley's reception myth.

At this point, I pause to offer a note of… caution. **Liber L. vel Bogus** is not an easy book to read. It was not an easy book to write. In fact, in places it is comprehensively heavy going! What follows is a dense cross-referencing of sources, timelines, personalities and often contradictory accounts. A comprehension of this material is dependant upon a general knowledge of Crowley's life and an intimate familiarity with the details of alleged occurrences in Cairo during the early spring of 1904. As I discovered, the Devil is very much in the detail. 'Sustained Attention' is a mandatory requirement of participation in this convoluted paper-trail. It is futile to surf the following material with the same robotic level of auto-acceptance as that apportioned to a TV listing, or Facebook page. Did you, for example, notice that the Content page lists two items labelled "*E*" in the Introduction? Are you paying attention? Are you wondering why my hypothetical 'high-ranking saboteur' erased one 'toxic' notebook (OS23) from the record, but not an equally damaging specimen (OS27 appears on the Warburg microfilm and was available, albeit briefly, in Marcus Katz's **The Invocation of Hoor**).

This question, I accept, crossed my mind. As a researcher, I follow a trail led by possibilities arising from the jigsaw pieces on my table. At times, fate's favouring of Crowley with respect to numerous coincidences seemed implausibly… fortuitous. For what it's worth, I would wager good money that (again, back in a hypothetical, parallel world) the saboteur didn't engineer the omission of OS27 from the Warburg microfilm because he, she or they, like everyone else, completely missed the significance of this material. Not even when Markus Katz shone a spotlight on the "*long, futile Tarot divination*" did anyone go beyond his perceptive observations and grasp the jaw-dropping conclusion. The discrepancies in OS23 glitter on its surface. Conversely, those in OS27 are subtle and only revealed with a sharp eye.

If allowed to meander one step further down this speculative avenue, I'd perhaps wonder why [according to a confidential source] repeated requests for permission to reprint portions of OS27 were ignored by (c)O.T.O. Inc.. Rather ungraciously, almost before the ink used to print its small run was dry, the publisher withdrew Markus Katz's book at the behest of the material's Copyright holders, namely (c)O.T.O. Inc.. Did 'someone' with prior knowledge of the cover-up suddenly realise the explosive nature of material 'just' hidden in the shadow of a long, futile Tarot divination, and 'pull the plug' with utmost haste? In a very short time, **The Invocation of Hoor** has become an almost impossible-to-obtain book.

Before moving on, I'll mention one further instance of a random incident of fate proving unfeasibly kind to Crowley. Amidst copious editorial content punctuating **Magick** (Liber ABA, Book IV, parts I to IV – Second Revised Edition, Red Wheel/Weiser, 1998), is a matter-of-fact footnote stating that "*Pipie & Sons*" manufactured the paper on which Crowley wrote **Liber L. vel Legis**. In this instance fate conspired with a printers' imp, and together they slipped a single, seemingly inconsequential typo into the mix. A half-hearted internet search of "*Pipie*" returns nothing of significance. However, speaking to a real person with knowledge of the early 20th Century papermaking industry rewards the stubborn researcher with a surprise:

> "*Never heard of 'Pipie,' Richard, but there used to be a big Scottish papermaker called Pirie & Sons.*"

Following this clue leads to a truly astonishing revelation concerning the manufacture date of a specific brand of Alex Pirie & Sons watermarked Standard Typewriting paper, in relation to Crowley's reception claims. Of course, the Devil's Advocate may well counter with a variant of the 'lost vellum notebook' trick, by suggesting an error in the records of a world-renowned paper manufacturer, in preference to countenancing a suspicion regarding Crowley's hoary ol' '*Waiter, there's a praeterhuman entity in my honeymoon suite*' routine.

Back in the real world, it is time to start digging. So, with sharpened pencils, straight backs, and brightest stick-on 'happy face' affixed securely, let us proceed. Hang on. It will be a bumpy ride.

666 A saviour is needed. What is the one thing certain about his qualifications? That he should not be an ordinary man. The saviour must be a peculiarly sacred person; that he should be a human being at all is hardly credible. At the very least, his mother must be a virgin; and, to match this wonder, his father cannot be an ordinary man; therefore, his father must be a god. But as a god is a gaseous vertebrate, he must be some materialization of a god. Very good!

Let him be the god Mars under the form of a wolf, or Jupiter as a bull, or a shower of gold, or a swan; or Jehovah in the form of a dove; or some other creature of phantasy, preferably disguised in some animal form. There are innumerable forms of this tradition, but they all agree on one point: the saviour can only appear as the result of some extra ordinary accident, quite contrary to whatever is normal. The slightest suggestion of anything reasonable in this matter would destroy the whole argument. But as one must obtain some concrete picture, the general solution is to represent the saviour as the Fool.

Aleister Crowley 999

06.08   Checkmate

The discrepancies discussed in this section are subtle. For ease of reference, I recommend their study in conjunction with the following documents:

1 -   Facsimile of Crowley's handwritten manuscript of **Liber L. vel Legis**
2 -   Typeset version of **Liber L vel Legis** (any edition)
3 -   **The Invocation of Hoor** (Marcus Katz)
4 -   **Equinox of the Gods** (Aleister Crowley, any edition)
5 -   **Equinox Volume I, Numbers 7, 8** and **10** (any edition)
6 -   (Ideally) **Facsimiles of OS23 and OS27**

▶◉◀

◉   **Point One** – Lost amidst numerous chaotic notes scribbled on the cover sheet associated with Crowley's 1907 Appendix version of **Liber L. vel Legis** is a brief clarification inserted between the original lines of text. It reads:

"**except the translations of the Stele inscriptions.*"

This correction relates to a patently absurd assertion made with reference to the manuscript's origin, which reads:

"*This is a highly interesting example of genuine
automatic writing. Though I am in no way responsible
for any of these documents*, I publish them among my works, because
I believe that their intelligent study may be interesting & helpful.
– A .C.*"

The amendment ("*except...*") is squeezed in, between lines, after the word "*documents*," as indicated by the '*.' Given the problematic nature of Crowley's declaration that '*a manuscript written in his hand, and addressed specifically to his alter-ego (The Beast), is not of his creation,*' it is hardly surprising that an incidental aside claiming authorship of the stele inscriptions is overlooked by researchers.

▶◉◀

◉   **Point Two** – Crowley's adjustment refers to the six verses of his poetic rendering of the stele translation. His typescript reproduces these in full, whereas (due to time constraints inherent within the dictation) Crowley's manuscript indicates verse placement by means of three short notes incorporated into the text. These are:

"37. I adore thee in the song –

> **[Manuscript omits the remainder of Verse 37, and gives:**
> *"I am the Lord of Thebes" etc. from vellum book unity etc. ~~~ "fill me"*]
>
> **I am the Lord of Thebes**, *and I..."*

and:

> *"38. So that thy light is in me; & its red flame is as a sword in my hand to push thy order. There is a secret door that I shall make to establish thy way in all the quarters, (these are the adorations, as thou hast written), as it is said:*
>
> **[Manuscript omits the remainder of Verse 38, and gives:**
> *"The light is mine" etc.*
> *from vellum book to "Ra-Hoor-Khuit"*]
>
> **The light is mine**; *its rays consume..."*

(III, 37 & 38)

These corrections are curious, because the note Crowley inserted into his cover sheet preface refers specifically to "*stele translations*" (i.e. the literal French translation of the stele hieroglyphs prepared for Crowley between 23 March and 07 or 08 April by staff at the Boulak museum). Yet, the manuscript refers to, and typescript reproduces, Crowley's versified paraphrasing and not the translation itself. Interestingly, the typeset version of the handwritten cover page (as prefaces the Appendix dropped from **Collected Works**) resolves this discrepancy by use of an extra word, "*verse.*"

This may be an incidental slip on Crowley's part, but does raise an interesting question – Did the document described on Crowley's cover sheet originally incorporate the text of Brugsch's French translation of the stele hieroglyphs? If so, the manuscript as we know it today is a later variant, with Crowley's paraphrase of the translation replacing his originally favoured literal translation. The cover sheet survives (at the Harry Ransom Institute) alongside an early typeset version of **Liber L. vel Legis**, but not the manuscript itself – This was allegedly rediscovered in the mid-1980s by US bookseller Tom Whitmore. There is, in fact, no reason to dismiss outright a notion that Crowley's cover sheet refers to an entirely different document to that tacitly presumed.

▶◉◀

◉ **Point Three** – The last entry in the third section of OS27, prior to the occurrence of five missing pages, reads *"General idea of a ceremony to become R.H.K., etc."* Whilst it is not possible to deduce the missing content with certainty, we can at least narrow down the field. The deleted content was positioned after Ouarda's alleged dictation (to Crowley) of the **Invocation of Hoor**, which Crowley's **Book of Results** placed as having taken place on 18 March 1904, and before the *"long and futile Tarot divination,"* which the same record dated to 23 March. This gives a window of only six days. It is natural to assume, given the alleged chronology of events, that the missing material contains notes Crowley made of stele imagery whilst at the Boulak Museum, on 21 March. In consideration of the title assigned to this missing material (*"General idea of a ceremony to become R.H.K., etc."*) it is also reasonable to suppose that the remaining (now-lost) pages may have contained portions of Crowley's poetic versification of the stele translation - Especially as this ends with *"Abide with me, Ra-Hoor-Khuit."* I note that 21 March falls outside the range of dates during which Crowley could have received the French translation from which he subsequently created a poetic interpretation. Furthermore, the three manuscript notes, at **I, 14, III, 37 & 38,** all refer to the (singular) ***"vellum book to Ra-Hoor-Khuit."*** Given that Crowley wrote *"Invocation of Hoor"* on the front cover of OS27, and prefaced the missing pages with *"General idea of a ceremony to become R.H.K.,"* it seems reasonable to consider Crowley's description of stele imagery and paraphrase of Brugsch's translation as prime suspects for the five pages crudely torn from OS27.

Incidentally, Crowley did record an account of stele imagery in OS27, though its placement after an entry dated 23 March in the **Book of Results** itself raises further challenging discrepancies. Indeed, the **Book of Results**' location within the context of OS27 evokes yet more issues – As described in subsequent chapters.

▶◉◀

◉ **Point Four** – Of the major events comprising Crowley's account of the reception, most but not all are recorded in OS27. A direct comparison between 'official' account as first published in **Equinox I, 7**

(March 1912) and corresponding vellum notebook, OS27, reveals several discrepancies. These are:

1. OS27 is missing fragmentary diary entries included in **Equinox I, 7**. However, Crowley acknowledged this material as deriving from his personal diary, not the vellum notebook (OS27) - A statement verifiable by reference to his journal of the period.

2. Also absent from OS27 (and all other primary sources) are notes relating to Crowley and Rose's fateful trip to the Boulak Museum. Given the significance of this excursion, it seems utterly inexplicable that Crowley's private notebooks make absolutely no mention of it. OS27 does however include Crowley's description of stele imagery – Which he surely wrote whilst physically present in the museum and looking at the artefact labelled "*666*."

3. OS27 does not include Crowley's versification of Brugsch's translation. This omission is curious. **Liber L. vel Legis** references this material and, therefore, Crowley's account is reliant upon it. Furthermore, Crowley prepared the versification with a notable sense of urgency - He must have written this poem down, somewhere… but where?

4. A record of Crowley's "*cross-examination of Rose*" (**Equinox of the Gods**, page 71) is also absent from OS27. Since Crowley bases the convoluted mathematical 'proof' of his wife's Magickal Link with Horus on this dialogue, it seems inconceivable that he would not have made extensive notes at the time (18 March 1904). The absence of this conversation, and stele versifications, and Boulak trip is (I accept) suggestive of a second (now-lost) vellum notebook. On this moot point, I'll note that - Crowley's personal diary makes no reference whatsoever to the reception, yet nobody has yet suggested the possibility of a 'now-lost' diary covering just the missing pieces. This is one of many longstanding oddities that all with an interest seem content to brush under the carpet.

Crowley's contemporary notebooks average twelve lines per page, and each verse of the paraphrase contains six lines. This equates to a scenario in which Crowley writes two verses on each leaf. Since he only wrote on the right hand page of notebooks, four are required (including a title page) to accommodate the versification. Interestingly, an examination of the five page stubs clinging to the spine of OS27 yields one clue. Slightly over half way down the first page fragment, a single word, "*gold*," is discernable. Not much to go on, I accept. Nevertheless, it is interesting to note that Crowley's description of stele imagery employs the same word, and its placement within this text falls exactly where one would expect if the first missing page contained a duplicate of notes scribbled in the **Book of Results**. Of course, even if my hypotheses suggesting that the five missing pages comprise a one-page description of stele imagery and four pages of stele versification is correct (as seems entirely likely), the record is still missing both Crowley's 'cross-examination,' and a minor mystery - The short "*Name-coincidences of Qabalah*" allegedly written between 23 March and 07/08 April.

Incidentally, OS27 may lack references to several key events, but does include material subsequently expunged from the record. The substantial section titled "*Ritual B2. To have any knowledge*" by Yorke, is never, ever, mentioned by Crowley.

▶◉◀

◉   **Point Five** – Given the placement, context, chronology and even description of the five missing pages, it seems likely that the extant void correlates with Crowley's description of stele imagery plus six verses of his stele paraphrase. Even if this supposition is inaccurate, the mystery of why 'someone' ripped five pages from Crowley's notebook lingers. Whilst I cannot definitively state OS27 as the solitary instance of literary vandalism extant amongst Crowley's copious legacy, I am unable to name a comparable instance. When preparing a typescript from handwritten notes, he habitually scored lines through passages subsequently omitted from published works, but never ripped chunks from notebooks.

A comment Gerald Yorke scribbled on a page preceding the missing section throws suspicion on Charles Stansfeld, but this is almost certainly erroneous.

> "*[missing pages torn out*
>
> *G.J.Y. by Charles Stansfeld Jones or Frater Achad?]*"

Crowley recruited C. S. Jones (also known in Crowley's mystical society as "*Frater Achad*") from the **Equinox**, which didn't appear until 1909 – Though he did have access to Crowley's private material after this date. It is more likely that Yorke's note refers to Crowley's old Golden Dawn chum George Cecil Jones, who was on the scene and working closely with Crowley during the period prior to and following the missing pages.

Crowley himself may have suggested C. S. Jones to Yorke as a dig at a man he claimed had "*gone insane*" - An issue discussed in subsequent chapters. On a personal note, I consider it unlikely, in the extreme, that anyone other than Crowley would have felt 'authorised' to remove material from the Master's private records.

►◉◄

◉   **Point Six** – I now consider the mystery of a "*long and futile Tarot divination*" that was nothing of the sort. Crowley's published accounts mention the divination only in noting the content is unworthy of inclusion:

"*23* [March 1904] *The Secret of Wisdom.*
(We omit the record of a long and futile Tarot divination.)"

In his 1951 catalogue, Gerald Yorke indexed corresponding material as:

"*4. The planets and the signs of the zodiac.*"

Crowley must surely have grasped a comprehension as to the import of his 'futile Tarot divination' – These three pages form the basis of what will, four decades later, blossom into **The Book of Thoth**. Why didn't he trumpet this material as part of the miraculous accomplishments in Cairo? Why did he describe this material so inaccurately then discard it? In fact, why mention it at all? Why draw attention to a piece that will inevitable provoke a flurry of questions from anyone curious enough to track it down?

Crowley wrote the three pages without preface or title and Gerald Yorke's catalogue entry is a 'best guess.' I wondered if entries written immediately prior to, and following them, would offer an insight into this curio. On looking, Crowley's account imploded.

As is natural to suppose, OS27 lists events in chronological order. It begins with material contemporary with the Cairo period. Following this is an account of work undertaken on return from Egypt, at Boleskine in the summer of 1904. Inexplicably, the notebook then zips back in time and location, to record the three pages written a month previously, on 23 March, in Cairo. If this impossible feat was not enough to cast serious doubt on Crowley's account, the remainder of OS27 is 'upside down!' On investigation, it transpires that, for whatever reasons, on completion of the section Yorke labelled "*The Planets and the signs of the zodiac,*" Crowley flipped over and rotated his notebook by 180°, then continued on what was originally the bottom of its last page. Bizarrely, three segments of OS27 (namely **The Book of Results**, Crowley's description of stele imagery and his *"Golden Dawn to be destroyed"* rant against Mathers) are positioned in the back of OS27, upside down!

◉

◉   **Point Seven** – On consideration of the above, it is impossible to escape a self-evident and, for Crowley, extremely inconvenient observation that the Tarot divination and five missing pages could not have been written, as Crowley claimed, in Egypt. When, on 23 March 1904, Crowley wrote about *"a long and futile Tarot divination,"* he was referring to events that did not occur until after he returned to Boleskine, at the end of April 1904 – A fact confirmed by:

1. The chronology of Crowley's original source material as recorded in his vellum notebook (OS27).
2. The index of this material prepared by Gerald Yorke, in a section of OS27 titled *"1904 Summer. Work at Bol (eskine) with Beel (zebub). 5 pages have been torn out."* A title Yorke based on:
3. A corresponding note, written in Crowley's own hand, stating *"1904 Summer. Work at Bol (eskine) with Beel (zebub)."*
4. The 2002 Warburg index of Yorke material, which gives:
   "(a) 'Invocation of Horus according to the Divine Vision of Ouarda the seer' 1904 (The dance, The Supreme ritual. To Invoke, To obtain)
   (b) Ritual B2. To have any knowledge.
   (c) Revelation of ritual to consecrate talismans of XXII [Note by Yorke: Summer 1904, Work at Boleskine with Beelzebub] [5 pages lost]
   (d) Notes on Tarot
   (e) The Book of Results (Cairo 1904.)"

This single discrepancy exposes a fatal flaw in Crowley's reception story. Moreover, once realised, the fissure splinters into a number of secondary fractures. Without seeming to state the obvious, everything written in OS27 after the section titled "3. *Summer. 1904*" recounts incidents that occurred after leaving Egypt. This means that The Tarot divination, plus whatever was written on the five missing pages (perhaps Crowley's stele versification), plus three inverted sections (including the **Book of Results**, which Crowley misleadingly described as *"unspoiled and authoritative"*) are not contemporary with Cairo! Unpalatable as this may be to some, large chunks of the purportedly dated evidence used to support his Master of the Universe fantasy, Crowley actually wrote at Boleskine.

▶◉◀

◉   **Summation** – Each stone turned thus far in my exploration of **Liber L. vel Legis** has uncovered a nest of snarling discrepancies. In addition to multiple dating issues, and Aiwass' rather glaring error, plus contradictory and patently absurd statements on cover sheet and typeset Appendix, plus the complete absence of diary references to the three-day reception event itself, plus Crowley's reliance on material not even extant in April 1904... Well, on presenting this already overwhelming list of curios and contradictions, it is tempting to draw a line under proceedings as matters stand. I continue because it is important to investigate the historical record further and attempt to deduce what did actually occur in Egypt. A praeterhuman entity did not dictate **Liber L. vel Legis** to Aleister Crowley on 08, 09 & 10 April 1904. The next challenge is one of establishing the circumstances by which he did come into possession of the manuscript.

By tracking clues scattered across unpublished works, it is possible to chart the outline of Crowley's clandestine activities between 1904 and 1910. During this period, he obsessively wove the remnants of a clumsy scheme devised merely to topple Mathers and place Crowley at the Golden Dawn's helm, into an impossibly audacious campaign revealing Crowley as nothing less than the a contemporary Jesus, armed with a new Bible, and tasked with guiding Mankind through the birth-pangs of a New Aeon!

A study of the circuitous route by which Crowley moulded, revised and, at times, simply fabricated records in accordance with the evolving scope of his 'master plan' is utterly compelling and, rather perversely, a testament to the man's qualities of resilience and adaptability. Unsurprisingly, this immense transition left a few scars - Notably, the crater dug by five pages torn from OS27. This jagged breach in the record pinpoints the single instance in which Crowley was unable to conceal stretch-marks, patches and the cumulative debris of several upgrades with guile and a few strokes of his pen. Whatever information the five missing pages did contain, it presented such a conflict to the version Crowley was then touting as to require not just an editorial crossing-out, but complete annihilation - As discussed further in subsequent chapters.

Crowley was, unquestionably, more aware than anyone of the 'wrinkles' in his account and throughout his life stood braced against a possibility that someone with a keen eye may well stumble upon material that raised questions he could not answer. As such, he must have spent untold hours praying for Ra-Hoor-Khuit to throw a cloak of invisibility over several unavoidable 'seams' for which he could not account. Well, not without exposing his great Cairo revelation for the fabrication it demonstrably was.

As events transpired, Crowley's 'crime' escaped detection. He died believing that his deepest, darkest secret went with him to the grave. He almost got away with it – Almost! For Crowley, these issues are long-since irrelevant, but for those with an interest, those with a commercial or spiritual investment, and especially converts to his New World Religion, Thelema, the bomb started ticking only a few moments ago.

Something doesn't quite add-up!

When correlated with their Hebrew equivalents the numeric values of letters comprising Crowley's original title, **Liber L. vel Legis,** total… 666! This does not hold true following his addition of an 'A,' which brings the sum to 667.

Crowley never mentioned this synchronicity and, given its significance, it is possible that he never noticed it. If so, he would have perhaps thought twice about changing the title (from '**L.**' to '**AL**') and so spoiling an otherwise elegant Qabalistic 'proof.' With a sense of irony, I'll note that Aiwass did warn Crowley against changing so much as the style of a letter…

ל	L (Lamed)	= 30
י	I (Yod)	= 10
ב	B (Beth)	= 02
ה	E (Heh)	= 05
ר	R (Resh)	= 200
ל	L (Lamed)	= 30
ו	V (Vau)	= 06
ה	E (Heh)	= 05
ל	L (Lamed)	= 30
ל	L (Lamed)	= 30
ה	E (Heh)	= 05
ג	G (Gimel)	= 03
י	I (Yod)	= 10
ש	S (Shin)	= 300
	Total	= 666

06.09 A coke AL bull story

I.	**Dazed and abused**	Page 105
II.	**Contradictions, omissions, alterations**	Page 108
III.	**The AL-man Cometh**	Page 116
IV.	**Poetic Licence**	Page 124
V.	**Liber L. vel Bogus**	Page 128
VI.	**I'm sick, sick, sick of six, six, six**	Page 135
VII.	**Darn that pesky Tarot divination!**	Page 142
VIII.	**A book of mixed results**	Page 146
	Sex, sex, sex with six, six, six	Page 149
IX.	**The heavenly, who?**	Page 160
X.	**OS23, the final nail**	Page 164
XI.	**Bollocks dropped at the Boulak**	Page 169
XII.	**A great cover story**	Page 174
XIII.	**When the Fat Lady Sins**	Page 183
XIV.	**ALmost fatAL case of genital disintegration**	Page 192
XV.	**A view from above**	Page 195
XVI.	**The Grate Beast**	Page 210

I. Dazed and abused

If Crowley didn't receive the sixty-five pages of **Liber L. vel Legis** from Aiwass on 08, 09 & 10 April 1904, how did he come into possession of this manuscript? Leaving aside the devastating consequences this bombshell has for Crowley's New World Religion, Thelema (an "*engine of world reform*" not transmitted by a messenger of the gods, in Cairo), I concentrate on a pragmatic reconstruction of the historical record.

Given the meagre and contradictory data available, it is impossible to deduce 'with certainty' an account of events that transpired over a century ago. However, when carefully examined, the evidence to hand reveals a 'balance of probabilities' alternate scenario to that narrated by Crowley. What emerges is a genuinely extraordinary depiction of the birth of a New Aeon, and one completely negating a necessity for the divine intervention Crowley felt essential to underwrite his monumental insight. I begin on 12 October 1903, Crowley's twenty-eighth birthday.

At this time, the newly-married Crowley is a man on the edge. Cracks are starting to show, as evidenced by a letter written to his brother-in-law, Gerald Kelly (see page 60). During the previous five years, Crowley unconditionally hurled his intellect, time, resources, soul and a good deal of his fortune at an obsessive crusade to form a Magickal Link with Secret Chiefs covertly governing the evolution of our species - Without success. His attempts to assume control of the Golden Dawn have brought that mystical fraternity to the edge of oblivion. It is in desperate need of reformulation under a new leader. Unfortunately, Crowley is ineligible (for a position he feels is his by right) in consequence of a failure to earn certain occult credentials.

Magickal issues are not the only concerns on Crowley's mind. He may want to play 'Master of the Universe,' but finds himself married, with a country estate to manage, responsibilities tugging at his coat-tails and a life sliding towards a desultory cesspit labelled 'banal normality.' Crowley was fast becoming the physical embodiment of everything he loathed.

A crumbling mass of neuroses named Aleister Crowley embarked on honeymoon carrying enough excess emotional baggage to sink a ship - A burden that was slowly dragging him under. For the sake of his sanity, Crowley must find a way of permanently banishing, or manifesting his delusions of grandeur. Time was against him and Crowley, perhaps intuitively, maybe in desperation, gravitated towards the womb of his occult tutelage, Egypt.

The newlyweds arrived at the City of Pharaohs in November 1903. Crowley was eager to 'make something happen' and not averse to nudging events in the right direction. As a 'grand gesture,' he arranged to spend the night of Sunday 22 November alone with his wife in the King's Chamber of the Great Pyramid. During this time, and allegedly to impress Rose, Crowley performed an occult ceremony titled the *Preliminary Invocation of the Goetia.* According to his memoirs, the ritual was a success:

> "...*by his invocations he filled the King's Chamber of the Great Pyramid with a brightness as of full moonlight. (This was no subjective illusion. The light was sufficient for him to read the ritual by.)*" (**Equinox I, 7,** page 361)

Impressive as this astral lightshow undoubtedly was, Crowley curled his lip and snarled, menacingly. 'A bit of a warm glow' hardly constituted promising material from which he could:

"...build a new Heaven and a new Earth. I want none of your faint approval or faint dispraise. I want blasphemy, murder, rape, revolution, anything, bad or good, but strong."

His frustration was evident:

"Only to conclude, 'There, you see it? What's the good of it?'"
(**Equinox 1, 7**, page 361)

Crowley then threw a major tantrum:

"So Fra. P., after five years barking up the wrong tree, had lost interest in trees altogether as far as climbing them was concerned."
(**Equinox 1, 7**, page 361)

'Tree climbing' is a reference to the Golden Dawn 'Tree of Life,' the boughs of which he formerly clawed at with such enthusiasm. To relieve the ache of disappointment, Crowley reverted to type and headed for Ceylon, where he took pot shots at whatever fell between the crosshairs of his rifle. When general slaughter failed to lift his black mood, Crowley inclined towards Rangoon to seek guidance and solace from his first occult mentor, the Buddhist monk Allan Bennett. However, at some point, Crowley's intense soul searching dredged up an incidental and almost forgotten recollection. In a flash of inspiration, or madness, Crowley perceived this memory fragment as a 'gift from the gods.' Inspired by the 'divine seed,' he preformed the Edwardian equivalent of a handbrake turn and headed back to Egypt - His mind collating and formulating the essential components of an immensely audacious plan to steal the throne of his despised occult boss, Samuel Liddel MacGregor Mathers.

Crowley wasn't interested in merely taking the reins of Mathers' second-hand Ascended Masters and Secret Chiefs, or frittering away the hours with jaded entities well past their 'venerate-by' date. Nothing less than the establishment of a new world order, with a fresh set of gods, and a new book of rules, devised by him, would appease Crowley's ego. To facilitate this miracle, he decided to perform an elaborate (Golden Dawn) occult ceremony, in Egypt, on the day of the vernal equinox. A ritual, he calculated, that must manifest 'The Mother of all New Equinoxes,' because the 'battery' powering it comprised nothing less than a 'stone tablet' inscribed with a New Covenant for Mankind!

Aleister Crowley, 'the man,' did not return to Egypt. In his place stood a contemporary Moses named Prince Chioa Khan (the Great Beast) - A modern prophet for whom the voyage to Egypt symbolised an ascent of

Mount Sinai to retrieve a divine artefact from a secret location revealed to him by the gods of a New Equinox. In many respects, this scenario represented Crowley's final throw of the dice. Failure saw him limp back to Boleskine as a mere mortal and domesticated 'daddy' of the child Rose was expecting. The stakes were massive. Crowley was risking everything on an impossible long-shot. Yet, failure was simply not a viable option.

II. Contradictions, omissions, alterations

According to **Confessions** (page 385), Crowley and Rose left Colombo on 28 January. Their ship docked at Post Said (via Aden) on Monday 08 February, and arrived in Cairo the next day. In total, it took thirteen days to travel the 5677km from Colombo, Ceylon (now Sri Lanka), to Egypt.

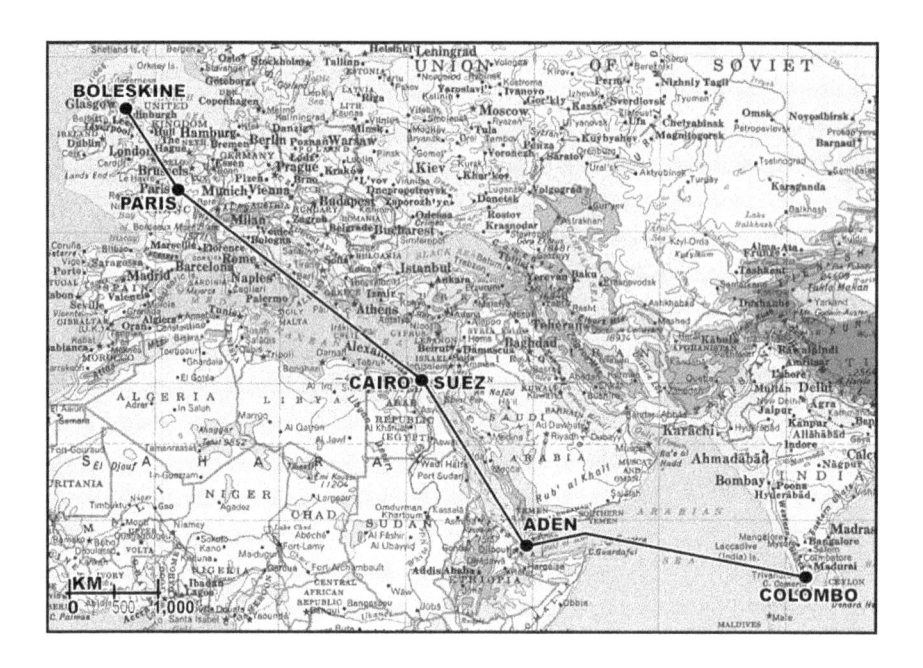

This statistic highlights a curious inconsistency in Crowley's recollection of leaving Cairo 'approximately a fortnight' after his reception of **Liber L. vel Legis**. The final day of dictation occurred on Sunday 10 April, suggesting a departure date of around 24 April. Yet, only two days later, they dined with Arnold Bennett in Paris (Bennett included an account of this in **Paris Nights: And Other Impressions of Places and People**, published in November 1913). Apparently, Crowley travelled the 3994km from Cairo to Paris at almost twice the speed of his previous journey from Colombo to Cairo – Highly unlikely! Unfortunately, this is merely one minor tripwire amidst a veritable minefield of contradictions Crowley laid to conceal his real agenda (see **AL cetera**).

Accounts of Crowley's adventures in Egypt appear primarily in three publications, **Equinox I, 7**, **Equinox of the Gods** and **Confessions**. **Equinox I, 10** reproduces a typeset version of **Liber L. vel Legis**, but without comment, as does the third volume of his **Holy Books**. The unpublished Appendix intended for inclusion in **Collected Works,** with its prototype version of **Liber L. vel Legis,** still accompanies the infamous cover sheet (Harry Ransom Center). Of these variations, all derive from just two fragmentary sources, namely his personal diary and its occult counterpart OS27, including the **Book of Results**. Both are problematic, as Crowley noted:

> "*This diary is extremely incomplete and fragmentary. Many entries, too, are evidently irrelevant or 'blinds.' We omit much of the latter two types.*" (**Equinox of the Gods**, page 67)

> "*Fra. P. never made a thorough record of this period. He seems to have wavered between absolute scepticism in the bad sense, a dislike of the revelation, on the one hand, and real enthusiasm on the other. And the first of these moods would induce him to do things to spoil the effect of the latter. Hence the 'blinds' and stupid meaningless ciphers which deface the diary.* (**Equinox of the Gods**, page 69)

His second source document, the **Book of Results**, Crowley describes in **Equinox I, 7** as:

> "*We have one quite unspoiled and authoritative document. 'The Book of Results,' written in one of the small Japanese vellum note-books which he used to carry.*"

Whilst this notebook certainly accompanied Crowley around Egypt, its various sections also record details of subsequent Magickal experiments at Boleskine in the summer of 1904. Crowley infers that he wrote the **Book of Results** in Cairo. However, its placement in OS27 is questionable. Crowley inverted the vellum notebook and started his **Book of Results** on what was originally its last page (upside down), but which now becomes its first page (the correct way up). Furthermore, and despite its dated sequence of entries, Crowley wrote the **Book of Results** with the same pen, in exactly the same style of handwriting. He also added the words "*1904*" and "*Cairo*" as an afterthought, at an indeterminate time.

It is entirely likely that Crowley wrote the **Book of Results** in a single session, and not between 16 and 23 March, in Cairo. The **Book of Results**' placement at the rear of his vellum notebook renders it difficult to ascertain exactly when Crowley wrote this chronicle, though, curiously, immediately following it is his description of the stele imagery, which begins with the words *"In the museum at Cairo."* Crowley *"fixed"* his visit to the Boulak as happening on 21 March. As such, this description (almost certainly written whilst standing in front of the stele) 'should' appear either towards the front of his vellum notebook (approximating to the placement of residual stubs from the five ripped pages), or between **Book of Results** entries made on 20 and 22 March. It doesn't!

> The Book of Results.
> 1904 ——— Cairo
> Mar 16. Did ♀. Invoke IAO.
> intuition to continue ritual day and night
> for a week

By Crowley's own admission, his personal diary (as reproduced below) for this critical period is *"... extremely incomplete and fragmentary. Many entries, too, are evidently irrelevant or 'blinds.' We omit much of the latter two types."* Moreover, not only is this material codified to cloak a hidden agenda, whilst editing it for publication Crowley made similar 'wholesale' deletions to those employed with the *"long and futile Tarot divination"* and, as discussed earlier, the single word, *"omit,"* concealed a multitude of sins.

Feb. 9	To Cairo
Feb. 11	Saw b.f.g.
	b.f.b.
	(This entry is quite unintelligible to us.)
Feb. 19	To Helwan as Oriental Despot.
	(Apparently P. had assumed some disguise…)
Feb. 20	Began golf.
March 16	Began INV. [Invocation] IAO [See Liber Samekh]
March 17	Thoth appeared.
March 18	Told to INV. [invoke] Horus as the Sun by new way.
March 19	Did this badly at noon 30.

March 20	At 10 p.m. did well – Equinox of Gods – Nov – (? New) C.R.C. (Christian Rosy Cross, we conjecture.) Hoori now Hpnt (obviously "Heirophant").
March 21	in . IAM (? One o' clock) [Sun enters Aries]
March 22	X.P.B.
	(May this and the entry March 24, refer to the brother of the A∴ A∴ who found him?)
	E.P.D. in 84 m.
	(Unintelligible to us; probably a blind.)
March 23	Y.K. done (? His work on the Yi King)
March 24	Met اجيحا again.
March 25	823 Thus
	461 " " = pfly2bz
	218
(Blot)	wch trouble with ds.
(Blot)	P.B. (All unintelligible; possibly a blind.)
April 6	Go off again to H, taking A's p.

Remarkably, his journal breaks off on 06 April. Even more astonishingly, it makes no mention of Rose, in any capacity. Nor is his cross-examination, Boulak visit, or three encounters with Aiwass noted, even in passing! The **Book of Results** is equally silent on the Aiwass front and only charts events between 16 and 23 March. In a comment made in **Equinox of the Gods**, Crowley asks, *"What happened between March 23rd and April 8th?"* He should be more concerned about 'what happened between 08 and 10 April!'

Reproduced below is a section of handwritten notes, titled the **Book of Results,** Crowley originally recorded this in his unpublished source document, the vellum notebook (OS27) named **Invocation of Hoor**:

Mar 16.	Die Mercury. I invoke IAO
	Intuition to continue ritual day and night for a week.
	*[Ouarda] says *"they"* are *"waiting for me."*
17 [Jupiter]	It's 'all about the child,' also 'all Osiris.'
	Thoth, invoked with great success, indwells us.
18 [Venus]	Revealed that the waiter was Horus, whom I had offended and aught to invoke. The ritual revealed in skeleton. Promise of success [Saturn] or [sun] and of Samadhi.
19 [Saturn]	The ritual written out and the invocation done – little success.
20 [Sun]	Revealed that the Equinox of the Gods is come, Horus taking the Throne of the East and all rituals &c are being

abrogated. Great success in midway of invocation. I am to formulate a new link of an order with the Solar Force.

7=4 [Note on opposite page]

21	Moon Sun enters Aries [Vernal Equinox]
22 Mars	The day of rest, in which nothing whatever of magic is ever to be done at all. Mercury is to be the great day of invocation.
23 [Mercury]	**The Secret of W, the seer.

1. Mercury of Ankh-f-n-Khonsu = [Ou Mh]
2. Mars in Libra = the ritual is of sex; Mars in the house of Venus exciting the jealousy of Saturn or Vulcan
3. Moon in Cancer the 4 of cups means purity in the path.

These produce

1	K of W	= Force
2	P of C	= Initiation
3	Mercury	= Wisdom in work

He that abideth in the midst is Mars in Pisces giving as the symbol of Horus as Kephra.

But 666 explains all this and more.

(… continues with "*In the museum at Cairo.*")

A comparison of the above with the elaborated version presented in **Equinox of the Gods** reveals numerous alterations and significant omissions.

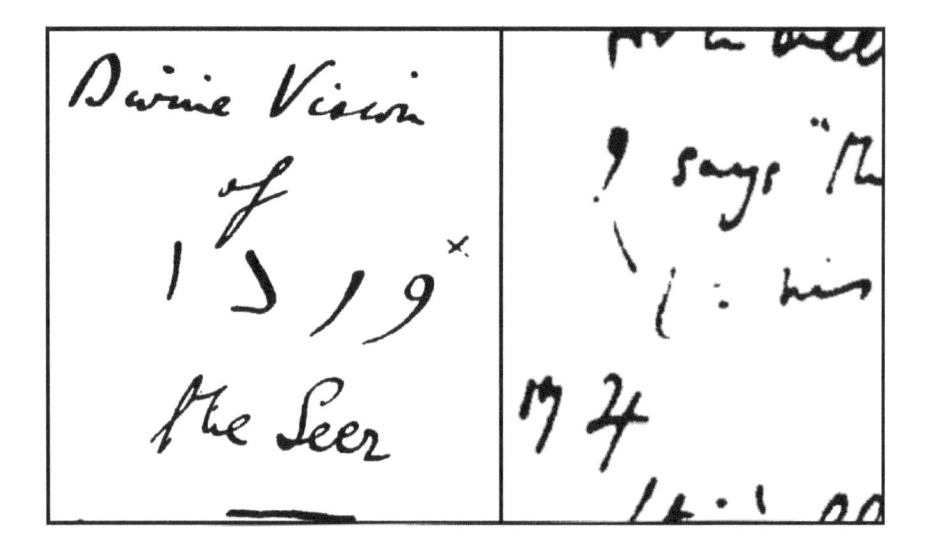

*Crowley's wife, Rose, plays a pivotal role in his 'official' version, but is actually referred to only twice in the **Book of Results**, and obliquely at that. In his 16 March entry, Crowley refers to her in the form of a symbol (resembling a '9') placed immediately to the left of "*Says*" (as shown in the right panel of the scan reproduced on previous page). A note by Gerald Yorke identifies this as "*his wife, Rose.*" The four symbols (left panel) comprise (right to left) the Arabic letters 'alif,' 'daa,' 'raa' and Waar, so giving 'Ouarda.'

Crowley's only other mention of Rose is absent from all published accounts. In **Equinox of the Gods, his (**Book of Results**) entry for 23 March reads:

"*23. The Secret of Wisdom.*
(We omit the record of a long and futile Tarot divination.)"

Conversely, the original (unpublished **Book of Results**) entry for 23 March suggests "*The Secret of W, the seer.*" Following this is another contentious item omitted from all published accounts, namely: "*the ritual is of sex.*" Somewhat bizarrely, the corresponding entry for 23 March in Crowley's personal diary reads "*Y.K. done (? His work on the Yi King).*"

It is also pertinent to note that the vellum notebook (OS27) in which Crowley wrote "*INVOCATION OF HORUS ACCORDING TO...*" is actually titled: "*INVOCATION OF HOOR.*"

▶◎◀

Even a superficial comparison of Crowley's source documents with published counterparts highlights numerous troubling issues:

♦ Crowley's personal diary (written in Cairo) contains coded references to meetings that he subsequently (in **Equinox I, 7** and **Equinox of the Gods**) denied ever took place. In **Equinox of the Gods** (page 114), Crowley adds a curious note to a list of people relevant to unfolding events:

"*Otherwise we knew nobody in Cairo* [...] *Contrary hints in one of my diaries were inserted deliberately to mislead, for some silly no-reason un-connected with Magick.*"

As with Crowley's insistence that 'coded' meetings referred to in his personal diary did not actually happen, it is reasonable to ask what he hoped to gain by this further deception.

♦ Neither his personal diary or **Book of Results** chronicle Crowley's cathartic visit to the 'Boulak Museum' (where Rose first saw the stele), or the preceding 'cross-examination.'

♦ Neither his personal diary or **Book of Results** mention the participation of Rose, in any capacity. Crowley's original notes only twice refer, in passing, to his wife:

A – A symbol (on 16 March)

B – Reference to a sexual rite omitted from all published accounts, and altered from the original *"The Secret of W, the seer,"* to *"The secret of Wisdom."*

♦ Neither his personal diary or **Book of Results** chronicle events that allegedly transpired on 08, 09 & 10 April.

►◎◄

The reason for these seemingly baffling contradictions, omissions and alterations is obvious and inescapable – The incidents described never happened!

Crowley's **Book of Results** represents a fledgling attempt to mould actual events, as recorded in his personal diary, around the myth he is weaving. Since all entries in the **Book of Results** were recorded with the same pen, in exactly the same style of handwriting, it is reasonable to suggest that all were written at the same time – Not over consecutive days, as is naturally assumed by the dated 'diary style' sequence and inferred by Crowley's euphemistic 'spin.'

Working with nothing more than scrappy diary entries and an obsessive lust for power, at Boleskine in the Summer of 1904 Crowley sketched a rough chronological outline (in his **Book of Results**) of the fabricated circumstances by which his occult prowess revealed an entirely new, and revolutionary Magickal technique. Of this, it is vital to remember that Crowley originally devised his scheme solely as a means by which to dispose of Mathers and assume control of the Golden Dawn. Precisely as is recorded in Crowley's primary source notebooks, he left Cairo with only the occult 'tool' required to destroy Mathers. This is explicitly clear from two deleted comments, *"the ritual is of sex"* and *"Revelation of ritual to consecrate talismans of XXII against G∴ D∴."* Only on completion of this precursor does Crowley get to form his own Magickal Link and, therefore, rightfully (in accordance with occult tradition) assume control of the Golden Dawn.

Crowley's diaries and notebooks of the period fail to mention numerous instances pivotal to the Cairo Revelation, because they never happened! At this time, Crowley's plan did not require such ornate garnishing. The three-day reception event and supporting cast he grafted on at a much later date, in response to a radical upgrade compelled by 'difficult' questions (relating to the seemingly trivial subject of occult seniority) posed by George Cecil Jones, in 1906. This sequence of events transformed **Liber L. vel Legis** from its original form, to the bare-bones, stripped down second version published in the **Holy Books,** and resulted in Crowley's reluctant sacrifice of five notebook pages.

III. The AL-man Cometh

The **Book of Results** begins on 16 March, whereas Crowley's personal diary records four events preceding this date, starting on 09 February. These are:

Feb. 9	To Cairo
Feb. 11	Saw b.f.g.
	b.f.b.
	(This entry is quite unintelligible to us.)
Feb. 19	To Helwan as Oriental Despot.
	(Apparently P. had assumed some disguise...)
Feb. 20	Began golf.

Skipping over, for now, the first two entries, I focus on his note of 19 February. To my mind, the feigned surprise is shallow and unconvincing. Crowley must surely remember the day he danced around Helwan adorned in the glittering attire of a noble Persian prince. Especially as he immortalised the moment in a holiday snapshot – Complete with industrial-strength halo!

"I wanted to swagger about in a turban with a diamond aigrette and sweeping silken robes or a coat of cloth of gold, with a jewelled talwar by my side, and two gorgeous runners to clear the way for my carriage through the streets of Cairo." (**Confessions**, page 387)

Following the brief entry of 20 February (*"Began golf"*) is a gap of almost a month. Crowley's personal diary resumes on 16 March, the date at which his **Book of Results** starts. Crowley's various accounts of events between 16 and 23 March are impossible to reconcile. The 'official' sequence appears to run as follows:

Wednesday 16 March
Preliminary Invocation of the Goetia (the "*Bornless*" ritual) performed. Rose suggests 'they' are waiting for Crowley.

Thursday 17 March
Preliminary Invocation of the Goetia repeated. Thoth "*invoked*," (**Equinox of the Gods**), or "*appeared*" (personal diary). Crowley gushes about "*great success*," but cannot recall what: "*Yes, but what happened? Fra. P. has no sort of idea.*" Rose whispers, "*It's all about the child. All about Osiris.*"

Friday 18 March
Ceremony repeated for a third time. Rose suggested that Crowley had upset the waiter, 'Horus,' and ought invoke this deity. After cross-examining Rose, she outlined the skeleton of a seemingly nonsensical ritual, which "*broke all the rules.*"

Saturday 19 March
Crowley fleshed-out and performed "*badly*" the new ritual at 12:30PM. **Confessions** (page 394) states this produced "*little success.*" A more promising result followed, in consequence of a second recital, undertaken at midnight. On this point, his diary and **Book of Results** are ambiguous. One suggests that the repeat performance happened at midnight on Saturday 19 March. The other gives 10PM on Sunday 20 March. Crowley noted this discrepancy in **Equinox I, 7** (page 375), though failed to clarify if both ceremonials happened on 19 March, or if he split them over two days (i.e. midnight on 19 March, and 10PM or midnight on 20 March):

> "*The other diary says 10 P.M. 'Midnight' is perhaps a loose phrase, or perhaps marks the climax of the ritual,*"

Sunday 20 March
Crowley notes "*Success in my invocation of Horus, by breaking all the rules,*" and "*Revealed that the Equinox of the Gods is come.*"

Monday 21 March
The Sun enters Aries at 1AM (i.e. the vernal equinox).
"*I should fix Monday, March 21, for the visit to Boulak*" (**Equinox of the Gods**, page 115). In other accounts, Crowley 'blurs' the date of this pivotal excursion between 20 and 23 March.

Tuesday 22 March
Crowley's personal diary gives *"X.P.B."* His **Book of Results** suggests 'a day of rest,' at the behest of Rose, and states: *"tomorrow to be the great day of invocation."*

Wednesday 23 March
1. Diary states *"Y.K. done (? His work on the Yi King)"*
2. Equinox of the Gods suggests *"23. The Secret of wisdom. (We omit the record of a long and futile Tarot divination.)"*
3. Unpublished notes in OS27 give *"The Secret of W. the seer,"* followed by the outline of a ritual of Sex Magick.

The common link in this nebulous cloud of material is 'a ritual' performed on Wednesday, Thursday and Friday. Then rewritten and tested on Saturday and/or Sunday. Success, by the new method (Rose's Invocation of Horus), is declared on Monday (the vernal equinox). In an attempt to deduce exactly what this ritual comprised, and when it was written or amended, I next focus on Crowley's original source document. His vellum notebook (OS27) entitled **Invocation of Hoor.** For anyone without access to this material (housed at the Warburg Institute, London), or scans of it, Markus Katz's 2010 publication **The Invocation of Hoor** is a reasonable substitute, though not infallible.

OS27 Page 1
This begins with a title and description of Rose's Invocation of Horus, as reprinted in **Equinox of the Gods** (page 77). On the opposite page 'someone' has written *"Skeleton?"* This refers to the skeleton of a new ritual Crowley mentioned on Friday 18 March. The two final words, *"Saturn"* and *"Die,"* suggest that the ritual will happen on Saturday and Sunday: *"Promise of success on Saturday or Sunday."* (**Equinox of the Gods**, page 79)

OS27 Page 3
Crowley's Preliminary Banishing is crossed-out and a note (on page 2) states: *"Use the sign of Apophis and Typhon,"* followed by a line to a second note, which reads: *"This written after, when preliminary opposite was cancelled."*

From this, it is clear that Crowley originally inserted a Preliminary Banishing into the new ritual proposed by Rose, though subsequently deleted this, allegedly at her command.

OS27 continues with the Invocation of Horus ritual reproduced in **Equinox of the Gods** (pages 77 to 84). In section three, Crowley changed a line in response to a minor hiccup: "*On Saturday the string of pearls broke: so I changed the invocation...*" (**Equinox of the Gods**, page 82)

This reference infers that Crowley performed Rose's **Invocation of Horus** (the new ritual) "*badly*" on Saturday 19 March, and repeated it with success ("*Success in my invocation of Horus*") on the same evening, or Sunday. He does not offer any rationale for the 'turn of fate.' From reading **Equinox I, 7**, it is reasonable to suggest that Crowley originally followed his Preliminary Banishing with a ceremonial titled **Festival of the Equinox** (on 16, 17 and 18 March). On 19 March, he dropped these in favour of Rose's new Invocation of Horus, though initially prefaced his new toy with a Preliminary Banishing, which, on 'third thought,' he also scrapped. Crowley insisted that Rose outlined a skeleton for the Invocation of Horus, which he later completed. Of this ceremonial, he dismissively explained his participation as:

"*...only agreed to obey her in order to show how silly she was, and he taunted her that nothing could happen if you broke all the rules.*"

Perhaps Rose did suggest the initial conditions ("*Lock Doors. White robes*" certainly sounds more 'middle-class housewife' than 'Great Wild Beast') and maybe she did contribute a few comments. Nevertheless, the resulting **Invocation of Horus According to the Divine Vision of W, the Seer** is unquestionably Crowley's work. Indeed, his assertion that Rose commanded him to scrap the Preliminary Banishing (i.e. "*omitted at W.'s order – P.*") was probably founded on a subsequent realisation that 'a nonsensical ritual, which broke all the rules,' probably wouldn't include a 'proper' occult component. **The Invocation of Horus** is pure Crowley and in perfect accordance with his occult thinking at the time. With reference to terminology, style and symbolism this is precisely what one would anticipate from a Neophyte of the Golden Dawn – With one exception. The ritual invokes Horus and not the traditional Osiris. This is the only departure from an otherwise typical rite constructed around the ancient Egyptian mythology favoured by occultists of this era. It contains none of the sexual elements alluded to in the unpublished B2 material, because Crowley has not yet written this.

Speaking generally, the Invocation of Horus, as printed in **Equinox I, 7** and **Equinox of the Gods,** matches notes Crowley penned in OS27. However, Crowley's unpublished (OS27) material continues, and a quite remarkable transformation happens – But not in published versions!

> Nuit
> Hadit
> R·H·K UNI A-?-...-K

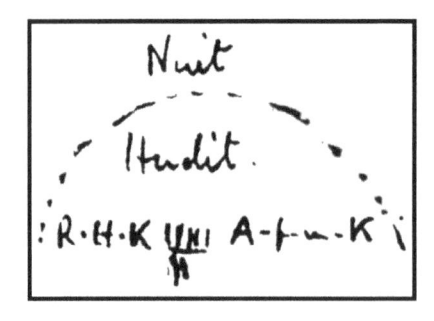

'Off-record,' Crowley's vellum notebook leaves the Golden Dawn far behind and charts entirely new territory. This radical material begins with *"The dance"* invoking *"O Nuit! O Hadit! O Ra Hoor Khuit!"* Following this is a short section titled *"The supreme ritual"* – To which Crowley appended a note of caution: *"But this is a secret as it is dangerous."* The page concludes with a diagram Crowley can only have sketched <u>after</u> viewing the Stele of Revealing. Yet, according to published accounts, this did not happen until his visit to the Boulak museum on 21 March, the next day.

Following these revelations, Crowley imported several new characters (Nuit, Hadit and Ra-Hoor-Khuit) into the Magickal formula of *"ABRAHADABRA."* Next is a spell *"To invoke,"* then another, *"To obtain LVX."* After this, Crowley pens an astonishing new ritual named *"B2. To have any Knowledge,"* that opens with **"Ra-Hoor-Khuit! I invoke thee!"**

A comparison of B2 material with his published description of stele imagery in **Equinox of the Gods** (page 74) leaves no doubt that when Crowley wrote the B2 ritual, on Saturday 19 or Sunday 20 March, he had seen the Stele of Revealing – Impossible according to his own published accounts. The similarities between certain lines are incontestable:

    B2:   *"Thou whose skin is of flaming indigo..."*

    Stele: *"His face is green, his skin indigo."*

    B2:   *"Thou whose garments are of green and gold, who bearest the potted skin of the fierce leopard."*

    Stele: *"His necklace, ankles and bracelets are gold. His tunic is the Leopard's skin, and his apron green and gold."*

Though steeped in Golden Dawn terminology, the B2 ritual and prefacing diagram are a tentative stepping-stone between Crowley's old ideology and the new concepts he is forming. The big problem is... Crowley is writing the soundtrack of a film he has not yet seen! The B2 material utilises stele imagery he does not see for twenty-four hours. It also celebrates the onset of a new *"Equinox of the Gods"* (a once every two thousand years event marking the sun's entry into a new astrological sign - In this instance to Aquarius from Pisces) a month before Aiwass informs him of the terrific news, on 08 and 10 April 1904. In March 1904, Crowley cannot possibly have any inkling as to the gods' intention of initiating a major cabinet reshuffle and must be equally oblivious to the imminent promotion of specific deities. Yet, the B2 material graphically depicts a contrary scenario and, again, one deeply problematic to Crowley's reception story.

With reference to the above, I return to Crowley's initial (and deleted from the record) insistence that his new ritual (whatever this actually comprised) is **1)** the occult tool with which to smash Mathers ("*Revelation of ritual to consecrate talismans of XXII against G∴ D∴*), and **2)** incorporates elements of sexual Magick ("*the ritual is of sex*"). In this context, three lines of the B2 material in particular stand out as being of especial interest. These are:

"*[As Horus, the God the Seer is worshipping, apply the [sword]]*

[Place hands on seers head, figuring her as Thoth & and filling her with [THOTH] fire]

The Enchanter invoketh and becometh [THOTH]."

This text clearly alludes to a ritual of Sex Magick. It also relates to the occult experiments Crowley and Rose performed later, back at Boleskine House: "*Arse very high*" (see page 84). The suggestive 'bending' position of Nuit, as depicted on the Stele of Revealing, provides a visual template for both. As noted by Markus Katz in his (2010) book, **The Invocation of Hoor**:

"*At this time, likely late April 1904, Rose would have been 5 months pregnant. The position indicated would seem to take this into account. It also accords with later rituals designed by Crowley to replicate the positions of Nuit and Hadit on the stele.*"

It is looking increasingly as though Crowley's rite of Sex Magick is not so much a case of '*lie back and think of England,*' as '*bend over and lie about Ra-Hoor-Khuit!*'

Astonishingly, Crowley omits from the record all traces of his pivotal shift in Magickal thinking – Why! He has stumbled upon a potent and innovative new occult methodology, Sex Magick, yet wholly fails to mention this in any published account! On this point, it is pertinent to note that Marcus Katz's 2010 publication reproduces this sensational material, but does so in a slightly incorrect order. Incidentally, the microfilm page files corresponding with OS27 do not reflect the inverse orientation of its final three sections. Only on inspection of the original notebook, or an identical facsimile, does the significance of its curious layout become evident.

Crowley's published accounts are incomplete and misleading. However, from a careful study of OS27 it is possible to deduce a probable chain of events, beginning on 16, 17 and 18 March when Crowley (as stated in published accounts) performed a selection from the Golden Dawn's greatest hits (including the Preliminary Invocation, Banishing and possibly Festival of the Equinox). Nothing of consequence happened and, on reflection, Crowley went out on a limb. He came to Cairo intent on manifesting (or fabricating) a New Equinox. To accomplish this, he reasoned, the outmoded Golden Dawn rituals needed updating in favour of the incoming hierarchy of deities and dogma. Herein is the genuine origin and intent of Crowley's Invocation of Horus.

According to its hieroglyphs, the stele depicts Osiris and Ankh-f-n-Khonsu, yet Crowley suggested that Horus and Ra-Hoor-Khuit were waiting for him. Furthermore, he described Rose's Invocation of Horus as nonsensical specifically because it invoked Horus, not Osiris. With this terminology Rose, or rather Crowley, audaciously suggested that Horus had assumed the throne of Osiris, and that a New Equinox had indeed dawned. Rather suspiciously, Crowley first allowed Rose to compose the elements of a groundbreaking new ritual then blamed her 'in advance' for its inevitable failure!

Crowley prepared the script of Rose's 'new method' on 18 and/or 19 March and performed the ritual at 12:30PM on 19 March, to "*little success.*" Crowley has now proved his point to Rose (i.e. "*nothing could happen if you break all the rules*"). Therefore, his decision to repeat the same ceremonial, either at midnight the same day, or between 10PM and midnight the following day, is ridiculous – Why repeat a ritual that was known to be duff from the outset? In fact, Crowley didn't repeat Rose's Invocation of Horus. Following the initial failure of his wife's 'nonsensical' ritual (on 19 March), Crowley seemingly plucked the B2 material from nowhere and immediately incorporated its radical new sexual aspects into his occult repertoire. He spent 19 March (and/or 20 March) writing the B2 ritual and performed it "*with great success*" on the evening of 19 or 20 March.

The dating discrepancy is equally curious and illuminating, for several reasons. Firstly, there is a slight divergence between the handwritten entry for Sunday 20 March in Crowley's **Book of Records**, and that published in **Equinox of the Gods**.

"Great success in midnight invocation." (**Equinox of the Gods**)

"Great success in midway of invocation." (**Book of Results**)

In all likelihood, Crowley enacted Rose's Invocation of Horus on Saturday, 19 March – With no result. Later that day, or possibly the next, he saw either the stele, or a photograph of it, experienced a revelation, promptly scrapped his wife's ritual and spent several hours, perhaps a whole day, preparing the sexualised B2 material in time for it to be employed, with great success, on Sunday 20 March. Unfortunately, circumstance compelled substantial revisions to Crowley's plan. Out of sheer necessity he was obliged to eradicate all reference to sex from the equation, and this was a big ask! Crowley hid the now-toxic B2 recital of 20 March beneath an alleged repetition of Rose's Invocation of Horus – Despite the absurdity of repeating an obviously defective ritual. Furthermore, it was not enough to gloss-over the B2 ritual itself. Crowley also needed to figure out a way of concealing the considerable time it took him to prepare this material. His initial solution was blunt. It involved nothing more sophisticated than rewinding the second, successful, performance back by twenty-four hours when roughing-out his prototype version of events in the **Book of Results** – A record created at Boleskine House in the summer of 1904. By doing this, Crowley greatly diminishes the time between first and second performances and 'seemingly' gives himself little if any time spare in which to tweak Rose's defective (at least on its first run) ritual.

Secondly, Crowley's evident 'twitchiness' about this discrepancy overspills into another facet of the reception story. In **Equinox of the Gods** Crowley published **a)** his cross-examination of Rose, **b)** a description of stele imagery and **c)** a translation of its hieroglyphs, between **Book of Results** entries dated 18 and 19 March. This makes absolutely no sense, whatsoever. What possible reason could Crowley have for sandwiching details of his visit to the Boulak Museum on 21 March, between diary entries dated 18 and 19 March? This, again, is an attempt to present the appearance of a day so full as to preclude any opportunity of repairing Rose's ceremonial prior to its second and 'miraculously' successful performance.

Strictly speaking, B2's sexual references were not themselves the primary cause of concern. When Crowley revised his plan, the previously inconsequential chronology of events suddenly assumed immense significance. In B2, and elsewhere, Crowley employs imagery, terminology and knowledge of which, according to published accounts, he is allegedly ignorant of until days and weeks later.

At this point, I restate a salient point by quoting Crowley's own words. On Sunday 20 March, following the success of whatever ritual, he wrote:

> *"Revealed that the Equinox of the Gods is come […] I am to formulate a new link of an order with the Solar Force."*

The operative phrase is *"I am to,"* future tense. Crowley departs Egypt with only the 'tool' required to sweep away the old order. In accordance with his instructions, Crowley returned to Boleskine and immediately launched a barrage of sex-tipped Magick missiles against Mathers. By his own admission, Crowley can only make the requisite Magickal Link on destruction of the now obsolete Golden Dawn. Since the demolition process had not even started whilst Crowley lingered in Cairo, it is utterly implausible that Aiwass or any other praeterhuman entity materialised to 'rubber-stamp' a job not yet even started! – A self-evident fact corroborated by the complete lack of any mention, whatsoever, of the three-day reception event in any of Crowley's contemporary writings.

IV. Poetic Licence

In the wake of his success on Sunday 19 (or Monday 20) March, Crowley's **Book of Results** states:

> *"I am to formulate a new link of an order with the Solar Force."*

He has not yet formed the link! The ritual of 19 or 20 March only points in the right direction. Though this was enough for Crowley to declare that a new *"Equinox of the Gods"* (a very 'old aeon' Golden Dawn term) was upon Mankind.

Crowley's diary notes only the vernal equinox on Monday 21 March. It is probably for this reason that he subsequently *"fixes"* 21 March as the date of his trip to the Boulak Museum. On Tuesday 22 March he declared, *"The day of rest, in which nothing whatever of magic is ever to be done at all. Mercury is to be the great day of invocation."* On Wednesday 23 March, Crowley's diary entry reads *"Y.K. done (? His work on the Yi King)"* whereas the (OS27) **Book of Results** gives *"The Secret of W, the seer,"* which was subsequently changed (in published accounts) to *"The Secret of Wisdom."* It must be emphasised that the

Book of Results is not a reliable or authoritative document with reference to events and dates. Crowley wrote this at Boleskine in the summer of 1904 and not, as he implied, in Cairo.

The **Book of Results** ends with Crowley's entry of Wednesday 23 March. His personal diary includes five entries after this date.

March 24	Met اجيحا again.
March 25	823 Thus
	461 " " = pfly2bz
	218
(Blot)	wch trouble with ds.
(Blot)	P.B. (All unintelligible; possibly a blind.)
April 6	Go off again to H, taking A's p.

As previously noted, neither his personal diary or occult record (**Book of Results**) mention Crowley's visit to the Boulak Museum, his cross-examination of Rose, or the three-day reception of **Liber L. vel Legis**.

The curious termination of Crowley's diary on 6 April may have an elementary solution. On first arriving in Cairo, on 9 February, he arranged a lease on the apartment he occupied on return, several weeks later. This short-term tenancy was, most likely, of a month's duration. Crowley took up residency on Monday 14 March and was due to vacate the premises on Friday 08 April. However, eager to return home and experiment with his radical new system of Sex Magick, Crowley probably left two days early, on Wednesday 06 April – The date of his final diary entry. Crowley's diary ends on 06 April, probably because on this date he packed it in a trunk in readiness for the return to Boleskine. At this time, Crowley had nothing more than the 'seed' of a new brand of occult methodology – Sex Magick. This, he believed, was the secret technique facilitating communion with the Secret Chiefs governing a New Equinox. Somewhat curiously, in **Confessions** (page 403), Crowley writes:

> *"I made a certain number of studies of The Book of the Law […] I had the manuscript typed. I issued a circular letter to a number of my friends, something in the nature of a proclamation of the New Aeon, but I took no pains to follow it up. […] I dropped the whole business, to all intents and purposes. I completely abandoned my diary. I even neglected a really first-rate opportunity for bringing The Book of the Law into public notice, for Mrs Besant was on the ship by which Ouarda and I returned to Europe. […] In Paris, I wrote a formal letter to Mathers informing him that the Secret Chiefs had appointed me as*

visible head of the Order, and declared a new Magical Formula. I did not expect or receive an answer. I declared war on Mathers accordingly..."

Given Crowley's capacity for self-promotion, the decision to avoid mention of his advancement to 'figurehead of a New Aeon' to either Annie Besant (who, in 1907, became President of the Theosophical Society), or author Arnold Bennett, is inexplicable. Unless, of course… He wasn't! In an unpublished document titled **Notes of conversations with Aleister Crowley concerning the Book of the Law, 1923, recorded by Norman Mudd.** (*"Dated Tunis, 1923, before the writing of the Comment called D."*), Crowley states that he advised fifteen associates of the New Equinox whilst still in Cairo (see below). So why remain silent on the boat home and, indeed, for several years afterwards?

"March 1912 ? No 7 Eqx. Published.
Quotations there form earlier than publication of facsimile.
In transcription of the MSS there appear passages not in the Mss
'I adore the in thee Song' 'Under curator' translation.
'Abstruction' Replica Made subsequently.
Image. Bronze hawk at Cefalu. Bought.
Wrote letter to fifteen people from Cairo 'Eqx. Of Gods come.'"

Of thirteen recipients named, Crowley's nemesis appears in thirteenth position. Beside Mathers' name is the word *"Probably."* In April 1904, Crowley writes *"circular letters,"* issues *"manifestos"* declares *"Eqx. Of Gods come"* and sends Mathers his occult P45, but does not actually mention **Liber L. vel Legis** or the specifics of his *"new Magical Formula"* to anyone, despite rumours to the contrary. On the next page of Mudd's notes, Crowley makes an extremely curious remark:

"What was sent to Fuller as Book of the Law? Presumably typescript."

Presumably! According to Crowley's official story, at this time the manuscript was misplaced and, therefore, he only possessed a typescript (and two carbon copies), or did he?

Whilst in Paris, Crowley collected newly-printed copies of *Why Jesus Wept* – A poem written in January 1904. The dedication, to his unborn child, reads:

"Arm! Arm, and out; for the young warrior of a new religion is upon thee; and his number is the number of a man."

Penned three months before his alleged revelation in Cairo, this is surely one of the most accurate prophesies ever uttered. Crowley's foresight borders on miraculous! On this subject, Crowley is curiously reticent. In **Confessions** (page 387), he defends another poem, **Ascension Day**, written late in 1903 and published in 1904:

> *"There was no doubt a certain brooding of the Holy Spirit of Magick upon the still waters of my soul; but there is little evidence of its operation. I have never lost sight of the fact that I was in some way The Beast 666. There is a mocking reference to it in 'Ascension Day,' lines 98 to 111. The Sword of Song bears the sub-title 'called by Christians the Book of the Beast.' The wrapper of the original edition has on the front a square of nine sixes and on the back another square of sixteen Hebrew letters, being a (very clumsy) transliteration of my name so that its numerical value should be 666."*

The passage Crowley contemptuously dismissed as a *"mocking reference"* actually reads:

> *"Yet by-and-by I hope to weave*
> *A song of Anti-Christmas Eve*
> *And First– and Second- Beast-er Day.*
> *There's one who loves me dearly (vrai!)* [A reference to his mother]
> *Who yet believed me sprung from Tophet,*
> ***Either the Beast or False Prophet;***
> ***And by all sorts of monkey tricks***
> ***Adds up my name to Six Six Six.***
> *Retire, good Gallup! In such strife her*
> ***Superior skill makes you a cipher!***
> ***Ho! I adopt the number. Look***
> ***At the quaint wrapper of this book!***
> ***I will deserve it if I can.***
> ***It is the number of a Man"***

From these references alone, it is evident that Crowley has adopted the mantle of 'Great Beast 666' and is intent on bringing his new religion to the world long before Aiwass appeared on the scene. In **Confessions**, he attempts to downplay and invalidate his own words (because they contradict the reception mythology), but is bolting the door long after his horse has departed its stable. Incidentally, Crowley's mother first nicknamed him 'The Beast' as a child, when she discovered him masturbating.

Before moving on, I note two further passages of interest. **Equinox of the Gods** (1936) adds a chapter to material first published in **Equinox I, 7** (1912). Written at Cefalu between 1920 and 1923, the new material begins with the words:

> *"Certain very serious questions have arisen with regard to the method by which this book was obtained."*

On a similar theme, a note in **Equinox I, 7** (page 385) reads:

> *"Similarly, with regard to the writing of Liber Legis, Fra. P. will only say that it is in no way 'automatic writing.'"*

Why did Crowley feel the need to publish a clarification referring specifically to *"automatic writing"* – A phrase that only someone with access to his long-since abandoned cover sheet or Appendix could echo?

> *"This MS. (which came into my possession in July 1906) is a highly interesting example of genuine automatic writing. Though I am in no way responsible for any of these documents, except the translations of the Stele inscriptions, I publish them among my works, because I believe that their intelligent study may be interesting & helpful. - A. C."*

'Someone' who had read Crowley's discarded notes (see above) and who could not reconcile these with the version of events Crowley was then touting. Not surprisingly, as far back as 1912, certain individuals were expressing doubts about Crowley's story - Questions that clung stubbornly to editions released during his life, and which have dogged his footsteps ever since.

V. Liber L. vel Bogus

Returning to a thread sewn earlier - In February 1904, Crowley steps onto Egyptian soil as 'a man on a mission' and almost ready to initiate his 'Grand Scheme' to assume control. Crowley is perfectly clear as to his objectives and wholly focussed on the fulfilment of three vital criteria. He must **1)** topple Mathers, thus succeeding him as head of the Golden Dawn, **2)** forge a new Magickal link with the Secret Chiefs and **3)** demonstrate, incontestably, the authenticity of his claim. Whether or not these objectives are actually accomplished is, to Crowley, incidental. One way or another, he *will* return as the spearhead of a *"new Magical Formula"* – All other priorities rescinded! In furtherance of his obsessive crusade, Crowley is prepared to *"break all the rules"* and fabricate any required 'evidence.' In this respect, he already has a secret weapon tucked discretely up his sleeve - The Stele of Revealing.

The date at which Crowley became aware of the Stele is open to considerable speculation, though certainly earlier than suggested in his official account (see Page 138). He could not have viewed it on first visiting Cairo (14 October to 05 November 1902) due to an ongoing relocation from the **Khedival Palace Museum** (closed in May 1902) to the **Cairo Museum** (opened on 15 November 1902). Incidentally, the actual '**Boulak Museum**' ceased exhibiting in May 1889 (See **AL cetera**). The artefact's ticket number '666' possibly caught his eye in consequence of its connection to the 'Beast of Revelation' – A term of endearment Crowley has been 'playing with' since childhood. Given his preference for anal intercourse, the suggestive manner in which the heavenly Isis is 'arched' over the starry vault of Heaven probably amused him, too. Only in late 1903 did Crowley begin to grasp the Stele's full potential. If carefully stage-managed, a scenario could be engineered in which this humble artefact is transformed into unmistakable 'proof' of his link to the Secret Chiefs and, therefore, a divine stamp of approval on whatever fable Crowley conjured to garnish his central sacrament.

Crowley's scheme to usurp Mathers has one inherent 'soft-spot.' Its successful implementation is reliant upon the seemingly accidental discovery of a specific artefact and subsequent, equally coincidental, revelation of its connection (via 666) to Crowley. This is the weak link in his blueprint to DIY deification, and he knows it. Even someone with Crowley's impressive powers of persuasion will have the Devil's own job convincing sceptics and believers alike that 'the Chosen One' blundered into incontestable proof of his own divinely-sanctioned mandate, as written by none other than himself!

In his first version of the Cairo Revelation, an interest in the stele leads directly to Brugsch's French Translation and the *"creation of the ritual by which Aiwass, the author of Liber L., was invoked."* This climaxes in the three-day reception of a text (by someone other than Crowley - Who only came into possession of the manuscript some two years after its creation) later revealed as the Founding Document of a New Aeon, with Crowley at its head. Everything rests on the stele and to bolster this Achilles Heel Crowley invents a subtle stratagem. He generates an aura (albeit thin) of credibility by distancing himself from the cathartic moment. Someone other than Crowley need discover the stele and make the initial connection. For dramatic effect, Crowley sneers and pours cynicism at all conjecture suggesting the involvement of Secret Chiefs. Though, ultimately, and begrudgingly, he will accept a god-sent invitation to assume the exalted role of 'Messiah.' Out of sheer convenience, Crowley tasks Rose, his wife (Ouarda the Seer) with the responsibility of inadvertently stumbling upon the sacred 'stone tablet.' Only later will Crowley decipher the cryptic clues to uncover a New Covenant from God. In other words, Crowley is attempting to emulate the same myth as worked so well with the Golden Dawn's Founding Documents – Initially discovered on a book cart and only later revealed as a skeleton ritual enabling suitably qualified 'adepts' to form a Magickal Link with the Secret Chiefs. These documents were fakes, but worked for the Golden Dawn. Crowley saw no harm in repeating the same trick. Crowley is also hedging his bets. Whilst in Ceylon, a minor altercation with a wounded bat precipitated an experience in which Crowley discovered his wife:

> "...*stark naked, hanging to the frame with arms and legs, insanely yawling.* [...] *When I got her down at last, she clawed and scratched and bit and spat and squealed, exactly as the dying bat had done to her.* [...] *It was the finest case of obsession that I had ever had the good fortune to observe. Of course it is easy to explain that in her hypersensitive* [pregnant] *state the incident of the day had reproduced itself in a dream. She had identified herself with her assailant and mimicked his behaviour.* [...] *The spirit of the bat had entered her.*"
> (**Confessions** page 380)

With reference to this occurrence, Crowley perhaps wondered if his wife possessed latent psychic abilities – Was she 'a bit of a seer?' Given this possibility, he may have wondered about initiating a sequence of experiments devised to test the extent of his wife's occult capabilities. It may even have crossed his mind at this time to outline a situation in which Rose seemingly 'finds' the stele whilst perusing exhibits at the Boulak Museum. This event certainly placed into his head the seed of an idea of Rose as a Medium – A role he exploited later in the reception myth.

The stele is an integral part of Crowley's 'Master of the Universe' scheme from the outset. The handwritten cover sheet and aborted 1907 Appendix both reference the artefact. Conversely, the 1910 **Holy Books** do not. The stripped-down version of **Liber L. vel Legis** published in **Volume Three** reproduces only the three chapters, without comment, explanation or introduction. The six verses of Crowley's paraphrase (of translated hieroglyphs) are the only stele-related material included in this version. Interestingly, between September 1907 and October 1909, Crowley decided to omit the distinction between material written by 'someone else' (i.e. *"Though I am in no way responsible for any of these documents…"*) and his *"translations of the Stele inscriptions."* The **Holy Books** reproduce **Liber L. vel Legis** as one, amongst a collection of 'inspired writings' Crowley feverishly churned out from 1907. Incidentally, the term *"inspired writings"* refers to material obtained in a trance-like state during which he acts only as an inert physical channel through which the will of the gods can pass. Of writing his Holy Books Crowley states:

> *"I was not wholly conscious at the time of what I was writing, and I felt that I had no right to 'change' so much as the style of a letter. They were written with the utmost rapidity without pausing for thought for a single moment, and I have not presumed to revise them."*

and

> *"…is wholly different from anything that I have written myself. It is characterized by a sustained sublimity of which I am totally incapable and it overrides all the intellectual objections which I should myself have raised. It does not admit the need to explain itself to anyone, even to me. I cannot doubt that these books are the work of an intelligence independent of my own. "*

Given the profound, even sacramental nature of this material, it is surprising to discover that the gods, completely independently of Crowley, encoded the name of his then mistress in section five, verse 43 of **Liber LXV: Cordis Cincti Serpente** (written in November 1907):

> *"**A**donai, **d**ivine Adonai, **l**et **A**donai **i**nitiate **r**efulgent **d**alliance! This O concealed the name of Her name that inspireth my rapture, the scent of whose body bewildereth the souls, the light of whose soul abaseth this body unto the beasts."*

The initial letters of Crowley's first sentence spell the name 'Ada Laird.' Some time later, the fair sex clearly still lingered in his mind, and pants. He again slipped another name into the proceedings. The initial letters of verses one and two of **Liber LXVI: Stellae Rubeae** spell out the name of Ada Leverson:

> *"1. **A**pep, **d**eifieth **A**sar,*
> *2. **L**et **e**xcellent **v**irgins **e**voke **r**ejoicing, **s**on of **N**ight!"*

Its preface describes this work as:

*"A secret ritual of APEP, the heart of IAO-OAI, delivered unto V.V.V.V.V. for his use in a certain matter of **Liber Legis**."*

'APEP' is an ancient Egyptian deity depicted as a snake or crocodile, who daily attempted to sink the boat of Sun-God Ra. The 'Star Ruby' is a heavily encrypted ritual of sexual Magick. On this theme, I note that Crowley inked the words *"Invocation of Hoor"* on the front cover of his vellum notebook. 'Hoor' is a coded reference to the anus (i.e. the Eye of Hoor). Assuming (as one naturally would) Crowley penned this title before adding content, his choice is highly-suggestive of advance knowledge relating to the outcome of a Magickal working which only later developed a sexual motif, and one styled on an occult methodology defined by its title – An invocation of the anus! Of course, the stele imagery on which Crowley configured his sexual rite includes three figures – One female and two males! Perhaps coincidentally, by rearranging one letter *"Ouarda the Seer"* becomes *"Our Ada the Seer."*

At this point, I pause to make an important point:

Crowley wrote the B2 material (subsequently eradicated from the record) with a knowledge of stele imagery, seemingly a day before he first saw it at the Boulak Museum. His description of stele imagery, beginning *"In the museum at Cairo..."* includes revised and upgraded details (see page 118) indicative that the B2 material was prepared from an earlier, less accurate source. To my mind, these subtle amendments are attributable to one of two possible scenarios. These are:

1) Crowley prepared the B2 material from rough notes already in his possession (from a previous trip to Cairo) and based the later description of stele imagery on a more accurate source (perhaps a visit to the Boulak, on 21 March).

2) Crowley prepared the B2 material from rough notes already in his possession, or made during his visit to the Boulak, and based his later and more accurate description on information and photograph of the stele accompanying the French translation.

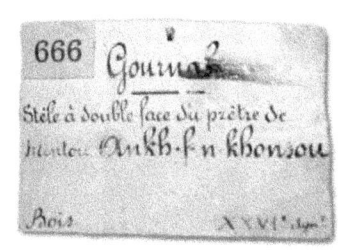

In this respect, Crowley's published accounts of his first glimpse at the stele are extremely problematic. The description, beginning, *"In the museum at Cairo,"* is the only occasion on which Crowley correctly identifies the stele's actual location.

In **Equinox of the Gods** and **Equinox 1, 7** he refers to the wrong museum (i.e. the Boulak) on five occasions! This is perplexing. The Boulak closed fifteen years previously and its successor, the Khedival Palace Museum closed prior to March 1902. Crowley can only have visited the Cairo Museum. So, why did he refer to it as the Boulak? Crowley's honeymoon coincided with the reinterment of Boulak founder Auguste Mariette's ashes at the Cairo Museum. This was a big event, made all the newspapers, and cannot have escaped Crowley's attention. Given the flurry of publicity, it is unlikely in the extreme that Crowley would have mistaken the Cairo Museum for one that closed in 1889. Yet, this is precisely what he did when he 'fixed' the date of his visit to the Boulak as 21 March (the vernal equinox).

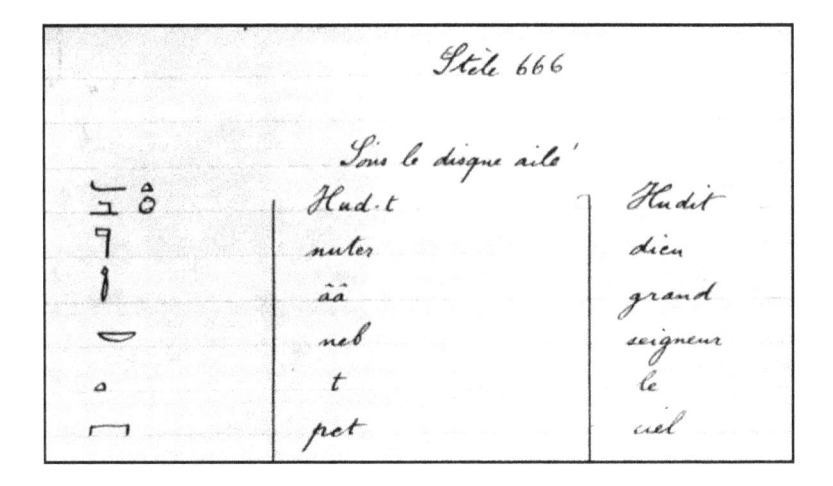

Stèle 666

Sous le disque ailé

	Hud.t	Hudit
	nuter	dieu
	āā	grand
	neb	seigneur
	t	le
	pet	ciel

On studying published accounts littered with irreconcilable discrepancies, and unpublished source material containing no mention of the alleged visit, it appears possible, even probable, that Crowley's fateful trip to the Boulak Museum on 21 March 1904 never happened! His recollection almost certainly derives from another visit to the museum, but when? The only correct reference to the artefact's actual location appeared in a section titled "*In the museum at Cairo*," as introduced with "*Here is P.'s* [Perdurabo - Crowley's occult name, meaning 'I will endure unto the end'] *description of the stele.*" Despite explicitly claiming authorship of the "*description*," Crowley actually extracted the text directly from material provided by (Émile Charles Albert) Brugsch Bey. In other words, Crowley got the answer right only once, in six attempts, on the occasion he copied from an unnamed French Assistant Curator of the Boulak Museum!

The Stele of Revealing – Exhibit number '666' in the Boulak Museum, as relocated to the new Cairo Museum in November 1902 - Inexplicably, Crowley alleges that he and Rose first saw the stele fifteen years after it had left the building! A reproduction of the original French stele translations, with a note of "*Acknowledgement,*" is included in **The Holy Books of Thelema**. This does not mention the Boulak Museum, at all. Curiously, a statement (by its editor) in **Magick** (page xxxviii) suggests otherwise.

134

References to the stele are present from the very inception of Crowley's plan, but an account of Rose's antics at the Boulak only materialises some eight years later (in **Equinox I, 7**). Indeed, with the exception of **Invocation of Hoor** and B2 material, there is no direct evidence contradicting a notion that Crowley penned the remainder of his vellum notebook (OS27) after leaving Egypt.

VI. I'm sick, sick, sick of six, six, six

Crowley landed in Port Said on 08 February and headed directly for Cairo, arriving the following day. Three days later, he made two coded entries in his personal diary.

Feb. 9	To Cairo
Feb. 11	**Saw b.f.g.**
	b.f.b.
	(This entry is quite unintelligible to us.)
Feb. 19	To Helwan as Oriental Despot.
	(Apparently P. had assumed some disguise…)
Feb. 20	Began golf.
March 16	Began INV. [Invocation] IAO [See Liber Samekh]

Unless a chance discovery sheds light on these enigmatic triplets, it remains a distinct possibility that Crowley's original intent is irrecoverable. As such, speculation is of limited value. Nevertheless, a smattering of informed deduction may prove somewhat instructive. For instance - If Crowley did indeed plan to covertly 'steer' his wife into the arms of the stele, it is reasonable to anticipate he'd first need to familiarise himself with the crime scene.

If he made an excuse to sneak away for a couple of hours and inspect the site, then Crowley's mood took a big hit on finding the Boulak boarded-up. He now has no idea where an artefact vital to his plan is currently displayed, if accessible at all. His grand scheme is in real danger of falling at the very first hurdle. Anxious to discover the stele's whereabouts, Crowley quickly arranges two meetings. Since he needs to keep a note of his activities (for later), but can't speak openly of efforts to locate a stele he's not even supposed to know about, Crowley writes in code. His diary entry of 11 February may refer to an encounter with "*Mr. Back, owner of the 'Egyptian News,' an hotel, a hunk of railways...*" In fact, Crowley provides incorrect information here. Mr Back was part-owner of not the *Egyptian News*, but Egypt's only English newspaper, the *Egyptian Gazette*. "*Saw b.f.g.*" may suggest that he saw '**M**r **B**ack **f**rom **G**azette,' who connected him with '**B**rugsch **f**rom **B**oulak.' The codified diary entry of Tuesday 22 March ("*X.P.B.*") may refer to an actual visit ('**X**' marks the spot of **P**erdurabo's visit to the **B**oulak, etc., etc., etc...)

The insurmountable obstacle inherent in this and all other scenarios, including Crowley's official version, is one of nomenclature. Had Crowley, alone or accompanied by Rose, actually viewed the stele, and if this event required a frantic scramble to discover its new location, he would most definitely not have erroneously referred to Cairo Museum as the "*Boulak*" on five separate occasions. Add to this the complete absence of any reference (in contemporary sources) to the excursion, and…

Whatever incidents and activities he veiled behind the letter-triplets, it seems that by 19 February Crowley had positioned his pieces and could relax. His palpable and growing sense of excitement is self-evident. He and his wife swaggered to Helwan not as ordinary old Mr. and Mrs. Edward Alexander Crowley, but in the guise of their regal alter-egos, Prince and Princess Chioa Khan. Rose also assumed the honorific title of '*Ouarda the Seer.*' A month later, Crowley took up residence at the Cairo apartment and immediately began his occult warm-up routine.

During his lifetime, Crowley published a multitude of accounts detailing occult adventures with a mindboggling cast of supernatural entities. In all instances, he tacitly assumes that readers accept 'at face value' his account – With one glaring exception! Even though Crowley employed Rose as an impartial and innocent bystander to catch his messiah-ball, he was still twitchy enough about unseemly 'connections' to the 666 stele as to barricade his mythical Boulak revelation behind an impregnable wall of mathematics – A tactic that is, put bluntly, ridiculous. Considering that a 'savagely sceptical' Crowley "*cross-examined*" (**Equinox of the Gods**, page 73) his wife's relations with the gods of a New Equinox to an absurdly hyperbolic degree, "*over the billion mark,*" it seems a trifle odd that he never bothered to record this momentous event in either his personal diary, or its Magickal counterpart, the **Book of Results!** I return to this point later.

From Crowley's perspective, the timing of Rose's alleged discovery of the stele numbered '666' is critical. Its narration needs handling with great sensitivity. In **Confessions**, he goes all round the houses to assure readers that a prior interest in the number 666 is but "*a mocking reference,*" despite several rather blatant contradictions of this assertion (see Section IV, **Poetic Licence**). If Crowley really was blasé about unseemly connections to 666, then why had he acquired a description of that particular stele's imagery and colouration days (and possibly over a year) <u>before</u> Rose allegedly first stumbled upon it! That Crowley possessed this information is unquestionable. He incorporated it into the unpublished and unacknowledged B2 material, written on 19 or 20 March.

Crowley's fledgling plan to smash Mathers begins with Rose's chance discovery of the stele. Its number, 666, Crowley assures us, represents a cast-iron guarantee that Rose has made a genuine contact with the Secret Chiefs and, therefore, he must heed her instructions. Well, that and the absurd (*"Over the billion mark"*) mathematical proof obtained during his earlier interrogation of Rose – The same *"cross-examination"* which does not appear in his notebooks until October 1907, three-and-a-half years later! Conversely, if Crowley's prior awareness of the stele is exposed, the 'true' inspiration behind his innovative occult methodology is also uncovered – Not so much a gift from the gods, as a creative, if lewd interpretation (in accordance with his preference for anal sex) of an ancient Egyptian 'saucy picture postcard!'

In **Confessions**, Crowley can't put enough distance between himself and 666. However, his (**Equinox of the Gods**) defence of the purportedly miraculous connection between Horus, Rose, the stele and Crowley's promotion to Messiah, tells a completely different story.

> *"666 had been taken by Fra. P as the number of his own Name (The Beast) long years before, in his childhood. There could be no physical causal connection here; and coincidence, sufficient to explain this one isolated fact, becomes inadequate in view of the other evidence."*
> (**Equinox of the Gods**, page 73)

As late as the 1920s, when Crowley wrote **Confessions**, his relationship with 666 and the stele is still problematic. On one hand, he must demonstrate a slight, *"mocking"* connection with 666 prior to Horus pointing Rose at the stele, but not enough as to arouse suspicion (i.e. collecting material prior to this event). On the other, since the stele's number essentially constitutes 'proof' of a genuine connection with the Secret Chiefs, (i.e. *"They knew his number"*), then 'suddenly' 666 becomes his lifelong best mate. Crowley can't have it both ways!

The two poems, **Ascension Day** and **Why Jesus Wept,** (see Section IV, **Poetic Licence**) emphatically demonstrate that by January 1904 Crowley had already decided he's the Great Beast 666, and *"the young warrior of a new religion is upon thee; and his number is the number of a man."* As previously noted, this line surely ranks as one of the most accurate prophesies ever uttered! Of course, Crowley knows exactly what will happen in Cairo, because he sketched an outline several months before. **Why Jesus wept** and **Ascension Day** celebrate Crowley's acceptance of a monumental promotion, three months before Aiwass offers him the position.

With reference to the stele, a post made (Friday 30 November) on his invaluable online Crowley resource (www.lashtal.com) Owner & Editor, Paul Feazey, makes a most insightful observation:

> *"Just a note of more general interest... The 'Paraphrase of the Inscription upon the Obverse' - i.e. the basis of Crowley's versification titled (it would appear) 'The Spell Called "The Song"' - is itself a paraphrase of Chapter 91 of 'The Book Of The Dead'.*
>
> *Readers of this thread will find much of interest in that short chapter, especially in the translation by Budge who was writing at a time that was roughly contemporaneous with AC's visit to Cairo. Note especially its mentions of 'Nu, triumphant', 'khu' and 'khaibit'.*
>
> *I suspect that 'The Spell called The Song' really is Crowley's title for the Paraphrase of the Inscription upon the Obverse of the Stele of Revealing. Verse 1 fits, of course, and the context in OS27 (adjacent to a mention of Ahathoor) fits the fifth verse, too.*
>
> *I've said it before, but: Egypt hides the keys to the gates of the city of Thelema! (Actually, I think I'll use that as the sub-title for my work on Ankhefenkhons, mentioned several times on this very site!)"*

Paul's remarkable statement suggests an alternate scenario in which Crowley's paraphrased versifications derive not from a French translation of the stele hieroglyphs (as explicitly stated), but rather from Wallis Budge's (1895) translation of the **Book of the Dead**, Chapter 91. Budge, like Crowley, was a member of the Golden Dawn. It is rumoured that he facilitated the performance of occult rituals in the British Museum's Egyptology rooms. He also traded antiquities with Brugsch. Interestingly, the man commissioned to undertake the stele's second translation, Babbiscombe Gunn, was a noted occultist with links to Waite, the Golden Dawn and Crowley. Maybe Crowley obtained both his initial insights of ancient Egyptian phallic symbolism and a connection to Brugsch through Budge. With reference to this point, I note that **Spell 93** states:

"O phallus of Ra, giving way, which destroys opposition."

Crowley was intent on destroying Mathers, and spent the summer of 1904 hurling sex-tipped Magickal missiles at his adversary. This ancient spell certainly appears to be a nod in the same direction. Perhaps coincidentally, the Magickal number of Crowley's New World Religion, Thelema is also set at ninety-three!

Crowley is acutely aware of his previous, albeit mocking correlation with the number 666. It is the weak link in his plan. For this reason, he invents the cross-examination of Rose and fabricates his ridiculous mathematical proof of her contact with Horus. Crowley claims this conversation took place on 18 March and, given its importance to his story (the precursor to him dragging Rose to the Boulak), he must surely have recorded the specifics 'at the time,' or soon after. Yet, as evidenced by a later notebook, OS23, Crowley does not actually write his account of this pivotal dialogue until late October 1907 – Three-and-a-half years later! Indeed, numerous items contradictory to Crowley's published accounts litter OS23, and this small vellum notebook holds at least one contemporary oddity. The Warburg microfilm index lists OS23, but this is absent from the reels. Somewhat mysteriously, the content of another notebook, namely OS21, appears in place of OS23 (see Section F – **What a Ferkukkle, it's the great OS23 shuffle!**).

Crowley's diary entries after 16 March are mostly encrypted and impossible to decipher with certainty. They may allude to clandestine liaisons with prostitutes, drug deals, or just about anything else he felt unable to write openly in a document his wife may chance upon. However, since he specifically draws attention away from certain "*unintelligible blinds*," I incline to a belief these refer to key events and experiences Crowley is anxious to gloss over. As, I suspect, do instances in which Crowley provides unnecessary and questionable clarifications. For instance, in **Equinox of the Gods** (page 73) he states:

> "*Fra. P. advanced to the case. There was the image of Horus in the form of Ra Hoor Khuit painted upon a wooden stele of the 26th Dynasty – and the exhibit bore the number 666!*[1]
>
> *(And after that is was five years before Fra. P. was forced to obedience!)*
>
> This incident must have occurred before the 23rd of March as the entry on that date refers to Ankh-f-n-khonsu.

666 had been taken by Fra. P. as the number of His own name (The Beast) long years before in His childhood. There could be no physical causal connection here; and coincidence, sufficient to explain this one isolated fact, becomes inadequate in view of other evidence."

The diary entry "*... on that date...*" is part of the "*long and futile Tarot divination*" omitted from all published accounts. As such, Crowley is the only person who read it. Why, then, did he feel a need to underline, in public, the fact of him using a particular name on 23 March after reading it in connection with an artefact he previously "*fixes*" as having viewed two days earlier, on 21 March? The 'issue' Crowley is evidently so twitchy about is touched on then casually dismissed in editorial notes published in **Magick**. These read:

"Another ritual, entitled "Ritual B2," was written in Cairo in this period, in the same notebook as the "Invocation of Horus" (Yorke MS 27). However, this could not be the invocation used on March 18th, as it uses elements from the translation of the Stele of Revealing, which they did not see until the 19th at the earliest, and which remained untranslated until at least March 23. Crowley annotated this ritual "NG" (possibly meaning "no good)." There is no clear record of its use in the Cairo Working, although it is an invocation of Ra-Hoor-Khuit. In a note to the translation Crowley thanked the staff of the Bulaq Mueseum for the "translation of the stele whose discovery led to the creation of the ritual by which Aiwass, that author of Liber L, was invoked. In light of this remark it is curious that while "Ritual B2" bears many signs of reliance on the translation, the "Invocation of Horus" does not."

Top Left – Ritual B2 (with the Hebrew letter Beth used in place of the English letter 'B') begins with the god name "*Ra-Hoor-Khuit.*"

Bottom Left – Section of Crowley's curious mysterious ritual entitled **The Great Invocation**, employing the word "*Ankh-f-n-khonsu.*"

Next page – **The Great Invocation** also includes Crowley's third incorporation of stele imagery.

A thorough comparison of these three rituals is highly recommended.

> *B, as priest. Signs of Enterer and Defence with each phrase.*
>
> O thou who art as an hawk of gold!
> Thee, thee I invoke!   *A ka dua, &c.*
> **O thou whose face is as an emerald, and thy nemmes as the night-sky blue!**
> Thee, thee I invoke!   *A ka dua, &c.*
> O thou who wearest the disk of flaming light upon thy brows, wrapped round with the smaragdine snake!
> Thee, thee I invoke!   *A ka dua, &c.*
> O thou whose eyes blaze forth with light! Whose eyes are as the sun and the moon in their courses!
> Thee, thee I invoke!   *A ka dua, &c.*
> O thou who bearest the Double Wand of Power, the Wand of the Force of Coph Nia!
> Thee, thee I invoke!   *A ka dua, &c.*
> O thou whose left hand is empty, for that thou hast crushed an universe, and nought remains!
> Thee, thee I invoke!   *A ka dua, &c.*
> **O thou who art girt about with the leopard skin: whose apron is of green and gold!**
> Thee, thee I invoke!   *A ka dua, &c.*
> **O thou whose heart is a secret sun in the caverns of thine heart: thou whose skin is of indigo as of the vault of night!**
> Thee, thee I invoke!   *A ka dua, &c.*
> O thou who hast formulated thy father and made fertile thy mother!
> Thee, thee I invoke!   *A ka dua, &c.*

Crowley's footnote ("*666 had been taken by Fra. P. as the number of His own name...*") is also most instructive. His repeated efforts to hammer home the supreme significance of what is, at best, a mundane coincidence, are questionable. Especially when compared with the "*mocking references*" flippantly laughed off in **Confessions**.

The entire weight of Crowley's plan pivots about the Rose-Stele-New Equinox axis. Not surprising, then, that Crowley overplays his hand. On a lighter note, it is perhaps fortuitous that the Boulak Museum's public toilets were not located in Room 666!

I hardly need mention that Crowley's diaries splutter out on 06 April, and omit any mention of the reception events.

VII. Darn that pesky Tarot divination!

In many respects, Aleister Crowley's vellum notebook, OS27, is a singularly remarkable document. Many spokes of **Liber L. vel Bogus** revolve around OS27. Markus Katz employed it to launch his 2010 publication **The Invocation of Hoor** and, excepting a few diary entries, this slim notebook comprises Crowley's only extant source material. From notes scribbled in OS27 arose the myth he fabricated around actual events in Cairo. This small Japanese vellum notebook is also a unique pictorial snapshot of the brief period in which Crowley's mundane and Magickal worlds inverted. Indeed, its physical composition reflects the monumental changes Crowley was experiencing at the time (i.e. midway through, he turns the book upside down, flips it over, and resumes on the back page) It is also the skid mark left by an emergency turn fate compelled Crowley to make in the autumn of 1907.

Aleister Crowley returned to Cairo in the spring of 1904 with several objectives in mind. By whatever means, he 'will' smash Mathers and his control over the Golden Dawn. He 'will' forge a Magickal Link with the Secret Chiefs and he 'will' receive the Magickal Formula of a New Equinox. Crowley is not merely referring to the bi-annual '*Word of the Equinox*' declared each spring and autumn. He is actually suggesting that the 26,500 year cycle of heavenly precession had transported the rising sun into Aquarius and, therefore, that the two millennia reign of Jesus (prophet of the epoch of Pisces) was over. Crowley's "*new Magickal Formula*" was, quite literally, the new 'Word of God,' and valid for two-millennia. As can be imagined, anyone making a claim of *that* stature requires hugely impressive credentials! Nevertheless, Crowley's ongoing psychological meltdown leaves him with no option other than to storm in 'all guns blazing.' He will return from honeymoon 'a god,' or a basket-case.

By a supremely perverse paradox, Crowley's single-minded focus and obsessive drive led directly to his most costly error, ever. In Cairo, Crowley was wholly preoccupied, engrossed, and otherwise submerged in the mechanics of manufacturing and concealing the stage, script, props and characters necessary to perform his 'divine pantomime.' As such, he almost completely overlooked a uniquely rare singularity, at which he did indeed make, in whatever sense, a genuine contact with the primeval 'Magickal Current' that will shape our planet for the next two thousand years. Alas, Crowley was so busy trying to fake it that he never noticed the moment when Horus really did offer him 'a light!' (I present a comprehensive analysis of this matter in the third part of this work.)

Crowley sailed away from Cairo not as the divinely-sanctioned "*Prophet of a New Aeon*" (decreed by Aiwass and validated by the **Liber L. vel Legis** manuscript). By his own admission, he hadn't yet even forged the prerequisite Magickal Link. Crowley reckons that he must first employ his new occult weapon (Sex Magick) to destroy the old order (Golden Dawn), thus paving the way for his subsequent initiation of the new Word. As noted in **Confessions**, Crowley dispatched Mathers' Magickal redundancy notice from Paris. Shortly after this, he arrived back at Boleskine House and opened his vellum notebook (OS27). Crowley flipped through its opening document, the Invocation of Horus and glances at B2 – The (unpublished) notes penned in response to his literal interpretation of stele imagery (i.e. the sexual aspect). On the next page, he writes:

> "*Revelation of ritual to consecrate talismans of XXII against G∴ D∴*"

'This' is the real Cairo Revelation! Not the lamentable fantasies Crowley subsequently wove.

Next, he sketched an outline of what is clearly a rite of sexual Magick including a technique utilised in the preparation of charged talismans. He then fired a Magickal barrage at Mathers.

> "*We therefore employed the appropriate talismans from The Book of the Sacred Magic of Abra-Melin against him, evoking Beelzabub and his forty-nine servitors.*"

Following the five pages torn from this notebook is the problematic "*long and futile Tarot divination.*" Why did Aleister Crowley make an inaccurate and misleading reference to material that, if viewed in the context of his vellum notebook (OS27), was almost certain to prompt questions to which he had no answers? The solution to this perplexing enigma is elementary, and an unfortunate instance of Crowley shooting himself in the foot in consequence of trying to be 'too clever' for his own good!

His **Book of Results** entry for 20 March succinctly encapsulates Crowley's self-inflicted dilemma - "*All rituals etc. are being abrogated.*" Here, Crowley is unequivocally stating that the old aeon system employed by Mathers and the Golden Dawn is obsolete. Unfortunately, he has not yet manufactured the upgraded package! Crowley has dispensed with the old favourites (Isis, Osiris et al), but has not yet created the essential liturgy and dogma required to kick-start his New Aeon. The preparation of this material is a huge task and undoubtedly a pressing issue – Crowley announced that the "*Equinox of the Gods has come*" in April 1904, so needs to produce 'something.' However, he can brush enquiries aside for a year or so - Which is precisely his intent.

Behind the scenes, Crowley spent the next three years refining his fledgling occult construct - By the summer of 1907 he had encapsulated its essential precepts into a contemporary equivalent of the Golden Dawn Foundation Documents and titled his variant **Liber L. vel Legis**. Crowley intended to drop this incidental item ("*automatic writing*" penned in April 1904, but which Crowley only received in July 1906) quietly into the next available publication. In the autumn of 1907, an opportunity presents itself and a typeset (with errors) version of **Liber L. vel Legis** is scheduled for inclusion, as an appendix, in the third volume of his **Collected Works,** though is omitted at the last minute.

The reasons Crowley pulled the debut outing of **Liber L. vel Legis** I describe in a subsequent chapter. For now, it is important to remember only that, at the time, he intended to publish this material in the aborted 1907 Appendix. Crowley's hidden agenda becomes clear on reading this, or its handwritten precursor, the cover sheet:

"*I publish them among my works, because I believe that their intelligent study may be interesting & helpful. – A. C.*"

With this publication, Crowley sets in motion a self-fulfilling prophecy. An intelligent study of this "*highly interesting example of genuine automatic writing*" will indeed be "*interesting and helpful,*" because Crowley himself will be undertaking the intelligent study, and Crowley himself will ultimately realise the immense significance of material he originally overlooked. Including a contemporary **Book of Thoth** that Crowley initially considered so trivial as to dismiss the material outright ("*We omit the record of a long and futile Tarot divination*").

In essence, Crowley's **Mk1** version of **Liber L. vel Legis** is simple, as evidenced by his contemporary diary entries (see page 110). We have a 'ritual' that is subsequently revised ("*by new way*") and which leads to Crowley declaring the onset of a new "*Equinox of the Gods.*" Notes written in the **Book of Results** echo this sequence, with one slight enlargement – Rose plays a small, incidental part not mentioned in his personal diary. Indeed, the **Book of Results** is an intensely curious document, as explored in the next chapter.

At the time of its creation (probably the late summer of 1904), the **Book of Results**' questionable position at the rear of OS27 is not fatal to

Crowley's **Mk1** version. In this context, the timing of events is not of particular significance, with one exception, the *"long and futile Tarot divination"* that wasn't. As described by Marcus Katz:

> *"... Crowley described as 'a long and futile Tarot divination' we see that is hardly a divination [...] These lines here are the precursor to the establishment of The Book of Thoth as a pictorial narrative of the Thelemic cosmology developed by Crowley."* (**The Invocation of Hoor**, page 39)

The material Crowley omitted from all published accounts was neither long, nor futile. In fact, it wasn't even a Tarot divination and, to confuse matters further, there were two of them! The Tarot divination referenced by Marcus Katz comprises a section of OS27 Gerald Yorke labelled "*4. The planets and the signs of the zodiac.*" The Tarot divination omitted by Crowley relates to material written as a diary entry, on 23 March, in the **Book of Results** (see page 110). This *"long"* divination comprises only eighty-seven words. Its layout and notation are suggestive of symbolism employed by the I-Ching, not the Tarot. Curiously, Crowley's personal diary entry for 23 March states "*Y.K. done (? His work on the Yi King).*" Given this, it appears reasonable to suggest that the Tarot divination Crowley omitted was actually an I-Ching oracle. If so, this mystery gains an additional layer of complexity – Why, in a journal written at Boleskine, did Crowley graft an I-Ching reading onto a Tarot divination that his published works describe misleadingly, and mention only in noting the omission?

Crowley's original plan saw him return from Cairo at the helm of a New Equinox, with a contemporary version of the **Book of Thoth** underwriting his claims. In this scenario, Crowley plays the ultimate sceptic begrudgingly thrashed into submission by unwieldy gods. Of course, once he's made an *"intelligent study"* of **Liber L. vel Legis**, and realised its significance, Crowley can backtrack and declare:

> *"Not only was Rose's seemingly nonsensical ritual actually a genuine instruction from the gods, the notes I initially dismissed as 'futile' are a skeleton of the legendary (and long-lost) Egyptian **Book of Thoth**. This proves that a New Equinox has dawned and that I, Aleister Crowley, am the Chosen One!"*

Crowley would love nothing more than to point triumphantly at three pages of notes relating to Tarot card correspondences now revealed as a contemporary **Book of Thoth**, and which underline his occult credentials. Well, he'd certainly like to, but can't. Since this material appears in OS27 <u>after</u> his return to Boleskine, Crowley can't pass it off as part of the Cairo Revelation. This places him in a difficult position. He needs an incidental hint in published works (i.e. a passing reference to the futile Tarot divination), the significance of which is only revealed later, but is reluctant in the extreme to draw attention towards material clearly not written in Cairo. To solve this conundrum, he adapts the **Book of Results**. However, his solution is not without inherent issues.

The **Book of Results** is Crowley's first attempt to draw together the threads of his New Equinox fabrication. Crowley cannot simply weave **Book of Results** entries around material written at Cairo, because there's not enough available space. Nor can he pen the **Book of Results** on the vellum notebook's next available page, because its inclusion after his "*summer work in 1904*" is absurdly suspicious. Crowley's only solution is to flip the notebook upside down and back-to-front, and start afresh on its last page. With this inventive sleight-of-hand, he provides himself with a plausible, albeit indirect means of referencing vital, though toxic material (i.e. The **Book of Results** appears 'on its own' at the rear of the vellum book. As such, its date of origin is open to a good degree of latitude). His published entry dated 23 March reads:

"*The Secret of Wisdom.*
(We omit the record of a long and futile Tarot divination.)"

In the event of anyone asking to view the omitted material (the skeleton **Book of Thoth**, lost for five millennia, and initially overlooked), Crowley points at his unpublished "*Tarot divination*" and suggests:

"*This is the material I initially thought futile. However, after intelligent study, back at Boleskine, these notes evolved into three pages of Tarot correspondences unveiling the **Book of Thoth**.*"

Some may question 'who,' exactly, had cause to request a loan of Crowley's unpublished notes. In reply, I suggest that perhaps the same individual(s) whose nagging suspicions dogged Crowley's publications from the very outset (see page 128). Crowley's **Mk1** plan is far from perfect, but good enough. He certainly 'got away with it' for over a century. However, a close inspection of his vellum notebook (OS27) reveals a catalogue of extremely dubious anomalies, as illustrated in the next segment.

VIII. A book of mixed results

For ease of reference a selection of scans from Crowley's vellum notebook titled **Invocation of Hoor** (OS27) are included in this section.

These do not include all pages, but merely outline the sequence of its various sections. Markus Katz's 2010 publication **The Invocation of Hoor** reproduces a full transcript of this material. As such, his book would be an invaluable resource in the study of these issues - Had it not been withdrawn from circulation.

In **Equinox I, 7** and **Equinox of the Gods** (pages 69 and 70), Crowley writes *"We have one quite unspoiled and authoritative document, 'The Book of Results,' written in one of the small Japanese vellum note-books which he used to carry."* Over the next few pages, I demonstrate that it is nothing of the sort. The **Book of Results** is Crowley's Magickal diary, as recorded in a small Japanese vellum notebook labelled OS27. I note that Crowley wrote all entries in this dated journal (16 to 23 March) with the same pen, in exactly the same style of handwriting.

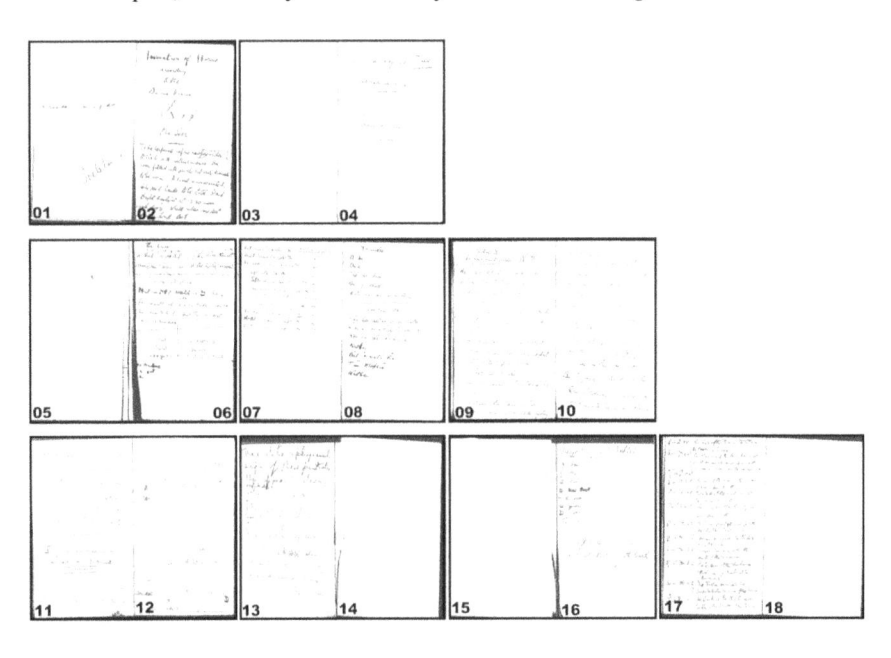

01 – First page of the *Invocation of Horus* (Rose's 'break all the rules' ritual)
04 – Final page of the *Invocation of Horus* (Rose's 'break all the rules' ritual)
06 – Diagrams (based on stele imagery)
07 – Page of occult computations
08 – Page of occult computations
09 – First page of unpublished and unacknowledged B2 Ritual
11 – Last page of B2 Ritual
12 – Method for charging 'sexual talismans' to wage war on Mathers, and dividing line between Cairo material (previous pages) and Boleskine work (subsequent pages)
13 – From *"There is to be a physical sign,"* to *"General idea of ceremony to become R.H.K."*

Five missing pages torn out at this point

16 – Page of occult computations
17 – The last page of Crowley's three page Tarot attribution notes

Thumbnail images 19 to 23 illustrate the arrangement of material Crowley wrote in the back of his vellum notebook.

20 – First page of the *Book of Results*
21 – Second page of the *Book of Results*
22 – Starts with "*In the museum at Cairo. Number 666 is the Stele...*" and ends with "*There is one other object to complete the secret of wisdom.*"
23 – Starts with "*Golden Dawn to be destroyed.*" Bottom half of page contains a brief description of four elemental "*Rituals of Initiation.*"

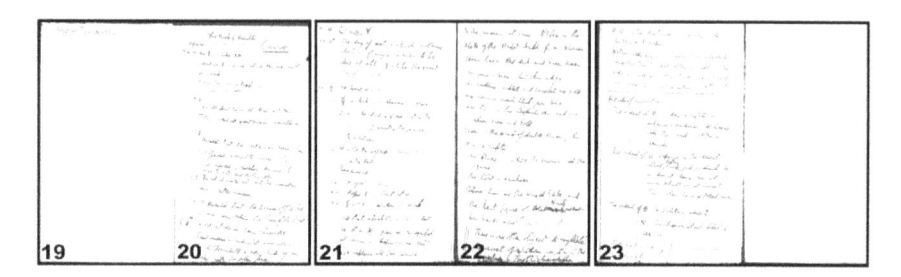

Since Crowley's Magickal adventures began on 16 March, it is natural to suppose that OS27 'should' open with his **Book of Results** entry for 16, 17 and 18 March. After this 'should' follow the nonsensical ritual (Invocation of Horus) Crowley penned, as per Rose's instructions on 19 March (with "*little success*"). Next 'should' be Crowley's record for 20 March (the successful performance). His notes for 21 March 'should' mention a visit to the Boulak Museum. Following this 'should' be the 22 March ("*Day of rest*") entry, with the (23 March) "*Secret of wisdom,*" plus long and futile Tarot divination completing the journal. None of which applies! Bizarrely, Crowley turned his vellum notebook upside down, flipped it over and scribed the **Book of Results (20 & 21)** on what was formerly its back page. A description of the stele's imagery ("*In the museum at Cairo*") follows this, with his "*Golden Dawn to be destroyed*" rant as the last item (**23**).

Regardless of its orientation, if Crowley wrote the **Book of Results** on the dates stated, then his description of the stele 'should' sit between entries of 20 and 22 March. It does not. Crowley's account fixes '21 March' as his first visit to the Boulak Museum (**23**). He must have written a detailed description of the stele imagery whilst viewing the item. Yet this comes after the **Book of Results** (the dated entries of which cease on 23 March). Indeed, it seems unusual to begin a Magickal endeavour with a document titled **The Book of Results!** How did Crowley know that anything would happen? How did he know that the "*Results*" would end on 23 March – The last dated entry recorded in the

Book of Results. Immediately following this is Crowley's description of the stele (which 'should' appear two days earlier, on 21 March).

Appearing first in the **Book of Results** is Rose's nonsensical Invocation of Horus **(02 to 04)**. Crowley claims he wrote this at the behest of his wife, on 19 March, and performed it at 12:30PM, to "*little success.*" Having made his point (i.e. "*Nothing could happen if you broke all the rules*"), what possible reason could Crowley have for then firing the same blank? His repetition of this rite, either at midnight on the same day (19 March) or between 10PM and midnight on the next, makes absolutely no sense, whatsoever!

In published accounts, Crowley lumps his cross-examination of Rose, description of the stele imagery and French translation of its hieroglyphs together between **Book of Results** entries for 18 and 19 March. Indeed, amidst his **Book of Results** entry for 18 March, Crowley states: "*It was probably on this day that P. cross-examined W. about Horus.*" Three days later, on 21 March, they visit the Boulak **(22)**, and later still (between 23 March and 07 April) Crowley comes into receipt of the French stele translations. Why does his vellum notebook not reflect this sequence? The **Book of Results (20 to 22)** makes no mention of either Crowley's cross-examination, visit to the Boulak, his receipt of the French stele translations, or the reception event itself!

To my mind, the big question is "*What changed between Invocation of Horus and B2?*" The text of Rose's nonsensical Invocation of Horus leaves no doubt that on 19 March Crowley had already decided (three weeks before Aiwass issued the press release) that a 'New Equinox' had dawned, with Nuit on the throne of Isis and Horus on that of Osiris. The Invocation of Horus is Crowley's fledgling expression of the new order, as decreed by him! Unfortunately, as narrated by Crowley, it didn't really go anywhere. Then, miraculously, it did!

Sex, sex, sex with six, six, six

After writing the Invocation of Horus and before penning the radically different B2 material, Crowley experienced quite a revelation. At some point between 19 and 20 March, he formed a notion of replacing figurative representations of phallic symbolism employed by the Golden Dawn and ancient Egyptian rites, into actual rituals of sexual magick, utilising a ceremony imitative of imagery painted on the Stele of Revealing. Of course, this depicts three figures, one female and two males.

Crowley's 'big issue' is that of his bisexuality. Regardless of supposed genius, wealth, power and influence, Crowley must conceal this sizeable facet of his life or face abject damnation by his contemporaries. Not surprisingly, the protocols of Crowley's New Equinox address the problem by elevating all aspects of sex to the status of sacraments. Under Crowley's new regime, the only *"sin"* is *"restriction,"* and he is elevated to the status of 'normal.' Indeed, overt references to Sex Magick litter the unpublished (and erased from the record) sections of Crowley's Cairo diaries.

I have a great deal of admiration for the sheer audacity of Crowley's plan. His intent was that of initiating a 'golden age' of unconditional sexual liberation upon a deeply repressed culture that perceived any suggestion of sexual irregularity as an indelible brand of Satan. In this respect, Crowley was most definitely a vanguard of sexual freedoms decades ahead of his time. Alas, back in 1904, the task of converting Mankind to the unimaginable joys of sexual ambivalence was asking a lot. To test the waters, Crowley elected to begin on a much smaller scale. He persuaded his new wife, whilst on honeymoon, to participate in a 'threesome' featuring Crowley and another male. This radical endorsement of the ultimate taboo must have sent Crowley's ego, confidence and ambition soaring into orbit! It must also have reinforced a suggestion that, on some level, the gods approved of his scheme to usurp Mathers.

As events transpired, and perhaps realising the impossibility and danger of imprisonment inherent in his dream, Crowley retreated from all hint of sexual shenanigans. By September 1907, he had expunged all reference to sex from the version of **Liber L. vel Legis** intended for inclusion as an Appendix in the third volume of **Collected Works**. Understandably, this major revision tossed a spanner or two into the machine. When Crowley squeezed sex out of his equation, the B2 material had to go. His seeming confusion relating to whether the second and, unbelievably, successful performance of Rose's Invocation of Horus took place on 19 or 20

March is a result of attempts to whitewash the sexualised B2 ritual out of his evolving scheme.

Incidentally, the honorific title of "*Ouarda the Seer*" bestowed on Rose by Crowley, in consequence of her alleged psychic talents, may veil a more literal interpretation – i.e. she who saw! Crowley must have been acutely aware that the highly sensitive information Rose possessed presented considerable danger to his liberty, if ever it became public knowledge. On this theme, it is interesting to note that the first exposition of **Liber L. vel Legis**, with frills, did not appear until March 1912, in **Equinox 1, 7**, after Rose was institutionalised, and not published in full until 1936, in **Equinox of the Gods**, after her death.

The B2 material is also problematic with reference to Crowley's description of the stele. This incorporates subtle refinements to imagery utilised in the B2 material, and is highly-suggestive of 'two' stele events, neither of which necessarily involves a trip to the museum. Crowley's cathartic impulse to experiment with sexual Magick explodes onto the scene immediately after the first, unsuccessful recital of Rose's Invocation of Horus. Sex saturates the remainder of his notebook, OS27. Whilst it is relatively simple to pinpoint the moment at which the realisation 'dawned' on Crowley, the question of when he actually came into possession of information relating to the stele is open to debate. He could have penned the B2 material using his own notes. He could have obtained it via his Golden Dawn contacts, or even from Brugsch himself. It is reasonably certain that Crowley did not visit the museum in 1904. If so, he would not have repeatedly stated that he visited the stele years after it left the building he described. To some degree, published accounts tacitly acknowledge Crowley's awareness of the stele prior to 21 March (the date 'fixed' for his visit to the Boulak). **Equinox I, 7** and **Equinox of the Gods** reproduce information relating to the stele between **Book of Results** entries for 18 and 19 March.

According to Crowley's story, notebook entries immediately after the undeclared B2 material 'should' continue with a chronicle of events between 20 and 23 March, culminating with the "*long and futile Tarot divination*." However, and quite inexplicably, the vellum notebook jumps forward in time to Crowley's barrage of Mathers, using sex-tipped Magickal missiles (**12 & 13**). It is certain that Crowley did not initiate these experiments until after his return to Boleskine and, since these notes begin on a right-hand page and utilise blank space on the previous left-hand page (beneath the end of the B2 material written on 19 or 20 March), no pages have been lost or removed **(13)**. The five (now) missing pages originally followed his description of the sexual rite utilised to charge talismans (ending with the "*Tell Jones this*" note) **(13)**. Following this are several pages of Magickal workings **(16)**, and only after this material does Crowley record a "*long and futile Tarot divination*" that is nothing of the sort **(17)**. Crowley's three-page Tarot divination marks the final entry in the vellum notebook, and this he definitely penned after he returned from Cairo. Crowley's claim to have written this material on 23 March is patently erroneous.

Put bluntly, Crowley's published accounts are completely at odds with the sequence of entries recorded in his vellum notebook, **Invocation of Hoor** (OS27). If, however, we accept that Crowley wrote the **Book of Results** 'after the fact,' on return to Boleskine, and that it represents a fledgling attempt to force the myth he is developing around events recorded in his personal diary, its seemingly contradictory order makes perfect sense.

Crowley probably left Cairo with a justifiable sense of excitement. A lateral insight led directly to what he clearly perceived as a general curative for all ails – Sex Magick. This monumental realisation provided him with the 'engine' required to destroy Mathers, formulate a new Magickal Link and receive a new rulebook for Mankind, valid for two-thousand years. Given this, Crowley may have considered a possibility that the Gods of a New Equinox had indeed taken him seriously and shuffled their game-plan in accordance with his needs.

After five years of costly failures and frustration, Crowley's occult machinations have seemingly precipitated something of major significance. He has not yet formed a Magickal Link with the Secret Chiefs, but is confident enough of its precursor as to inform fifteen acquaintances that "*Eqx. of Gods come,*" and notify Mathers of his redundancy. Crowley is one small step away from accomplishing the major goal of his life – Deification! Not surprisingly, he raced back to Boleskine (quicker than was physically possible) to begin an occult onslaught against Mathers at the earliest possible moment - Exactly as suggested by the sequence of his vellum notebook **(12 & 13)**.

As previously noted, Crowley intends to plant **Liber L. vel Legis** in the final volume of **Collected Works** (as an incidental specimen of automatic writing), and 'realise' its immense significance later (once he's destroyed Mathers and upgraded the *"abrogated"* Golden Dawn material). Whilst it is not possible to deduce the precise nature of Crowley's original scheme (since he never implemented it), the single factor responsible for precipitating a hugely-problematical second revision is clear.

In 1906, Crowley's former occult boss, George Cecil Jones, begins to discuss the formation of a new mystical order and Crowley senses an opportunity to improve his master plan. Rather than stumble over a self-planted seed himself, he decides to let a third-party, and an experienced occultist, unveil his revelation. This cunning tweak inherently imparts an aura of authenticity onto **Liber L. vel Legis,** and significantly enhances its impact. Crowley plays on Jones' fervent desire to become part of the 'next big thing' and incorporates him into the revised New Equinox scheme. Unfortunately, this minor adjustment backfires spectacularly, because Jones' occult seniority presents Crowley with a major and unanticipated problem.

Remember that the new Magickal Link with the Secret Chiefs opens only on destruction of the old regime. Since this has not happened when Crowley pitches the scheme to his former Golden Dawn mentor, Jones will surely insist that he (the superior occult officer) and not Crowley should be conversing with praeterhuman entities, when they arrive! Crowley's diary entry of 29 July 1906 graphically illustrates his problem:

"Sunday night. D.D.S. [Jones] *and P.* [Crowley] *discuss a new O∴* [mystical Order].

D.D.S. wants Authority."

26th.	Went down to stay with G.H.F∴ D.D.S. 7°=4▫.
27th.²	I, Perdurabo, a member of the C∴C∴ do hereby solemnly obligate myself etc. to lead a p∴ and unselfish life; and will entirely devote myself to raise etc. myself to the K∴ of my higher and d∴ G∴ that I shall be Him. In witness of which I I∴ the great A∴ אוו to give me a proof of his existence.
	Complete and perfect visualization of C∴ as P∴ on ✝.
	"The low dark hill, the storm, the star". But the [portal — artwork] of the Camel open and a ray therein; [...] a certain vision of A∴ remembered only as a glory now attainable.³
29th.	Sunday night. D.D.S. and P. discuss a new O∴.
	D.D.S. wants Authority.
	I should write and say "Perfect the lightning-conductor and the flash will come."
	[P.S.] Dec. 31. Very true; but there need not be hesitation any more.
30th.	Returned to London. No more definite A∴ driven from 12 to 12.
August 3rd.	Left for Eastbourne.

Crowley has no answer to Jones' legitimate claim, and has not come this far to secure only a silver medal. With reference to this point, I note that Crowley dropped the Appendix from **Collected Works Vol. III** at some point between September (galley proofs) and November 1907 (publication). In November 1907, Crowley and George Cecil Jones established an initiatory order and successor to the Golden Dawn – Coincidence… I think not!

To circumvent Jones' perfectly valid assertion Crowley needs something quite sensational, and does not disappoint! He transformed a pending Magickal Link accessible only to the occult world's Top-Dog (Jones), into an extant channel, with Crowley pre-designated as sole terrestrial authority and voice. He moulded a potentially "*interesting and helpful*" specimen of "*automatic writing*" penned by another and which only came into Crowley's possession two years after its (dated) origin, into a divine revelation and mandate personally received by the New Messiah. In other words, Crowley grafted the three-day reception component onto his evolving fable. The meeting with Aiwass he fabricated solely as an audacious and emphatic means of telling Jones:

> "*Sorry, mate. I know you 'should' get to chat with ET. It's so unfair, and all, but for whatever reasons they picked me. Life's a bitch!*"

Crowley's fateful decision to initiate his New Equinox scheme by proxy (i.e. steer Jones into a realisation of **Liber L. vel Legis**' supreme importance) utterly transforms the significance of his vellum book (OS27) and **Collected Works** Appendix. It also sheds much light on the baffling notes made on the handwritten cover sheet.

1)   *"M.S. (which came into my possession in July 1906)"* - Added at a time when Crowley, after *"intelligent"* study, reveals the wonders encoded in a manuscript penned by a mysterious Egyptian Adept. It is important at this point for Crowley to emphasis that he is not the author of **Liber L. vel Legis**. Otherwise, Crowley has to defend a ludicrous claim that *he* wrote a text that *he* later revealed as the Foundation Document of a New Aeon, of which *he* was supreme leader.

2)   *"...except the translations of the Stele inscriptions"* – At this point, Crowley was reeling Jones into the scheme. He is still presenting **Liber L.** as the work of another and intent on slipping it discretely into the next available publication. Inconveniently, for Crowley, this is the third volume of his own works, but what the hell.

Crowley realised that Jones would recognise the stele versifications incorporated into **Liber L.** as being written by him. The pair worked closely together since Crowley returned to Boleskine in the summer of 1904. Jones must be intimately familiar with Crowley's poetic versification. Indeed, the final entry, prior to the five torn leaves, in Crowley's Cairo notebook (OS27) is a note exclaiming: *"Tell Jones this."* To overcome the versification problem, Crowley appends a note explaining why his poetic rendering appears within the typeset transcript of a manuscript overtly stated as authored by someone other than Crowley. Jones cannot have seen the manuscript itself at this time. If so, he would undoubtedly have posed a question that Crowley could not possibly blag his way around:

> *"How is it possible that a work purportedly written on 08, 09 & 10 April 1904, can directly reference material written two years later* [when the manuscript allegedly came into Crowley's possession] *by a man of whom the author of **Liber L. vel Legis** had absolutely no awareness?"*

With a simple adjustment, Crowley kept his New Equinox scheme rolling along, with Jones on board. The third, and perhaps most inexplicable note is neatly explained as a consequence of Crowley's second modification, in which Jones rather than Crowley will stumble upon the full glory of what Crowley innocently assumed was nothing more than an *"highly interesting specimen of genuine automatic writing."*

3)   *"I meant I could be its master from that date a. c. oct '09"* – At this point, Crowley's New Equinox plan has undergone a significant revision. A manuscript originally touted as the work of another and which Crowley only acquired two years later has transformed into a document penned by Crowley himself. This amendment is not included in the typeset 1907 Appendix, as Crowley had not yet written it.

> LIBER L. VEL LEGIS
>
> GIVEN FROM THE MOUTH OF AIWASS TO THE EAR OF THE BEAST ON APRIL, 8, 9, AND 10, 1904.
>
> [This MS. (which came into my possession in July 1906) is a highly interesting example of genuine automatic writing.* Though I am in no way responsible for any of these documents, except the verse translations of the stele inscriptions, I publish them among my works, because believe that their intelligent study may be interesting and helpful.—A. C.]

4) It is interesting to note that **Liber L. vel Legis** made its debut public appearance three years later, in the third volume of **THELEMA - The Holy Books**. In this, Crowley presented **Liber L.** without introduction or explanation, as merely one of a sequence of "*inspired writings*" churned out in 1907. Given the supreme importance of this work to Crowley's new order and Mankind in general, it is inexplicable that Crowley did not splash both it and the reception story as a preface to the first volume, rather than a bare skeleton tucked quietly in the third. The reason for Crowley's questionable presentation of **Liber L.** in the **Holy Books** is simple. When published, Crowley had shifted responsibility for the 'great reveal' from his shoulders and onto those of Jones. As such, he can't extol the virtues of **Liber L.** until after Jones has pointed them out, and Jones can't do that until after Crowley slips it discretely into one of his books.

In essence, these four points outline the subtle modifications Crowley incorporated into his New Equinox scheme between 1906 and 1910. Neither Crowley's trip to the Boulak or three-day reception appears in the **Holy Books** because, at this time, the question of Jones' mystical seniority has not become critical. Only after Jones (nudged by Crowley) realises that **Liber L.** is the skeleton of a methodology facilitating communication with the Secret Chiefs does his extra occult 'stripe' become problematic. When this happens, Crowley is compelled to rewrite the record, again, and usurp Jones by fabricating the reception event. Of course, this major revision evoked multiple discrepancies, anomalies, contradictions and the general ambience of 'fuzziness' Crowley imparted on his account out of sheer necessity.

In consequence of implanting the reception component and its associated mythology, the chronology of his vellum notebook **Invocation of Hoor** (OS27) falls apart. Crowley's biggest problem is his mention of the sexualised Golden Dawn destroying talismans **(12)**. **Confessions** explicitly stated that he undertook this work at Boleskine. Therefore, his corresponding notes in the vellum notebook represent a clear division between Cairo material (on previous pages) and Boleskine notes (on subsequent pages).

Realistically, the **Book of Results** entries dated 16, 17 & 18 March 'should' appear before Invocation of Horus (written on 19 March). However, Crowley's (enforced) decision to fabricate the **Book of Results** at the back of his vellum notebook **(20 & 21)** renders the Invocation of Horus **(02 to 04)** dateless and 'safe' (i.e. he can incorporate it into the updated myth).

The B2 material is problematic **(06 to 11)**. Extant diary entries Crowley is working around cannot accommodate his rewrite of Rose's **Invocation of Horus** (resulting from the insight regarding stele imagery and Sex Magick). Crowley's solution is quite blunt. He omits all mention of the B2 material and glosses over it, sloppily, in published accounts. However, since the B2 material is undated, and falls on the right side of the Boleskine talisman division **(12)**, it is also 'safe.'

The Tarot divination's placement on the wrong side of the Boleskine line also presents challenges **(17)**. Crowley needs to reference this material later (as the rediscovered **Book of Thoth**), but without exposing its placement on the wrong side of the Boleskine dividing line. His solution is very clever. He takes a Yi King divination (referred to in his legitimate diary entry of 23 March) and mutates this into the bogus Tarot divination (as recorded beneath "*The Secret of Wisdom*") reproduced in his unpublished **Book of Results** entry for 23 March **(21)**. By doing this, Crowley can point anyone who asks to see the unpublished Tarot Divination (and soon-to-become the **Book of Thoth**) at his **Book of Results** entry, and not its toxic counterpart on the wrong side of the line. With this sleight-of-hand, Crowley nudges the Tarot material into a position in the vellum book that he can explain.

The Book of Results is the first material encountered on flipping and inverting Crowley's vellum notebook **(20 & 21)**, and its 23 March entry ends with "... *but 666 explains all this & more*." Immediately following this statement is the stele description **(22)** Crowley published in **Equinox of the Gods** (pages 73 and 74). Since this material derives from notes made during his (21 March) visit to the Boulak, it 'should' appear between **Book of Results** entries dated 20 and 22 March, but doesn't! Its actual placement after the **Book of Results** is curious, but not necessarily damning. Unfortunately, an unpublished correction Crowley made to his description of stele imagery is catastrophic **(22)**. He initially wrote "*the heavenly Isis,*" though, on second thought, changed this in preference to "*Nuit.*" On publication, Crowley reverted to his original choice (Isis) and his reason is elementary. When (on 21 March) Crowley wrote his stele description, Nuit was nothing more than fluff on the periphery of the Golden Dawn pantheon of gods. Crowley referred to her previously only once, in passing, (***The Soul of Osiris,*** Litany, 1901):

"*My sorrows are more manifold
Than His that bore the sins of man.
My sins are like the starry fold,
My hopes their desolation wan.
O Nuit, the starry one arise,
And set thy starlight in my skies!*"

In making the unpublished correction, Crowley inadvertently revealed (on 21 March) his awareness that Nuit had assumed the throne of Isis. Knowledge allegedly first imparted to him by Aiwass on 08, 09 & 10 April – Three weeks later! Indeed, the transfer of power from Osiris to Horus and Isis to Nuit is the Cairo Working's 'big thing.' Yet, Crowley's slip demonstrates prior knowledge of Heaven's new sleeping arrangements weeks before the official proclamation.

I now turn to five leaves torn crudely from OS27. A note preceding the missing pages reads "*General idea of ceremony to become R.H.K.* [Ra-Hoor-Khuit] *also to devote oneself to him by a Grand Method; thence directly to vivify Avenger.*" The paraphrased verses Crowley used in **Liber L.** end with "*Abide with me, Ra-Hoor-Khuit!*" Furthermore, notes written on the **Liber L.** manuscript refer to a (singular) "***vellum book to "Ra-Hoor-Khuit.***" According to the timeline of Crowley's official story, immediately after the unacknowledged B2 material should follow his "*cross-examination*" of Rose, description of stele imagery, stele versification and "*Name-coincidences of Qabalah.*" Inexplicably, OS27 omits mention of these vital components of Crowley's story. The **Book of Results** is equally blank, with one exception. It clumsily tacks a description of stele imagery (as published) after the **Book of Results** entry for 23 March.

Of these surprising omissions, both "*Name-coincidences of Qabalah*" and "*cross-examination*" Crowley recorded in another small vellum notebook, namely "*OS23.*" This notebook is definitely post-Cairo, as its entries run from the summer work at Boleskine to late 1907. The placement of these two items is questionable. Crowley states that he wrote the *"Name-coincidences […] between 23 March and 08 April."* Yet these handwritten notes appear in a journal not started until well after his return to Boleskine. Moreover, the placement of *"cross-examination"* notes in a section titled *"(i) How the Scarlet Woman knew R.H.K.,"* some three-and-a-half years after the events described is, with respect to the reception fable, utterly nonsensical. The 2002 Warburg catalogue divides OS23 into ten sections (labelled 'a' to 'j'). Since "g" states *"(g) Rose Skries for Capt Rost, 19 Oct 1907,"* it follows that Crowley wrote *"i"* at some point afterwards.

Hardback notebook, Japanese vellum notebook, 1904-7, in A. C.'s hand
Contents page by Yorke
(a) The Rituals, ordeals and rites of the secret and public worship of Ra-Hoor-Khuit
(b) Name-coincidences of Qabalah
(c) Notes
(d) The initiation message for Mabel Maryham
(e) Notes
(f) 'Correct designs of Tarot Trumps' as published in 777 col. CLXXXI.
(g) Rose Skries for Capt Rost, 19 Oct 1907
(h) Notes
(i) How the Scarlet Woman knew R.H.K.
(j) Notes, including temple ground plan and illustration of painting, the sign of night, the dark waters. ???
[Mic. 66pp]

On examination of this puzzle's various pieces, the single glaring absentee is Crowley's versification, or paraphrase, of stele hieroglyphs, plus, of course, five missing pages. What circumstances prompted 'someone' to hack this from the record? The answer, again, relates to 'timing.' As originally conceived, the sequence of events recorded in his notebook was not of particular significance. However, when Crowley introduced Aiwass, he also imparted a critical relevance on chronology. The reception event is reliant upon Crowley's versification (Aiwass referenced it on three occasions).

If Crowley did record this on the five missing pages demonstrably written long after leaving Cairo, then his whole fable falls apart. If 'someone' with access to his unpublished notes, and 'someone' already questioning Crowley's story, and 'someone' looking for a reason to bounce back from a sneaky 'three-Aiwass card trick' notices the discrepancy, well... How could Crowley answer the inevitable accusations and remain flavour of the New Equinox! He couldn't, simple as that! In consequence, the stele versification had to go, as did his equally belated description of stele imagery. As previously noted, a small stub approximately two-thirds down the first missing page survives. On this, a single word is written, "*gold.*" Tantalisingly, the word appears exactly where one would expect if the missing text did comprise a version of Crowley's description of stele imagery:

> "*His tunic is the Leopard's skin, and his apron green and gold.*"

If this word did once form part of Crowley's stele description, its original placement in OS27, adjacent to his paraphrasing of stele hieroglyphs, makes perfect sense.

To keep his scheme afloat, Crowley had one, last-ditch' option open to him. After ripping the five toxic pages from his notebook (and blaming Jones), he replicated the stele description in the only place available – After the **Book of Results** entry dated 23 March. Ideally, he 'should' also have copied his stele versifications here. This would have detoxified both items, by smudging them into the safe 'who can say for sure when it was written' **Book of Results**. Alas, he ran out of spare pages!

I close this chapter with a speculative intuition. It is likely that Crowley retained the five torn pages for reference and sentimental value. If he did indeed tuck these discretely away, somewhere, they probably survive. One day, perhaps soon, a researcher investigating an entirely unrelated facet of Crowley's legacy may uncover them.

IX. The heavenly, who?

The scan (below) derives from an unpublished page of Crowley's vellum notebook (OS27) beginning with the words "*In the museum at Cairo.*" He initially wrote "*the heavenly Isis,*" then crossed through this and inserted a substitute name, "*Nuit,*" above the deletion. When Crowley published this material (**Equinox I, 7** and **Equinox of the Gods**), he reverted to his original choice of 'the heavenly Isis.' Again, as with his "*Tell Jones this*" note, a few moments spent in consideration of this seemingly trivial adjustment reveals deeper layers of meaning.

Crowley 'fixes' the date for his cathartic visit to the Boulak Museum as Monday 21 March. As one would expect, on viewing the stele (allegedly for the first time) he writes a detailed description of its imagery. In doing this, he places Nuit on the throne of Isis (albeit as a correction). Crowley can't read hieroglyphs, so has no reason whatsoever to suppose that the arched figure is anything other than the traditional goddess, Isis. Crowley's use of "*Nuit*" in his description of stele imagery directly contradicts an assertion that he received news of the 'transfer of power' from Aiwass, three weeks later. Yet, despite correcting his source notes, Crowley inexplicably reverts to his first (wrong) choice, "*the heavenly Isis,*" in published accounts.

Of course, the initial (Isis to Nuit) correction could have happened after Aiwass' visitation. However, this scenario is even more questionable with reference to Crowley's decision to publish his original choice ("*the heavenly Isis*"). Imagine that you visit a museum and make notes relating to an artefact you erroneously believe is a statue of Edward Alexander Crowley. Some time later, a friend mentions that the exhibit actually depicts Winston Churchill. In response, you probably correct your notes. If subsequently you publish these, it would be nonsensical to reproduce your original, incorrect, text – Especially as you are aware of the error. Yet, that is precisely what Crowley did... and for self-evident reasons.

Appended to the bottom of his stele description is an exceedingly curious footnote. A distorted version of which appears in published accounts:

> "*There is one other object to complete the secret of Wisdom – (P. notes "perhaps a Thoth") or it is in the hieroglyphs. (This last paragraph is, we suppose, dictated by W).*"

Crowley's original (unpublished OS27) note (see scan on previous page) differs from its published counterpart in several important respects:

> *"There is one other object to complete*
> *the secret of Wisdom. – or, it is in the*
> *(perhaps a Thoth.) hieroglyphs."*

As published, this passage is nonsensical. However, a close look at the text, in context, reveals Crowley's chain of thought. He initially wrote:

> *"There is one other object to complete the secret of Wisdom."*

On review, Crowley realised that he could not possibly 'know' that only "*one*" object was required to complete the puzzle – Who told him? To sidestep the niggle he 'separated' this paragraph by means of parallel vertical lines and suggested it was "*dictated by Rose*" (who would know, because Horus was whispering in her ear). Having corrected a serious continuity error (Isis/Nuit) and delegated advance knowledge of the 'one' missing piece to Rose, Crowley amends his footnote as a means of reminding both his audience and himself, that 'at this point he did not have a translation of the stele hieroglyphs.' It now reads:

> *"There is one other object to complete the secret of Wisdom. – or, it is in the hieroglyphs."*

Crowley's adjustment is an overstatement of the 'bleeding obvious.' Why would anyone have reason to believe that he had a translation of the stele hieroglyphs when standing in front of the artefact on 21 March? - A translation naming Nuit and not Isis as the blue figure arched over the canopy of heaven. Actually, the first translation gives "*Nout*" whilst the revised attempt (quoted in **Equinox of the Gods**, page 74) suggests "*Nut.*" Neither of which fit the Qabalistic correspondences Crowley is attempting to graft onto his evolving construct.

A striking parallel of Crowley's inexplicable awareness that 'only one other object is required to complete the secret of Wisdom' occurs in the infamous **II, 76** 'riddle.' Immediately following this mysterious sequence of numbers and letters is a forthright statement aimed directly at **The Great Beast**:

> *"What meaneth this, o prophet? Thou knowest not; nor shalt thou know ever. There cometh one to follow thee: he shall expound it."*

Despite its overwrought phraseology, the intent is perfectly clear – Crowley won't solve the riddle, ever. Yet, in **Magical and Philosophical Commentaries on the Book of the Law**, he boldly declares:

> *"Be ye well assured all that the solution, when it is found, will be unquestionable. It will be marked by the most sublime simplicity, and carry immediate conviction."*

Once again, it is pertinent to ask 'how' Crowley knew this. If he can't solve the puzzle, how can he comment, subjectively, on its answer? He can't, obviously! Well, not unless Crowley wrote it.

Of various amendments, Crowley's final adjustment is singularly curious. His addition of three words degrades the text to a level comparable with the nonsensical and contradictory cover sheet:

> *"There is one other object to complete the secret of Wisdom. – or, it is in the (perhaps a Thoth.) hieroglyphs."*

By slipping in *"a Thoth,"* Crowley is setting the scene for the sexual revolution to come. As evidenced by his description of the Sex Magick ritual, 'Thoth' clearly refers to a penis (*"Place hands on seers head, figuring her as Thoth & and filling her with [THOTH] fire"*). Remember also that stele imagery incorporates three figures, one female and two males. The suggestion they are 'a Thoth short' may be a direct, though cryptic allusion to a ritual involving Crowley, Rose, and another male (waiting in the wings).

Crowley makes one further premature 'leak' of the big news he allegedly does not yet know. In the unpublished and unacknowledged B2 material Crowley writes *"...through the heaven of Nuit."*

Earlier in this chapter, I suggested - *"This small Japanese vellum notebook is also a unique pictorial snapshot of the brief period in which Crowley's mundane and Magickal worlds inverted."* By sharpening the focus of this observation by one degree, it is possible to identify the exact moment when Crowley's world changed. In the final two paragraphs of his unpublished ritual, B2, he writes:

"O Thou light in darkness who sheddest thy glory in the Abyss, so we adore thee in the midnight temple. Thou hast lightened our darkness. Thou has brought forth knowledge. Thou hast appeared, Though we invoked Thee not. Hail unto Thee, that travellest under heaven in Thy Bark, O Kephra. Thou that ridest through the heaven of **Nuit** *in Thy strength – Thou that bearest the head of the beetle and thou that controls the mysterious rites of midnight, we adore Thee and we invoke thee.*

We bow down before Thee. Is there any of the Gods like unto Thee, Our Lord? Be graciously pleased to abide with us in the darkness of earth, making the ways light unto us until we come into the everlasting kingdom of the light where the shadows have no place and the lamp of the highest is exalted in the temple; until the gloom of the veil of **Isis** *is dispersed and beauty of Ahathoor is the delight of her servants,"*

In this passage, the old aeon goddess, Isis, and the figurehead of Crowley's new world religion, Nuit, pass like ships in the night - Separated by only the width of ninety-four words. It is an exquisitely poignant moment. Albeit irrevocably marred by Crowley's knowledge of a once-in-an-aeon transition he will not actually learn of for three weeks.

X. OS23, the final nail

In certain respects, this book likens Crowley's unpublished material to 'evidence' seized by authorities, and published accounts with his 'defence' statement. A direct comparison exposes multiple examples of misinformation, misdirection, omissions and falsifications. It also reveals numerous instances in which Crowley references material that he does not yet possess. In one notable instance five pages of incriminating material vanishes from a vellum notebook. The single fact that Aiwass (a "*praeterhuman entity*" and 'herald of the gods') is demonstrably unable to count, or remember that 'two' comes between 'one' and 'three' is, alone, ample to discredit Crowley's alibi.

As discussed in my Introduction, William Breeze supported his 'f-k' change with a bewildering supposition about what 'may' have been written in a lost notebook of which no duplicate, index, or reference to is extant (well, *that* plus a scribbled 'k'). Indeed, Crowley never once bemoaned his loss of 'a Cairo' notebook. Nevertheless, with reference to his defence, the importance of this mythological vellum notebook cannot be overstated. If the five pages torn from OS27 comprise Crowley's versification, then his entire reception myth hangs on this being merely a later copy of material originally written in the lost vellum notebook. Disregarding any inconclusive stele versification issues, the existence of 'another,' earlier notebook would conveniently resolve numerous other instances of material written absurdly out-of-sequence. With respect to a second Cairo notebook, the highly suspicious arrangement of material in OS27 is also resolved in consequence of it being 'a later duplicate' of Cairo material - Though, the minor issue of why Crowley duplicated this in a seemingly haphazard way remains unresolved.

The content of OS27 begins with Rose's nonsensical Invocation of Horus and incorporates material unquestionably written at Boleskine during the summer of 1904. The inclusion of his **Book of Results** (irrespective of its actual time of writing) suggests that Crowley was keen to confine all Cairo-related material to a single source. Of three notable omissions, two are located in a vellum notebook labelled OS23 (the same specimen as vanished from the Warburg microfilm). The chronology of events recorded in OS27 covers the period from May 1904 to November 1907. Curiously, Yorke's 1951 typescript references this material in the wrong order (see scan below). His doodle beneath the word "*May*" is suggestive of a cryptic reference to the sexual nature of this material.

```
✓
 23.Small Japanese vellum notebook (1904 - 7)
     1.The rituals ordeals and rites of the secret and public worship of Ra-Hoor-Khuit
       Hadit and Nu.
   ✓ 2.Rough pencilled qabalistic workings and comments on the Book of the Law May 1904.
     3.How the Scarlet Woman knew Ra-Hoor Khuit.
     4.Name coincidences of Qabalah.
     5.Correct designs of Tarot Trumps as published in 777 Col. CLXXXI.
   ✓ 6.Rose skries for Capt Bost. Oct 1907.
```

The corresponding 2002 Warburg catalogue indexes OS23 in its correct sequence (see scan on next page), though the microfilm actually replicates the content of OS21. Of this, Item '**b**' states:

"*Name-coincidences of Qabalah*"

Anyone familiar with **Equinox I, 7** or **Equinox of the Gods** will recognise this title as a reference to material Crowley states:

"During the period March 23rd – April 8th [...] Perhaps then, perhaps later, he made out the name-coincidences of the Qabalah." (**Equinox of the Gods**, page 84)

OS 23

Hardback notebook. Japanese vellum notebook. 1904-7, in A. C.'s hand
Contents page by Yorke
(a) The Rituals, ordeals and rites of the secret and public worship of Ra-Hoor-Khuit
(b) Name-coincidences of Qabalah
(c) Notes
(d) The initiation message for Mabel Maryham
(e) Notes
(f) 'Correct designs of Tarot Trumps' as published in 777 col. CLXXXI.
(g) Rose Skries for Capt Rost, 19 Oct 1907
(h) Notes
(i) How the Scarlet Woman knew R.H.K.
(j) Notes, including temple ground plan and illustration of painting, the sign of night, the dark waters, ???
[Mic. 66pp]

When preparing the **Equinox I, 7** Crowley must have constantly referred to his handwritten source notes. It is inconceivable that he erroneously apportioned material written at Boleskine to a date of *"23rd March - April 8th."* The inclusion of this material in OS23 certainly quashes any suggestion that Crowley wrote it during the period between 23 March and 08 April, and before his alleged reception of **Liber L. vel Legis**. Crowley unquestionably wrote his 'Name-coincidences of the Qabalah' at Boleskine, not Cairo.

Item '**g**' states:

"Rose Skries for Capt Rost, 19 Oct 1907."

For what it's worth, Rose was a terrible clairvoyant. I note this listing as a benchmark for what follows. Item '**i**' states:

"How the Scarlet Woman knew R.H.K."

The placement of this material is exceedingly problematic, to say the least! It, of course, relates to Crowley's cross-examination of Rose.

"It was probably on this day (18 March) *that P. cross-examined W. about Horus. [...] Here therefore we insert a short note by Fra. P.* **how W. knew R.H.K** *(Ra-Hoor-Khuit)."* (**Equinox of the Gods**, page 71)

Given the singular importance of Rose's astral contact with Horus (or Ra-Hoor-Khuit), Crowley must surely have made notes of his pivotal cross-examination on the day in question (i.e. 18 March), or very soon afterwards. Yet, this crucial jigsaw piece lurks amidst the pages of a notebook that Crowley started on return to Boleskine, and which follows an entry dated "*19 Oct 1907.*" It is inconceivable that Crowley wrote an account of this hugely significant precursor to the couple's Boulak trip, from memory, three-and-a-half years after the conversation to which it relates.

The single omission from the extant record is Crowley's handwritten versification of the French stele translation (plus whatever he wrote on the five missing pages). The manuscript references this material on three occasions:

"***V. 1. of spell called the Song.***"
(I, 14)

"***I am the Lord of***" *etc. from vellum book unity etc.* ~~~~ "***fill me***"
(III, 37)

"***The light is mine***" *etc. from vellum book to* "***Ra-Hoor-Khuit.***"
(III, 38)

Remember that a note prefacing the five torn pages states "*General idea of ceremony to become **R.H.K.**,*" that the stele versification (as used) ends with "*Abide with me, **Ra-Hoor-Khuit***" and that Aiwass instructed Crowley to insert verses with specific reference to "***Ra-Hoor-Khuit.***" It is also pertinent to note that the B2 ritual opens with "***Ra-Hoor-Khuit! I invoke Thee!***" - However, Crowley's manuscript note can't be referring to this material, as (according to his version of events) it doesn't exist. Interestingly, the aborted 1907 version of **Liber L. vel Legis** includes **The Great Invocation**, which opens with "*Unity uttermost showed,*" the third segment of Crowley's stele paraphrase and the verse originally referenced (though later corrected) in **III, 37**. This curio raises a tantalising question: '*Did Crowley's original paraphrase begin with its third verse?* If so, was **Liber L.** 'Chapter Three' actually the first written? Think about this – Of three chapters, only the third concerns itself with the stele. If Crowley penned the last chapter, first, (and his versification originally began with its third verse) then it makes perfect sense that **III, 37** originally referenced the word "*Unity.*" This scenario also explains why material referred to obliquely on the third day of dictation (III 37 & 38) Aiwass specifically named in a chapter supposedly written two days previously (I, 14).

> ### APPENDIX
>
> ### THE GREAT INVOCATION [1]
>
> *A, as priest. Sign of "Enterer."*
>
> Unity uttermost showed!
>   I adore the might of thy breath
> Supreme and terrible god,
>   Who makest the gods and death
> To tremble before thee!
>   I, I adore thee!   ("*Sign of Defence.*")
>
> *A ka dua*
> *Tuf ur biu*
> *Bi aa chefu*
> *Dudu ner af an nuteru!*
> Abrahadabra!
>
> *B, as priest. Signs of Enterer and Defence with each phrase.*
>
> O thou who art as an hawk of gold!
>   Thee, thee I invoke!   *A ka dua*, &c.
> O thou whose face is as an emerald, and thy nemmes as the night-sky blue!
>   Thee, thee I invoke!   *A ka dua*, &c.
> O thou who wearest the disk of flaming light upon thy brows, wrapped round with the smaragdine snake!
>   Thee, thee I invoke!   *A ka dua*, &c.
> O thou whose eyes blaze forth with light! Whose eyes are as the sun and the moon in their courses!
>   Thee, thee I invoke!   *A ka dua*, &c.
> O thou who bearest the Double Wand of Power, the Wand of the Force of Coph Nia!
>   Thee, thee I invoke!   *A ka dua*, &c.
> O thou whose left hand is empty, for that thou hast crushed an universe, and nought remains!
>   Thee, thee I invoke!   *A ka dua*, &c.
> O thou who art girt about with the leopard skin: whose apron is of green and gold!
>   Thee, thee I invoke!   *A ka dua*, &c.
> O thou whose heart is a secret sun in the caverns of thine heart: thou whose skin is of indigo as of the vault of night!
>   Thee, thee I invoke!   *A ka dua*, &c.
> O thou who hast formulated thy father and made fertile thy mother!
>   Thee, thee I invoke!   *A ka dua*, &c.

Rose 'finds' the stele. In response, Crowley acknowledges the '666' connection and arranges a French translation of its hieroglyphs. This he receives "*between 23rd March and 08th April,*" and immediately pens a poetic versification just in time for Aiwass to incorporate it into **Liber L. vel Legis**. Unfortunately, 'someone' slips-up and the second verse is forgotten. Crowley, at some unknown time afterwards, corrects the error and is twitchy enough about his praeterhuman blooper as to specify a source ("*from vellum book*"). The next verse contains a further instruction to insert segments of the versification. Even though this is correct, Crowley feels a need to hammer home his reference material ("*vellum book to Ra-Hoor-Khuit*"). Chapter I, 14 incorporates a third reference to the versification, and this is quite specific – "*V. 1. of spell called the Song.*" The ink is not yet dry on a versification he undoubtedly rushes through the process, yet Crowley evidently needs to remind himself as to its location. How many versions did he prepare, and where are they? The extant record is missing Crowley's handwritten stele versification(s) and/or *"spell called the Song/Joy"* and, for that matter, its corresponding typescript(s). No rough notes or prototype version of the stele versification exists, anywhere. Crowley's paraphrase first appears, fully formed, in the **Liber Legis** typescript allegedly prepared whilst still in Cairo. The same version as was used for the 1907 **Collected Works** and 1910 **Holy Books**.

In closing, I will note that the historical paper-trail is bereft of only a stele versification approximating to five notebook pages, and the notebook (OS27) is missing five pages.

XI. Bollocks dropped at the Boulak

Of many mysteries shrouding Crowley's reception of **Liber L. vel Legis**, his multiple references to the Boulak Museum is a hoary ol' chestnut. For reasons discussed earlier in this work (see also **AL cetera**) Rose cannot have accompanied Crowley on the fateful excursion during which his wife discovered the Stele, because the museum in question did not exist in March 1904!

Equinox of the Gods reproduces several mentions of the Boulak originally published in **Equinox I, 7**, plus other instances in an additional section, written at Cefalu in the early 1920s – Beginning: *"Certain very serious questions have arisen with regard to the method by which this Book* [**Liber L. vel Legis**] *was obtained."*

    1 - *"This refers to the striking scene in the Boulak Museum."* (Page 71)

    2 - *"To test 4, Fra. P. took her to the museum at Boulak."* (Page 73)

    3 - *"In the museum at Cairo."* (Page 73)

    4 - *"It differs slightly than that used by Fra. P., which was due to the assistant curator of the Museum at Boulak."* (Page 73)

    5 - *"Brugsch Bey of the Boulak Museum dined with us."* (Page 114)

    6 - *"I should fix Monday, March 21, for the Visit to Boulak."* (Page 115)

Crowley makes six references to the museum, and names it correctly only once. For too long, aficionados have swept this baffling discrepancy under the carpet, and for good reason. The implications for his reception fable are devastating. Crowley's account is reliant on visiting a museum that had, on the date stated, been closed for years. Yet, Crowley remains utterly oblivious to this. Furthermore, his suggestion of dining with Brugsch Bey, who would have undoubtedly corrected Crowley's misconception, merely adds a further layer of suspicion. On this single point, many of the flaws inherent in Crowley's fabrication are graphically exposed.

As previously explored, the question of where and when Crowley came into possession of stele-related information is open to considerable debate. The inclusion of stele imagery in the B2 material that is subsequently refined in Crowley's published description of the stele is suggestive of two stele events – Neither of which requires a physical viewing of the artefact in question. On this theme, it is noteworthy that material held at the Harry Ransom Center includes a photograph of the stele's reverse, but not its front. Crowley also commissioned a second translation (at an unspecified date). Did this material provide the additional information incorporated into Crowley's stele description?

A further clue to the Boulak mystery twinkles in Crowley's description of the stele, beginning *"In the museum at Cairo."* Of this, Crowley writes; *"Here is P.'s description of the stele."* In published editions, readers are 'groomed' into a tacit belief that Crowley wrote this text whilst physically in the presence of the artefact. To reinforce this notion he referred to an arched figure as *"the heavenly Isis."* Rather inexplicably, his unpublished handwritten notes (in OS27) state *"Nuit"* in preference to the crossed-out 'heavenly Isis' (see page 160). Had Crowley published his text with the corrected *"Nuit"* it is arguable that he innocently employed information retrospectively (i.e. He initially assumed the figure was Isis, though on receipt of the French Translation and Aiwass' New Equinox declaration, realised his error, so backdated the correction). However, **Equinox I, 7** and **Equinox of the Gods** revert to *"the heavenly Isis,"* which makes absolutely no sense, whatsoever. Unless... Crowley did not pen his description of the stele whilst physically in its presence, but rather the text is a paraphrase or loose transcription of notes received later, perhaps months later.

Crowley's **Book of Results** description of the stele concludes with a note omitted from all published editions:

"Above him are the Winged Globe and the bent figure of ~~the heavenly Isis~~ Nuit, her hands and feet touching earth.

There is one other object to complete the secret of Wisdom. – or, it is in the (perhaps a Thoth.) hieroglyphs. GD to be destroyed ie: publish its history & its papers. Nothing needs buying. I made it an absolute condition that I should obtain samhadhi, in the Gods' own interest. My rituals work out well, but I need the transliteration."

It seems to me quite extraordinary for Crowley to make a correction reliant upon a translation (or "*transliteration*") of hieroglyphs he twice emphasised, in the next paragraph, were not yet in his possession!

Crowley's first exposition of **Liber L. vel Legis** (the aborted 1907 Appendix) does not mention Rose or the fateful Boulak visit. This merely states:

"We are indebted to the kindness of Brugsch Bey and M. Delormant for the above translation of the stele whose discovery led to the creation of the ritual by which Aiwass, the author of Liber L., was invoked."

Crowley only named the correct museum once, in six attempts, and this in a text derived from notes supplied to him by Brugsch – Though misleadingly presented as Crowley's own words, as written in the Boulak Museum on 21 March 1904. A visit that was physically impossible anyway, due to the closure of that museum and relocation of its artefacts. Neither Crowley's mundane nor Magickal diaries note the Boulak visit, and the cross-examination of Rose (a vital precursor to and catalyst of the alleged Boulak visit) he does not record in OS23 until three-and-a-half years after the event.

It is not coincidental that Crowley removed the Appendix from **Collected Works Vol. III** (post-September 1907) just as he started portraying Rose as a psychic ("*Rose Skries for Capt Rost, 19 Oct 1907*") and penned the fictitious cross-examination, titled "*How the Scarlet Woman knew R.H.K.*" in OS23. At this time, Jones' occult seniority compelled a modification of **Liber L.**, from '*The work of another (a* *mysterious Egyptian adept) subsequently revealed by Crowley as the skeleton of new system affording communication with the Secret Chiefs governing the evolution of Mankind,'* to *'A personal mandate specifically announcing Crowley as the new Messiah.'*

Incidentally – Even though Crowley has calculated the basic Rose-Boulak-Stele-Horus connection by late 1907, he elects not to use it when premiering **Liber L.** (as one amongst a series of inspired writings 'Channelled' in 1907) in the third volume of his **Holy Books**. Crowley reproduced only the three chapters, without fanfare, explanation or introduction in this publication because, at this time, he had elected to delegate responsibility for the discovery of **Liber L.** from himself, to Jones. Consequently, he can't 'make a big thing' out of something he doesn't yet know is 'a big thing!'

In all probability, Crowley's description of the Boulak Museum and stele derive from different sources, as does material used to create the B2 ritual. His (**Equinox I, 7**) description of the stele originates from Brugsch's supplemental notes, and not necessarily a trip to the museum. Chances are the fabled Boulak visit never actually happened. The events Crowley described are a fiction grafted onto his Master of the Universe scheme in response to changes compelled by unforeseen circumstances.

Before moving on, I'll note one further Boulak mystery. In **Confessions** (page 421), Crowley briefly describes a "*week in Cairo*" beginning on 23 May 1905:

> "*I fed up and lounged about and told stories till the twenty-third, when I arrived in Cairo. The city is abandoned by tourists by this time of the year on account of some superstition about the climate; but to me Cairo at the end of May was more pleasant that I had ever known it. I joined the P&O on the thirty-first.*"

Rather oddly, he omits mention of an excursion noted in John Symonds' **King of the Shadow Realm** (page 80):

> "*He spent a week in Cairo, visited the Boulak Museum to see the stele of Ankh-f-n-Khonsu.*"

Was it on this occasion that Crowley actually procured stele information from which he created a versification? Why does he still refer to this museum as the "*Boulak?*" One further 'oddity' tips its cap in the direction of 1902. This derives from Crowley's '**Old Comment**' on **Liber L**. Though first published in **Equinox I, 7** (March 1912), Crowley spent several years preparing the comment. His diary entry of 02 May 1906 states:

> *"Working at comment on Liber Legis with (as usual) lamentably little result."*

Crowley's comment on **III, 39**, as published, reads:

> *"This being done; but quickly? No. I have slaved at the riddles in this book for nigh on seven years; and all is not yet clear."*

On first or even second look, nothing about this phrase appears suspicious. However, a comparison with Crowley's handwritten notes tells quite a different story. In its original form, the comment was dated (see scan below). The strange figures in brackets represent Crowley's unique dating system. When 'translated' these specify a period between 22 August and 22 September (Virgo) 1909 (the fifth year of his New Aeon). This simply does not add up!

If Crowley has (as is explicitly stated) slaved at *"the riddles"* for *"seven years,"* in September 1909, then his thraldom began approximately in September 1902. In other words, Crowley admits to working on a commentary eighteen months before receiving the text on which he's commenting! That all published editions of the **Old Comment** omit the incriminating date is not accidental. The bracketed date vanished from the record because it directly contradicts Crowley's assertion that he received **Liber L.** from an angel, on 08, 09 and 10 April 1904. In recent years, numerous researchers, biographers and assorted Thelemic academics have studied this material in furtherance of their own literary projects. Why has this serious glitch in Crowley's reception myth gone unnoticed, until now? Why has nobody previously raised this issue in the public domain? On a theme, it is worth noting that another ritual in the same notebook (titled **The Ceremony of the Equinox**) is dated '21 March to 20 April (Aries) 1909.' Strangely, again, despite predating the

Old Comment material by approximately six months, Crowley wrote his **Ceremony of the Equinox** after this, in the notebook – A chronological impossibility.

XII. A great cover story

At this point, I return to the lesser mystery of contradictory and nonsensical comments scribbled on an overlooked cover sheet.

> *"Given from the mouth of Aiwass to the ear of The Beast on April 8, 9 & 10, 1904."*

Crowley conceived these words as a preface to material he intended to slip quietly into the final instalment of **Collected Works**.

> *"This is a highly interesting example of genuine automatic writing. Though I am in no way responsible for any of these documents, I publish them among my works, because I believe that their intelligent study may be interesting & helpful - A. C."*

As written, the above description emphasises a declaration that Crowley was not the author of **Liber L. vel Legis,** and included it amongst his own writings out of curiosity and a 'hunch.' To underline and highlight his assertion, Crowley elaborated:

> *"This **item**, (which came into my possession in July 1906) is a highly interesting example…"*

He then appended a further proviso:

> *"…example of genuine automatic writing. Though I am in no way responsible for any of these documents, **except the translations of the Stele inscription**, I publish them…"*

The typeset (1907 Appendix) version of this states "*MS.*" not "*item,*" and includes one more caveat:

> *"This **MS.** (which came into […] except the **verse** translations of the Stele inscription…"*

It is also instructive to note that the cover sheet's final adjustment "*i. e. I meant I could be its master from that date*" is dated "*Oct 09.*" This suggests that in late 1909, when preparing the **Holy Books** for publication, Crowley still intended to preface **Liber L.** with material included in the earlier Appendix. As events transpired, **Holy Books Vol. III** reproduced only the three chapters of **Liber L.**, with associated frills and embellishments conspicuous by their total absence. This edition also discretely slides authorship of the manuscript away from a mysterious Egyptian Adept and into Crowley's lap. Though, inexplicably, places absolutely no emphasis on the text's especial significance.

The numerous adjustments littering Crowley's cover sheet trace boundary lines between different versions of **Liber L. vel Legis.** All of which, I may add, were precipitated in direct consequence of Crowley's involvement with a man named George Cecil Jones.

Crowley first encountered George Cecil Jones, Magickal name *"Frater D.D.S.,"* in 1898. Along with Allan Bennett, Jones was Crowley's main tutor throughout his Golden Dawn period. In the summer of 1906, he and Crowley were still working closely, exploring occult themes. The note Crowley penned in his vellum notebook (*"Tell Jones this"*) is a reference to George Cecil Jones. At first glance, Crowley's crude 'memory jogging' tool seems perfectly innocuous. However, on consideration, this initial presumption may not necessarily be accurate.

Crowley wrote the note in a distinctly different style to all other entries in his vellum book, and what he says is, in reality, nonsensical. Think about this… He writes 'a reminder' on the item he needs reminding of. This is akin to printing *'Don't forget to take my dinner out of the freezer'* on a post-it note, then affixing this to the meal in question! One glance at his vellum notebook will serve as an adequate reminder. If Crowley misplaces this, he also forfeits his knotted handkerchief. The note is patently not intended to fulfil its apparent purpose, so what did Crowley have in mind when he wrote it?

The formative years of **Liber L. vel Legis'** evolution, from 1904 reception to 1910 first publication, features three key players. Foremost is Crowley's former mentor in the Golden Dawn, George Cecil Jones (Frater D.D.S.). On 18 November 1906, Crowley wrote a poignant *"Epilogue & Dedication"* to Jones (**Collected Works Vol. III**). Jones also co-founded Crowley's fledgling mystical order, the A∴ A∴.

J. F. C. Fuller is the second major player. Fuller enters the picture as winner of Crowley's 'essay' competition (**Collected Works**) around 1906. Crowley published Fuller's hyperbolic and 'prize winning' critique, entitled **The Star in the West**, in 1907. Charles Stansfeld Jones

(Frater Achad) arrives last. He is recruited from the **Equinox** (1909) and is the twentieth member admitted to the A∴ A∴.

George Cecil Jones and Fuller quickly vanish from the scene following the infamous (1911) *"Looking Glass"* libel trial. Fearing that Crowley's nefarious reputation may stain his career aspirations, Fuller jumped ship first. Of this major rebuttal, Crowley wrote in **Confessions** (Chapter 67):

> *"...to my breathless amazement he fired pointblank at my head a document in which he agreed to continue his co-operation on condition that I refrain from mentioning his name in public or private under penalty of paying him a hundred pounds for each such offence. I sat down and poured in a broadside at close quarters.*
>
> *"My dear man," I said in effect, "do recover your sense of proportion, to say nothing of your sense of humour. Your contribution, indeed! I can do in two days what takes you six months, and my real reason for ever printing your work at all is my friendship for you. I wanted to give you a leg up the literary ladder. I have taken endless pain to teach you the first principles of writing. When I met you, you were not so much as a fifth-rate journalist, and now you can write quite good prose with no more than my blue pencil through two out of every three adjectives, and five out of every six commas. Another three years with me and I will make you a master, but please don't think that either I or the Work depend on you, any more than J.P. Morgan depends on his favourite clerk"."*

Not content with a private separation, Crowley also lobbed a brace of very public mud-balls at his former associate. **Issues I, 9** and **I, 10** of **The Equinox** (1913) included general directions advising against the acceptance of occult instruction from a *"former member,"* with 'questionable' occult credentials. Perhaps surprisingly, Fuller maintained an unhealthy obsession with the occult, and Crowley. The extensive archive held at the Harry Ransom Center derives from his estate.

Crowley bumped into G. C. Jones a decade later, on 30 December 1919. Of this meeting, his diary notes:

> *"It was a sad interview. He is the same dear man as he was, strangely gray for 46, but his turning back from the Abyss is evident. He is just a nice, simple bourgeois, interested in the number and quality of his offspring."*

George Cecil Jones outlived Crowley by six years. He died in 1953.

Charles Stansfeld Jones broke from Crowley (in 1912) to form his own branch of the A∴ A∴, in Canada. In 1917, he spent a brief period in jail following his arrest, in a hotel room, under suspicion of feigning insanity to avoid conscription (a 'draft dodger'). Kenneth Grant's book **The Magical Revival** includes an alleged incident (related to Grant by Crowley) in which Jones returns to Vancouver, in 1930, wearing only a raincoat, which he proceeds to remove in a railway station prior to *'performing a certain Magical operation.'* This is most probably Crowley's mischievous 'dig' at Jones, who resigned from the A∴ A∴ in 1918, and who Crowley 'formally' expelled eighteen years later.

This chronology is important as it relates directly to the five missing pages torn from OS27, and to Gerald Yorke's accompanying note naming C. S. Jones as the culprit. The missing pages become toxic only after Crowley modifies his scheme and assumes responsibility for the authorship of **Liber L.** (albeit in the inert capacity of *Channeller*). This change occurred within the brief period between October 1909 cover sheet note and 1910 publication of **Holy Books Vol. III**. On this theme, it is useful to note that the (post-Cairo) placement of Crowley's stele versification becomes problematic from the moment he incorporated this material into the September 1907 Appendix. At this time, Crowley was compelled to explain how his stele versification is included in the "*automatic writing*" of another (someone who could not possibly know Crowley) and a manuscript that Crowley only came into possession of two years after its creation. On these points, Crowley's own words are unmistakable:

> "...*which came into my possession in July 1906* […] *I am in no way responsible for any of these documents*..."

Crowley elegantly sidestepped this thorny issue with just eight words:

> "...*except the verse translations of the Stele inscription.*"

The chronological placement of items in OS27 only becomes critical once Crowley claims authorship of **Liber L. vel Legis**, and this doesn't happen until around 1910. At this time, George Cecil Jones, Fuller and Charles Stansfeld Jones were active on Crowley's scene and could have ripped the pages. However, C. S Jones and Fuller are newcomers to Crowley's mystical meanderings, whereas G. C. Jones and Fra. Perdurabo have been working together for almost a decade. Indeed, G. C. Jones' awareness of Crowley's revolutionary Sex Magick workings compels one of the cover sheet adjustments. Ultimately, Jones' occult reputation convinces Crowley to delegate responsibility for unveiling the wonders of **Liber L.** to his former Golden Dawn tutor – Which leads directly to him pulling the Appendix from **Collected Works Vol. III**.

In April 1906, Crowley and G. C. Jones begin to discuss a reformulation of the Golden Dawn. By November of the following year, just after Crowley scraps his Appendix, the pair found A∴ A∴ (Astrum Argenteum, or Silver Star). This mystical fraternity serves as the primary vehicle for Crowley's exposition of Thelema and cites "*Aiwass*" as its authority, but not **Liber L. vel Legis**! Somewhat inexplicably, the new Order's charter seemingly derives from Jones' acceptance of Crowley's attainment of the trance of Samadhi and 1907 "*inspired*" writings. The trance of Samadhi marked Crowley's 'spiritual promotion' from "*Adeptus Minor*" (a grade he revisited, under Jones, on 27 July 1906) to "*Magister Templi*," accompanied by the Magickal motto "*Vi Veri Vniversum Vivus Vici*" (meaning "*By the force of truth, I, while living, have conquered the universe)*" and usually abbreviated to "*V. V. V. V. V.*")," on 10 October 1906.

Between April 1906 and November 1907 Crowley played a classic 'Triple Samadhi' manoeuvre, by **1)** Convincing Jones as to the genuine nature of his contact with the Secret Chiefs, **2)** Leapfrogging his former occult boss' seniority and **3)** Reformulating the A∴ A∴ whilst retaining Jones' support and loyalty, in the lesser role. By 27 December 1906, Crowley had Jones eating out of his halo!

> 27th. Back to Town. Broke down myself.[1]
> Appear to have got into the Fruit of which Jones' "Hail! All Hail!" was the Blossom. In short, recognizing that *I am He* in the same way that I recognize "Snow is white" — not arguing it, nor announcing it triumphantly. I acted on that basis without self-consciousness, and wrote various letters.

At this time, as evidenced by the September 1907 Appendix and October 1909 cover sheet note, Crowley was still touting **Liber L** as the work of another (albeit with *his* stele versifications). This means that Jones awareness of it originates in the period between Crowley withdrawing his Appendix (September 1907), and cutting prefacing material from the version published in **Holy Books Vol. III** (1910). Had Jones seen this earlier prototype (including "*Given from the mouth of...*"), Crowley could not subsequently transfer authorship, backdate ownership and morph "*automatic*" to "*inspired*" (as reproduced in **Holy Books**).

On a general theme of 'when,' it is most curious that the very first instance, ever, of Crowley referring directly to **Liber L. vel Legis** does not happen until 18 April 1906. That's two years after its creation and two months before Crowley came into possession of it – Depending on which version of the reception fable you believe. His diary entry of this date reads:

*"Studying **Liber Legis**: decide to ask A. to invoke Aiwass."*

Incidentally, "*A*" is Elaine Simpson, one of Crowley's casual mistresses of the period – Ironically, the relationship seemingly conflicts with her Golden Dawn motto "*Semper Fidelis*," meaning 'always faithful.' In connection with this theme, it is useful to quote a passage from **Equinox of the Gods** (page 127), in which Crowley states:

*"I lay claim to be the sole authority competent to decide disputed points with regard to the Book of the Law, seeing that its Author, Aiwaz, is none other than mine own Holy Guardian Angel, to Whose Knowledge and Conversation I have attained, **so that I have exclusive access to Him**. I have duly referred every difficulty to Him directly, and received His answer; my award is therefore absolute without appeal."*

If, as explicitly stated, Crowley enjoys "*exclusive access*," then the diary entry noting his request that Elaine Simpson invoke Aiwass is nonsensical. Moreover, in the same publication (page 118) Crowley states:

"I now incline to believe that Aiwass is not only the God or Demon or Devil once held holy in Sumer, and mine own Guardian Angel, but also a man as I am, insofar as He uses a human body to make his magical link with Mankind."

Is it a bird? Is it a plane? No, it's Super-Aiwass! As evidenced by his own words Aiwass is anything Crowley wants him to be, as best fits his motivation at the time. Indeed, a tendency to 'make it up as he went along' is a habitual trait proliferating Crowley's writings. In **Equinox of the Gods** (page 110) he declares:

"Morality – Sexually powerful and passionate. Strongly male to female; free from any similar impulse towards my own sex."

This utterance falls squarely into the category of 'misdirection by means of omission with intent to deceive.' Given the era's associated prejudices (and laws) relating to sexual deviance, a modest silence would be understandable, even forgivable. However, Crowley's unprovoked and overt portrayal of himself as a textbook example of normal heterosexuality is ludicrous - Especially as this blatant falsification appears in a book extolling the wonders of his New World Religion and his suitability as a spearhead of Mankind's third epoch.

The next diary reference occurs on 02 May 1906:

> *"Working on Liber Legis with (as usual) lamentably little result."*

If we take Crowley at his word, then his reception fable crashes at this point, because *"Working on **Liber Legis**"* two years after its dictation really isn't the way forward. So, if only to prevent this book from abruptly stopping here, let's ignore yet another unfortunate instance of ambiguity and assume Crowley meant to write 'Working on **Liber Legis Comment**.' On this subject, it is important to revisit five specific instructions dictated by Aiwass:

> ***I, 36.*** *My scribe Ankh-af-na-khonsu, the priest of the princes, shall not in one letter change this book; but lest there be folly, he shall comment thereupon by the wisdom of Ra-Hoor-Khuit.*
>
> ***I, 52.*** *If this be not aright; if ye confound the space-marks, saying: They are one; or saying, They are many; if the ritual be not ever unto me: then expect the direful judgments of Ra Hoor Khuit!*
>
> ***I, 54.*** *Change not as much as the style of a letter; for behold! thou, o prophet, shalt not behold all these mysteries hidden therein.*
>
> ***II, 54.*** *The stops as thou wilt; the letters? change them not in style or value!*
>
> ***III, 47.*** *This book shall be translated into all tongues: but always with the original in the writing of the Beast; for in the chance shape of the letters and their position to one another: in these are mysteries that no Beast shall divine.*

As evidenced by his published and unpublished works, in the five years between 1904 and 1909 Crowley spent much time creating a complex mat of rituals, occult computations and dogma. All of which are reliant upon the mysterious shape and style of letters within a lost manuscript. A single transcription error in the typed copy Crowley worked from had the potential to spoil weeks, if not months of toil. He is allegedly working on the new Bible for Mankind, yet Crowley lays its foundations on a surface he knows is flawed.

Between 18 April and 02 May, his 1906 diary contains two astonishing entries – Both of which I reproduce in full on the following two pages.

Diary entry for 20 April 1906

> A∴I∴ with A. in her temple. Aiwass invoked appears, of brilliant blue as when she saw him as guardian of my sleep. He has followed me ever, wishing me to follow his cult. When A. took wand, he grows brilliant and breaks up into a formless light: yet she feels him as an enemy. He seems entangled in a mesh of light and to be trying to escape. I warn him that if he goes away he cannot return. (A. in herself is hostile) "Return to Egypt, with different surroundings. (This misheard: he said *same*.) There I will give thee signs. Go with the S.W. this is essential: thus you shall get real power, that of God, the only one worth having. Illumination shall come by means of power, pari passu. Live in Egypt as you did before. Do not do a G.R. Go at once to Egypt: money troubles will be settled more easily than you think now. I will give you no guarantee of my truth." He here turned blue-black. "I am loath to part from you. Do not take A. I do not like the relations between you; break them off! If not, you must follow other Gods. Yet I would wish you to love physically, to make perfect the circle of your union. A. will not do so, therefore she is useless. If she did, she would become useful. You have erred in showing her the true relation between you on spiritual planes. Having burst that, she will remain by her sense of power over you (?) She is spiritually stronger that you. You should have dominated her by your superior strength on other planes. She will give you much trouble though eventually she may become a great aid. But your shorter path lies by Egypt and S.W. though she is not spiritually your equal. S.W. has become your enemy; but you having conquered, she is bound to aid you as you will. She has been your enemy and that of A. but you returned her hatred, hence her seeming power over you in the present. (Qy. this hearing.) I will give you a sign when alone and away from present medium. You must recognize the sign by your own intuition. Do not part from S.W. Use her. (Here S.W. appears with an evil look. She glitters like a jewelled serpent. Strange bands of light scintillate between her and Aiwass. A. now takes wand again: still feels animity on spiritual planes. Aiwass banished; S.W. has disappeared. A. tries to speak to A∴: He wants G. Retirement: does not mind whether S.W. is with me or not; but I should use *brahmacharya* (? if with her, or anyhow) I shall be guided as things turn up, as to the truth or falsehood of Aiwass, who is not to be altogeter distrusted (I think the opposition is Aiwass' limitation as a servant). A∴ will give us a sign: A's freedom. (I reply that if this comes about in a miraculous manner, well and good.) Close.

Brief synopsis of significant events between 1904 and 1910

1904 April 08/10	Reception event, manuscript written
1904 April/May	Manuscript lost. Typescript plus two carbon copies
1906 July	Came into possession of manuscript
1906 April 18	First mention of Liber Legis (typescript)
1906 April 20	Discusses formation of a new order with Jones
1906 May 02	Diary entry: "*Working on Liber Legis*"
1906 July 27	Samadhi attained, with promotion to Magister Templi
1907 September	Appendix withdrawn from Collected Works Vol. III
1907 November	Crowley and Jones reformulate A∴A∴, citing Aiwass
1909 June 28	Manuscript found in attic at Boleskine
1909 October	"*I meant I could be...*" cover sheet amendment made
1909 December	Accepts the promotion offered in 1906

Diary entry for 21 April 1906

> I∴ of R.H.K. gives glorious material flashes of light, akasic and lilac. The God, beheld, will not speak. Asked for a messenger, Aiwass appears. A. suspecting him, puts a ב on him; he blurs and becomes dirty and discrowned. A. takes wand; but this dissipates him. His real name she says is האראי (270=INRI) A. uses [artwork] and shrivels him to a black charred mass. I ask her to invoke something genuine; a white figure without a face and with little shape mounts throne. It has a glittering rayed corona. Says: "I am the God of Vengeance. I am thy Guardian Angel. I would have thee seek thine own soul in silence and alone. Take no aid with thee: take no mortal soul but retire away and depart from mankind." ב makes him brighter: he grows firmer. Repeated, form vanishes and only brightness remains. Asked for a sign or his name ה is written on throne. "I will give no other signs: you must learn to trust your own intuition."
>
> A.'s intuition tells her that he is genuine. As to our relations, he wishes us to work together (A contradiction very supra) "I do not wish you to go too far in work with S.W. She will dazzle you and be apt to lead you astray. You must always remain as armed when you work with her, as a man in full armour. I could wish you to strengthen the link between you and A. on all planes. You are very needful to each other, and can only accomplish G.W. together. (This clearly OO. I take wand and curse him by Him whom he hath blasphemed, invoking, however, A∴. The light becomes more brilliant. To V.N. it disappears here. Voice continues: "You must go and do a G.R. after which you shall get a sign" (Clearly due to A. knowing my wish; but he is clumsy. Will anything now convince A? I take serious measures to banish all but A∴. Voice silenced: and she doubts if voice is from brilliance. A. feels me absolutely necessary for her. I not. Voice is *from her* so cannot be banished and it goes on:) "There shall be short period of work? *not*? done in actual unison; after which your powers join irrevocably together. There is no escape from that; you are bound to work together; and the fitting time and hour for this shall come simultaneously to you both. There will then be no doubt in either of your minds: there will be no obstacle to this union ... you must look towards this time and towards a beacon light. Never lose sight of that, You and O.M. will meet with subtle temptation from this object — promises of great power and illumination; but heed them not. A. is your true helper from whom you have right to look and demand help. You must never cease to demand this aid, and by your demand strengthen and aid your comrade. I your Guardian Angel tell you this."
>
> (The falsity of all this patent more at the time than now — I foresaw what follows)
>
> I ask for proof that he *is* Guardian Angel — it is clear that Voice and Brilliance are distinct. A. however feels that this rigmarole is true. Hence we discuss our relations and the Great Invocation degenerates. This however is checked by my will and her own feeling that we have done enough for honour. I am not exhausted after all this, as I was yesterday. Is this a proof that all is Right Magic, or that little force was expended? Where am I, in fact? O Holy Exalted One, do Thou illuminate my mind!

Crowley's final diary entry of 1906, made on 28 December, is... utterly enigmatic.

> "*Beginning to see possibilities of scheme (i.e Truth Scheme).*"

XIII. When the Fat Lady sins

Crowley devised **The Equinox** as a public mouthpiece and recruiting ground for the new Order he and Jones formed in November 1907. He described it as *"THE OFFICIAL ORGAN OF THE A∴ A∴."* Given the mandate of this bulky periodical, it is surprising to find that neither the opening *"Editorial"* section, or *"AN ACCOUNT OF THE A∴ A∴"* or recommended *"Course of Reading"* mention **Liber L. vel Legis**, in any capacity! Though its title page states the date in both Roman Numerals and Crowley's New Aeon dating system.

The typeset material was available from September 1907. Why didn't Crowley launch **The Equinox** with a big 'Horus is here' type fanfare, accompanied by the Appendix version of **Liber L. vel Legis**? On publication of its third volume (March 1910) Crowley has accepted both his occult advancement to Magister Templi and **Liber L. vel Legis,** why then does **Equinox I, 3** omit mention of these momentous events? Why does Crowley wait until the March 1912 publication of **Equinox I, 7** to premiere his reception story, and why is the 1910 **Holy Books** edition bereft of this?

These conundrums, and all other discrepancies outlined in this book, arose in consequence of a radical change in Crowley's thinking as precipitated by his involvement with George Cecil Jones. Though Crowley took great pains to conceal his tracks, the extant record indirectly marks the exact day on which his mystical construct pivoted on its axis. For Thelema, 28 June 1909 is 'ground-zero.' Consider the following dilemma – If G. C. Jones saw the 1907 Appendix, then Crowley couldn't subsequently reinvent **Liber L.** as one of the *"inspired"* works he 'channelled' in 1907. Once Jones has seen the **Holy Books** version of **Liber L.**, Crowley can't back-track it to Cairo, 1904. Of the other significant player, Fuller, Crowley asks (in 1923) *"What was sent to Fuller as Book of the Law? Presumably typescript."* This question relates to whether or not Fuller received the prefacing (cover sheet) material. Whatever variant Fuller did study, Crowley recounted his response in **Confessions**, Chapter 60:

> *"In a spirit of mischief I sent him a typescript of The Book of the Law and asked him to tell me what he thought of it. I wanted to disgust him with myself; I wanted him to class me finally as a hopeless crank. His answer came in the course of two or three days: I could not believe my eyes. This, he wrote, is the utterance of a Master. What did he know about Masters, confound him! It was as if I had sent a copy of Tit-Bits to the Archbishop of Canterbury, and he had reverently pronounced it to be the authentic Logia of 'our Lord'."*

Crowley published Fuller's prize-winning *"critical essay"* entitled **The Star in the West** in 1907. Bizarrely, and as noted by Crowley:

> *"It is a very complete and just exposition of my views, and it is especially to be noticed that within the one hundred and thirty-three pages there is no reference to* **The Book of the Law**.*"*

To this curious omission, Crowley adds:

> *"So late as October 1908, I was carrying out a Retirement (see "***John St. John***"), and invoking my Holy Guardian Angel, without any reference to* **The Book of the Law**. *Fuller and I had gone to work to edit my magical diaries and present to the world the story of my magical career in* **"The Temple of Solomon the King"**, *as if the Cairo working were a mere episode of that career. We were carrying out the orders of the Secret Chiefs by exposing the G∴ D∴ and publishing its Ritual."*

In this passage, Crowley acknowledges his seemingly pathological aversion to mention **Liber L**, and confirms my suggestion that the Cairo revelation pertained exclusively to a destruction of the Golden Dawn. Interestingly, Crowley admits (in 1923) that **Liber Legis** was not to Jones' liking, *"on grounds of Chap III. Suggested a dirty type of Allah or Jehovah."*

John St. John is in itself a fascinating document. First published in **Equinox I, 1** (March 1909) it records a twelve day *"magical retirement"* beginning on 01 October 1908. As stated by Crowley, *"It is a very complete and just exposition of my views."* The Magickal techniques employed by Crowley are principally Yoga (asanas, pranayama) and sex with Maryt Waska (which he describes as *"performing the Vajroli Mudra"*) underpinned by invocations of Adonai from the Goetia as well as ideas drawn from Abramelin and the Golden Dawn. He alludes to and quotes from the Christian Bible (and Fuller's **The Star in the West**) and gives illustrations from Islam, Hinduism, Zoroaster, the Arthurian legends and the Greek myths… but does not mention **Liber L.**, at all.

Crowley also frequently refers to the gods and myths of ancient Egypt, but uses the traditional names and spellings as they were then generally understood, not the idiosyncratic **Liber L.** versions. For instance, the sky goddess is always Nu not Nuit:

> "*…the Sun in His strength that travelleth over the heaven of **Nu** in His bark in the mid-career of Day.*"

On comparing his present results with previous experiences, he finds them **exceeding** those obtained in Egypt!

> "*….the 'ultra-violet' or 'astral' light in the room was such that it seemed bright as daylight. He hath never seen the like, even in the ceremony which he performed in the Great Pyramid of Gizeh.*"

No reference is made to Aiwass, or the reception of **Liber L. vel Legi**s. In fact, when Crowley says "*My Holy Guardian Angel,*" he is speaking specifically of Adonai. A chronological list of attainments twice extols the virtues of Port Said's Duty-Free store, though his third visit in February 1904 (i.e. Aiwass and the reception) doesn't rate a mention:

> "*It is in any case remarkable that I was born in October (1875); suffered the terrible mystic trance which turned me toward the Path in October (1896); applied for admission to A∴ A∴, in October (1898); opened my temple at Boleskine in October (1899); received the mysteries of L.I.L. in October (1900);* **first landed in Egypt in October (1902); landed again in Egypt in October (1903)**; *first parted from…*"

Moreover, on page 451 of **Confessions**, Crowley laments yet another missed opportunity to introduce Thelema. Of his spectacularly obscene publication **Bagh-I-Muattar**, or **Scented Garden**, published in 1910, he observes:

> "*It is especially to be noted that, although I have packed every kind of magical and mystical lore into the volume, there is nowhere any reference to* **The Book of the Law**.*"

The dated "*Oct 09*" cover sheet amendment suggests that Crowley intended to include this material in **Holy Books Vol. III** until very close to its publication. At this time, it contains a scribbled note claiming authorship of the stele paraphrase and another dating his possession of the manuscript to "*July 1906.*" The 'Oct 09' adjustment modifies this stance to suggest, rather bizarrely, that Crowley actually meant he could be "*its master*" from that date, and not that he came into possession of the document, as explicitly stated. Put bluntly, the 'Oct 09' note is nonsensical because Crowley is asking readers to forget that that he previously said that the manuscript was the work of another and ignore a suggestion that his only contribution was that of the stele versification, and accept now that he wrote the whole thing! To compound this mystery, Crowley repeatedly demands that he ignored **Liber L. vel Legis** between 1904 and 1909. A passage in **Confessions** (page 541) encapsulates his alleged position:

> "*Here was the Book which I hated and feared, the Book from which I was desperately trying to escape...*"

In fact, nothing could be more divorced from reality. Far from a 'desperate escape attempt,' Crowley's diary records extensive work with both **Liber Legis** and its accompanying comment throughout 1906. He spends considerable time in 1907 editing it in readiness for inclusion in the third volume of **Collected Works**, and handing out copies for comment. His Magickal notebooks between 1904 and 1907 comprise little else other than material revolving around **Liber L. vel Legis,** and he undertakes further editing in preparation for its debut appearance in **Holy Books Vol. III**. Given the context of this publication, Crowley's inflammatory statement in **Confessions** (page 540) is patently absurd:

> "*I determined, in a mood which I can only describe as a fit of ill temper, to publish* **The Book of the Law***, and then get rid of it for ever...*"

The one 'certainty' in this bewildering mass of contradictions is Crowley's **Jekyll & Hyde** mentality with reference to **Liber L. vel Legis**. In the public domain, he's preaching a radicalised message of '*lambaste, lose, loathe and leave well-alone.*' Conversely, behind-the-scenes he's frantically '*AL-ing it to the max!*' Interestingly, and irrespective of all contributing factors, six long years elapsed between the alleged reception event and first publication. Following a long period of seeming inactivity, the lost manuscript's rediscovery lit the fuse on a quick-fire sequence of events that would – finally – detonate Crowley's mind-bomb. In just a few short months, Crowley **1)** Finds the lost manuscript, **2)** Accepts (after a three year hiatus) his occult promotion, **3)** Revises the material prefacing **Liber L.**, **4)** Scraps this, **5)** Claims authorship of **Liber L.** and **6)** Publishes a typescript as one of his "*inspired*" works, in **Holy Books Vol. III**. That's one Hell of a metamorphosis, and one precipitated by a fortuitous rediscovery of the long-lost manuscript. Of this, Crowley's gushing account borders on mythological. He doesn't stumble over it down the back of his sofa or bureau. Nothing 'ordinary' will suffice and in emphasising the extraordinary, Crowley completely overplays his hand. The miraculous event he narrates in **Equinox I, 10** (October 1913):

> "*The house was ransacked by the three men and by the servants; no trace was discovered, and the search was abandoned. On June 28, we find this entry -*
>
> *Glory be to Nuit, Hadit, Ra-Hoor-Khuit in the Highest! A little before midday I was impelled mysteriously (though exhausted by playing fives, billiards, etc. till nearly six this morning), to make a final search for Elemental Tablets. And lo! when I had at last abandoned the search, I cast mine eyes upon a hole in the loft, where were ski, etc., and there, O Holy, Holy, Holy! were not only all that I sought, but the manuscript of Liber Legis!*"

As noted in my Introduction, and in stark contrast to Crowley's self-evident whoops of joy, the Magickal Record of his pupil Victor Neuburg tells a very different story - As succinctly encapsulated by eminent Crowley aficionado "*the_real_simon_iff*" (aka "*Lutz*") in a post made on www.lashtal.com:

> "**Crowley and his discrepancies** - *Reply #93 on January 17, 2013.*
>
> *It seems to have been quite an event for him. But now it happens that we have Neuburg's very detailed Record of his Magical Retirement which lasted until June 27. This record was studied and then commented on by Crowley and then to be rewritten by Neuburg "in a neat and legible handwriting", appended with "a fragment of biography" and finished on June 30 when they left together for London. Neuburg's entries record every little detail of his retirement and of his surroundings in the house, the mood-swings in his "Most Holy Guru", the tea he was served by his "Guru's slave" (Ward), reading and playing and meal times with Crowley, everything. It seems highly unlikely that Neuburg wouldn't mention this event, which must have changed the atmosphere at Boleskine considerably. It is even more unlikely that he did not draw any highly meaningful connections between his Initiation and the finding of the manuscript. What's even more puzzling is that it seems that the manuscript of Neuburg's Record housed at the Harry Ransom Center appears to be written in Crowley's hand (this is a private conclusion, maybe both men had quite similar handwritings, but Neuburg's signature on his*

Probationer Oath suggest a totally different style) which - if true - would mean that Crowley himself left out the event while rewriting the Record (for whatever reasons)."

Two discrepancies for the price of one – Bargain! Neuburg's journal casts serious doubts over Crowley's euphoria. If Crowley wrote (for whatever reasons) this material, his omission is wholly inexplicable and deeply suspicious. Crowley's handwritten diary for this period is currently missing. As such, it is not possible to cross-reference what he wrote at the time with the published account. On this theme, it is curious that Crowley reproduced a 1909 diary entry trumpeting the manuscript's rediscovery in a periodical published over four years later. Why wasn't it featured in **Equinox I, 2** (Sept. 1909), or any of the other seven numbers issued prior to his disclosure in **Equinox I, 10** (Sept. 1913)?

That the historical record is missing a handwritten diary for this period is not particularly questionable. Crowley himself noted the loss of numerous items during his lifetime and often referenced material no longer extant. Conversely, the lost manuscript story is highly suspect. Its alleged 'absence' is not questionable in itself. However, the complete absence of contemporary records lamenting its absence is extremely dubious. Prior to his euphoric declaration, Crowley never mentioned the loss, or the obstacles this presented him. In April 1906, Crowley bemoaned a *"lamentably little result,"* but did not cite his separation from the manuscript as a cause.

Crowley's Magickal notebooks between the summer of 1904 and late 1907 are filled with Qabalistic mathematics, ritual elements and garbled snippets relating directly to **Liber L. vel Legis**. On studying these complex occult records, it is easy to conclude that **Liber L.** represents the culmination of this work, rather than Crowley's insistence of the converse. For example, the use of *"Do what he will"* is a clear precursor of *"Do what thou wilt."* Similarly, he wrote *"Name-coincidences in Qabalah"* and *"cross-examination of Rose"* years after the events described – Events on which Crowley's reception myth is reliant. Not once does Crowley refer to **Liber L. vel Legis**, or its derivatives.

Of innumerable twists, turns, misdirection and outright falsifications woven into the saga that is **Liber L. vel Legis**, we can at least pinpoint the moment of its debut public appearance to the early part of 1910, in **Holy Books Vol. III**. At this moment in time, Crowley tacitly presents **Liber L.** as nothing more than one amongst numerous *"inspired"* writings penned in 1907. Inexplicably, not only did Crowley forget to include the Rose, Boulak, reception saga, he also broke Aiwass' fundamental command:

> ***III, 47.*** *This book shall be translated into all tongues:* ***but always with the original in the writing of the Beast;*** *for in the chance shape of the letters and their position to one another: in these are mysteries that no Beast shall divine.*

Crowley has allegedly rediscovered his manuscript by this time, so why didn't he include a facsimile, as explicitly instructed? It must be emphasised that Aiwass represents the gods of a New Aeon. Yet, again, Crowley evidently preferred his own agenda to that of a purportedly divine mandate – '*Like, whatever…*'

Crowley's reticence to follow commands is even more curious in consideration of his occult relationship with G. C. Jones, co-founder of the *A∴ A∴*. Jones is strictly 'old school,' and intimately familiar with Crowley's less savoury characteristics. Crowley echoes Jones' pedantic nature in a 1907 piece titled **Liber LXI vel Causæ**.

> ***20.*** *Thereupon these two adepts conferred together, saying: May it not be written that the tribulations shall be shortened? Therefore they resolved to establish a new Order which would be* ***free from the*** *errors and* ***deceits*** *of the former one.*
>
> ***21. Without Authority they could not do this****, exalted as their rank was among adepts. They resolved to prepare all things, great and small, against that day when such Authority should be received by them, since they knew not where to seek for higher adepts than themselves, but knew that the true way to attract the notice of such was to equilibrate the symbols. The temple must be builded before the God can indwell it.*

Jones won't sit easy on his throne until he's back in his Golden Dawn 'comfort zone,' with a proper Founding Document tucked in his robe. Beneath his beatific shield of indifference, Jones probably still feels a bit aggrieved about the way in which Crowley leapfrogged him to bag a place at breakfast with the incoming Secret Chiefs. As such, he will undoubtedly scrutinise Crowley's every utterance. Why, then, does Crowley not 'make Jones' day,' and get the man off his back, by revealing the very item Jones' ego demands? Why does Crowley wait another two years to 'show his hand?' Why at such a ludicrously small scale, accompanied by a wholly baffling note:

> *"The reproduction of Liber Legis has been done thus minutely in order to prevent the casual reader from wasting his valuable time over it."*

From Alpha to Omega, **Liber L. vel Legis** evolved in response to Crowley's changing aspirations and circumstances. I have little hesitation in suggesting that both the initial loss and subsequent rediscovery events are two further examples of fabrications woven into the myth as a patch over unforeseen eventualities. It is my personal feeling that 28 June 1909 marks not the date on which Crowley rediscovered his lost manuscript. Rather, it represents the time at which he wrote it! In support of this seemingly wild suggestion, I offer the following rationale:

1) The cover sheet (scribbled on paper originating from Cairo) states *"translations of the Stele inscriptions."* It also refers to *"documents,"* and the enclosed material only becomes a *"MS."* on Crowley overwriting the original term, *"item."*

2) Accompanying this (Harry Ransom Center) is not a manuscript, but a typescript, which reproduces Crowley's paraphrase, not a literal translation of stele hieroglyphs.

3) Crowley does not publish a corrected version of **Liber L. vel Legis** until the September 1913 issue of **Equinox I, 10**.

4) Crowley spends five years erecting the superstructure of Thelema on a typeset copy he knows is flawed.

5) Anyone (G. C. Jones, Fuller, Neuburg, C. S. Jones, etc.,) who sees the manuscript prior to Crowley's 'October 09' authorship switch (i.e. the Appendix version) will recognise Crowley's distinctive handwriting style and immediately contest multiple glaring contradictions. A typescript negates this formidable obstacle.

6) Standard Typewriting paper, originating from London, is the base material on which Crowley scribed his New Covenant.

7) The **Liber L. vel Legis** manuscript is Crowley's 'Trump' card. It is a textbook occult validation of both his genuine contact with the Secret Chiefs and their declaration of monumental changes to come. Why doesn't he use it?

To my mind, the only scenario capable of reconciling these anomalies is a heretical suggestion that Crowley guarded his manuscript so closely in consequence of him not actually writing it until around July 1909. Is the 'lost manuscript' story actually Crowley's way of stalling Jones' perfectly understandable request to see a proper, handwritten Founding Document? Does July 1909 mark the point at which Crowley caved-in to Jones' demands and delivered his best attempt to retro-engineer a manuscript from the extant typescript?

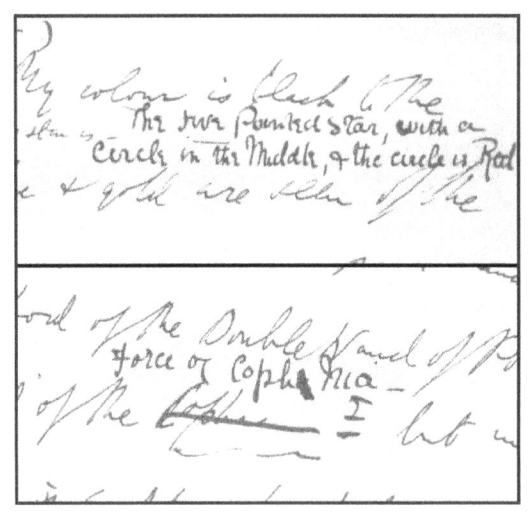

Two notes, in the distinctive style of Rose, written on the manuscript support this scenario. According to the official story, Crowley was alone in the room during the dictation, and Rose can't hear Aiwass (because Crowley has exclusive access), so how was she able to 'fill in the gaps?'

In many respects, the solution to this riddle encapsulates the 'essence' of multiple discrepancies outlined in this publication. Ultimately, it resolves into one, of two possibilities, which are:

1) Aiwass, by some nebulous praeterhuman process, instructed Rose.

2) Whilst replicating the reception conditions, Rose dictated (from a typescript) to Crowley, who scribbled furiously. On completion, Rose compared her typescript against Crowley's manuscript. She corrected two omissions, wrinkled her weary brow, and sighed - "*You still missed a few bits. We're going to need another go.*"

Is the extant manuscript Crowley's best effort (of several) to divert a calamity as the countdown on Jones' patience ticked ever-closer to zero? This scenario certainly explains his curiously overanxious attitude towards a few transcription errors littering the original typescript. Crowley's evident twitchiness is explicable if viewed in terms of a guilty reaction to the lie embedded at the heart of his New World Religion, and one that festered from the very first second of Crowley's New Aeon. In this respect, Crowley certainly appeared reluctant in the extreme to reveal his Founding Document. Eight years elapsed before he cautiously flashed the absurd 'Barbie Doll' scale facsimile in **Equinox I, 7**. Following this, another twenty-four years passed before Crowley felt able to provide a reasonably sized reproduction of the manuscript, in **Equinox of the Gods**. Incidentally, a long-standing rumour suggests that the treasure-trove allegedly unearthed by Tom Whitmore contained more than one handwritten **Liber L. vel Legis** manuscript.

XIV. ALmost fatAL case of genital disintegration

According to Crowley, but not Neuburg, the 28 June 1909 rediscovery of his lost manuscript was a glorious event. Alas, the euphoria was short-lived. Events culminating on 27 April 1911 gouged an almost bottomless pit into which the **Great Beast 666** and his mystical aspirations plummeted.

On 26 November 1910, a sleazy magazine named **The Looking Glass** published an article (one in an increasingly vitriolic campaign) that evoked several of Crowley's old friends, notably *"unnatural vice" "unmentionable immoralities."* Fuller demanded that Crowley sue on grounds of libel. He declined. Ultimately, Jones picked up the gauntlet and initiated another legendary episode in the riotous life of Aleister Crowley. On 25, 26 and 27 April 1911 Mr. Justice Scrutton presided over Crowley's trial by proxy. The jury retired at 2:58PM and took only half-an-hour to decide in favour of **The Looking Glass**, and damn Crowley – Of whom it was stated:

> *"...that Crowley is a man of notoriously evil character has been established. It is not even questioned. His literature shows it, the admissions of Jones himself shows it, and what was said to Jones's own solicitor shows it."*

Another decade will pass before fate crowns Crowley with his ultimate accolade, the title of *"Wickedest Man in the World."* Nevertheless, even at this early stage he's galloping in the right direction. Let us not forget that this *"notoriously evil character"* is enthusiastically touting himself as the *"Prophet of a New Aeon"* – Essentially a successor to Jesus. As if to underline a seemingly innate juvenile lewdness most unbecoming of the 'Chosen One,' Crowley sniped at the judge and trial itself, by noting that an anagram of the letters comprising his name described "*a fact of nature.*"

Having blown most of his inheritance, Crowley can't afford a costly litigation in defence of his reputation that he can't possibly win, and one certain to result in a public exposure of his "*unnatural vices.*" Nor can he take the stand in defence of Jones. Doing this would compel him to commit perjury, or destroy Jones' case by conceding he is an active sexual deviant – With its inherent penal consequences. Fuller considered Crowley's avoidance an act of cowardice and the pair never met again. Consequentially, Crowley forfeited his greatest ally. Incidentally, Fuller's departure inadvertently created an entirely unanticipated problem for Crowley. Fuller retained the 1907 Appendix version of **Liber L. vel Legis**., and his possession of this sensitive material significantly restricted Crowley's subsequent attempts to refine his master plan.

Following the Looking Glass trial, Crowley became radioactive and toxic even in small doses. Even his most loyal pet, Neuburg, went 'Absent Without Leave.' In October 1911, Crowley accused his lapsed disciple of accepting money in return for abandoning him. The bribe derived from a family increasingly concerned about Crowley's detrimental effect on their son's health, wealth and happiness. Indeed, Lawrence Sutin casts a further shadow on Crowley's character in his 2000 publication **Do What Thou Wilt**:

> "*Neuburg had, in past years, willingly placed his family funds at the disposal of Crowley and The Equinox. As Crowley was now beset by financial worries, the cut-off of funds could not have been pleasant. There is a startling story alleging the extent to which Crowley had gone to wring money from Neuburg's family. According to one family friend, during one of their trips to the Sahara, Crowley had sent Neuburg's mother a telegram reading 'Send £500 or you will never see your son again'.*"

In a very short time span, all of the major pieces in Crowley's cosmic chess game fell. A corresponding sense of dissatisfaction amidst the lower ranks Crowley addressed in a sneering piece entitled "*X-rays on Ex-Probationers,*" which venomously observed:

> "*Rats leave sinking ships; but you cannot be sure that a ship will sink if you see a rat running away from it.*"

Of this catastrophic period, Crowley laments:

> "*Yet hardly anyone had read any of my work and the intrigues of my enemies had made it impossible for me to make myself heard. I never cease to wonder at the persistence of malignant hostility on the part of people who have never met me or read a line of my writing. I cannot see why people should pursue me with secret slander, often of a kind which carries its own refutation with it. To give one instance: It was said it was my practice to lure men into the Himalayas for weekends ... I always returned alone!*"

By 1912, Crowley is a Messiah preaching to a global audience of one – Assuming Aiwass isn't still loitering around. Much to his credit, or desperation, Crowley picks up the pieces and carries on regardless. He works around the Appendix version of **Liber L. vel Legis** in Fuller's possession by fleshing-out the Rose-Boulak-stele-reception components. The latest upgrade he published in **Equinox I, 7**. (March 1912), safe in the knowledge that the only person able to contradict his fable is drying-out in a private institution. At Crowley's behest, his ex-wife, Rose (they divorced on 24 November 1909), was 'treated' during the autumn of 1911. Perhaps tellingly, the 'all-singing, all-dancing' version of **Liber AL,** accompanied by a decent sized manuscript facsimile did not appear until 1936, after the death of his first wife Ouarda the Seer, or Rose.

The rest, as they say, is history, or histrionics! Crowley 'pulls off' his spectacularly audacious plan and for the remainder of his life portrays himself as the god-appointed herald of a New Aeon. Since the AL reception fable is reliant on the miraculous appearance of Aiwass, Crowley did his utmost to eradicate all traces of intermediary stages from the record. The discrepancies analysed in this publication represent Crowley's failures in this respect. The remit of this book is one of demonstrating only that Crowley did not write **Liber L. vel Legis** on 08, 09 & 10 April, period. The 'alternate timeline' outlined is merely a 'best-fit' scenario of the probable sequence of events, based on a direct comparison of Crowley's published accounts and unpublished source material. Given an absence of hard evidence, though accepting a possibility that new material may emerge at any time, it may prove impossible to determine the true date(s) on which Crowley wrote the AL manuscript.

XV. A view from above

My exploration of the origins and genesis of **Liber L. vel Legis** has, I accept, barely scratched the surface of a complex, convoluted and genuinely baffling web of intrigue. It does however expose a multiplicity of glaring discrepancies in Crowley's account of the Cairo Revelation, and casts grave doubt upon the validity of his claims regarding Aiwass, Horus, Ra-Hoor-Khuit, Nuit, Thelema and the New Aeon.

To date, nobody has uncovered an outright 'confession' signed by Crowley. Nor, I suspect, would the appearance of such make an impression in 'blind faith' of the type demanded by religious doctrine, including that of Thelema. Indeed the appearance of a handwritten admission would evoke only a vociferous retort of "*Fake!*" from those terminally afflicted by 'Crow-Blindness.'

Incurables aside, "*Occult Detective*" **Bob Freeman** recently encapsulated the prevalent mindset regarding **AL**-related oddities in his blog of 04 January 2015:

"Anyone who hasn't questioned at least some of Old Crow's account haven't really been paying attention."

(https://authorbobfreeman.wordpress.com/2015/01/)

In many respects, **Liber L. vel Bogus** is an attempt to marshal known and previously unknown 'wrinkles' into a single mass, in hope of creating an unsightly hump under Crowley's carpet of such dimensions as to negate the default option of 'look away and skirt around.' Nonetheless, until resolved, a UCO (Unidentified Crowley Object) remains just that - Unidentified! The absence of definite proof affords ample scope for interested parties to arrange extant signage into a route best fitting personal preferences. To restate an earlier analogy (see **Supplemental Material – The Definitive R. T. Cole**): A tourist visiting relatives in Leeds and Manchester may well navigate around, rather than over the Pennines as a means of incorporating a spot of 'Monster Spotting' – Of an aquatic or otherwise nature. 'Uncertainty' is a fertile breeding ground. From 'Creationists' to 'Holocaust deniers' and all shades between, converts warp their faith around the most formidable obstacles. Even the seemingly cut-and-dried case of 'reality' itself remains open to infinite debate and conjecture. It is possible to debate the nature of anything until participants are blue in the chakras, and without the slightest progress towards a resolution. Over the years, I have repeatedly found that the only way of getting anything done is to strip the issues in play down to black and white, then visualise myself stuck between them in a real-world (with real consequences) scenario. For instance, the next time a smart arsed, self-appointed guru squawks, *"reality is an illusion,"* rap him/her smartly on the beak and ask, *"What hurts?"*

On reading a copy of this work, a good friend eloquently phrased the question of Crowley's reception of **Liber L. vel Legis** with an inspired remark. She said:

"Well, if I were on trial for a serious crime I certainly wouldn't hang the next twenty or so years of my life on a defence equivalent to Crowley's reception story!"

To my mind, that one sentence perfectly encapsulates the whole situation. Most who read this publication will have strong allegiances with Crowley. To counter any natural tendencies towards biased sentimentality I suggest that you read **Liber L. vel Bogus** then visualise yourself in the dock of the Old Bailey No 1 Court on charges punishable by a life sentence – 'Feel' the cold sweat running down your back.

Would you sit comfortably behind a defence so patently absurd that any third-rate prosecutor would tear to it shreds in minutes? Conversely, imagine you are a jury member. Would you believe Crowley's alibi? The simple, honest answer is *"Not a cat in Hell's chance!"* Why, because as the most entrenched apologist must reluctantly concede – Even if Crowley was telling the truth, his account is so laced with omissions, deletions, U-turns, contradictions and outright lies as to destroy any semblance of credibility. If the prosecutor in this trial calls Crowley's exploits, character and reputation to the stand as witnesses, well…

March 1912 ? No. 7 Eqx. Published.
Quotations there form earlier than publication of facsimile.
In transcription of the MSS there appear passages not in the Mss "I
"I adore thee in the Song" "Under curator" translation.
"Abstruction" Replica made subsequently.
Image. Bronze hawk at Cefalu. Bought.
Wrote letter to fifteen people from Cairo "Eqx. of Gods come"

1. Ivor Back probably has copy. Consulting surgeon London.
   His father a great explorer (?T.) of Egypt. In Cairo at time.
2. Searge Cecil Jones, Chemist
3. Gerald Kelly
4. Rev. F. F. Kelly
5. Norman Collie ?
6. Travers, Morris
7. A. Bennet
8. Ernest Radcliffe ? Commissioner in Cashmire
9. Edward Threnton Martin and Co., Calcutta
10. Eckenstein, Oscar. 7 years
11. Mathers. Probably
13. Elaine Simpson "Fidelis", Married

In B(agh)-i-M(uattar) account of 49 servitors of Beelzebub obtained sometime in 12 monts following (the writing of the Book of the Law. T)

Production of Beetles

A beetle sent to Jones from Boleskine to ask him to determine its species. He replied that at S. Kensington, they couldn't identify it. (June to Dec. 1904).

Three typed copies (of Liber Legis T.) made in Cairo. One used by publishers of Zaehnsdorf edition (Chiswick Press) previous to rediscovery of Mss. Erros in vellum books due to the fact that this typescript not properly checked from Mss. Two and three no memory.

Competition date leading to acquaintence with Fuller 1904-5. Met Fuller early in 1907. Star in the West published 1907/8 about.

What was sent to Fuller as Book of the Law? Presumably typescript.

Not been in Egypt since May, June 1905?

1904 Book of the Law
1604 Dee and Kelly working
1304 Jacques de B Molay
1004
 704 The Hegira?
At time of Christ there was a real Adept Apollonius of Tyana.

> Real difference with Jesuit that of SIN. Granting your God is
> everything you claim and granting that there is such a thing as sin
> against his law, my instinct will be to do that sin.
>
>   ASWA   --prick
>   THELEMA   --anus
>
> Arabic spellings required and find out Hebrew words with identical meaning
> and similar sounds.
>
> Greek for Restriction, Sin. List of such words in AL as suggest deeper
> meanings.

(Above) A small segment of the fascinating and still unpublished material entitled **Notes of conversations with Aleister Crowley concerning the Book of the Law, 1923, recorded by Norman Mudd. "Dated Tunis, 1923, before the writing of the Comment called D."** I don't recall any published work noting the 'ASWA [AIWASS] = prick' or 'THELEMA = anus' correlation. Beneath its pomp and ceremony, does Crowley's New World Religion amount to nothing more than an infantile and lewd intent to give everybody 'one up the backside?' If so, this notion does seem perversely apt with reference to the man's penchant for sadistic practical jokes, lifestyle choices, festering grudges, resentment, contempt, sense of injustice and pathological need for divinely-sanctioned acceptance and adulation.

As a means of drawing together various strands aired in this volume, and bringing it to a pause, I now sketch the outline of a scenario I believe best describes the origin and evolution of **Liber L. vel Legis**, as deduced from an investigation of the chaotic paper-trail left over a century ago. I'll also mention an exceedingly curious photographic oddity that has perplexed viewers for decades.

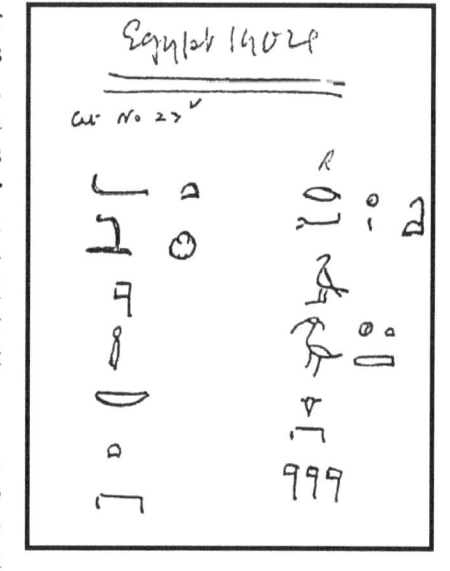

The story begins in late 1902, when Crowley first came into possession of stele material. He recorded its hieroglyphs in a notebook dated "*1902,*" and subsequently altered this to "*1904*" as a means of concealing prior knowledge of an artefact his evolving fable subsequently demanded was initially encountered some eighteen months later. He also transplanted memories from another visit to the Boulak and employed these as a foundation on which to forge a description of his fictitious 1904 visit – Which explains why Crowley repeatedly named the wrong museum. He was unaware of the artefact's relocation.

By late 1903, Crowley is desperate to validate five years spent chasing occult entities. He wants Mathers' job as head of the Golden Dawn, but cannot accomplish this without incontestable evidence of a Magickal Link to the Secret Chiefs. His whirlwind romance and marriage to Rose (itself an allegorical depiction of a ritual of sexual Magick) affords Crowley an opportunity to visit the ancient gods of Egypt and perhaps, 'make something happen.'

His evident disgust at the pitiful astral lightshow evoked in the King's Chamber suggests to me an expectation of more, much more – I would not be surprised to discover that Crowley wrote and utilized Rose's nonsensical Invocation of Horus (the first item in OS27) as part of the ceremonials enacted in the Great Pyramid. Crowley certainly departed Egypt enveloped by a dark, brooding storm cloud. Then, en route to visit Allan Bennett in Rangoon, something changed. This must have occurred around January 1904, since he wrote **Why Jesus Wept** at this time – In which he announces that, *"the young warrior of a new religion is upon thee; and his number is the number of a man."* When Crowley spun his ship on its anchor and steamed back to Egypt, he 'knew' exactly what was going to happen next, because he'd just experienced a 'spiritual intuition' that would define the remainder of his life.

Crowley's life-changing revelation gravitated around a notion of using stele imagery as the basis for a ritualised act(s) of Sex Magick. Having made this connection, his notebook continues with the B2 material (incorporating stele imagery he purportedly does not yet possess) and copious notes relating to Sex Magick. I suspect that, by whatever means of persuasion, Crowley lured his new wife into a threesome including Hamid, the couple's athletic male *"waiter."* If indeed Crowley did secure Rose's willing participation in a drama incorporating homosexual elements, then his sense of achievement must have felt boundless. He had broken his generation's ultimate taboo, whilst on honeymoon, and with his bride's cooperation and indulgence. If Crowley was looking for a convenient portent on which to hang his new crown, this was surely as good as it was ever going to get! The gods themselves had revealed to their 'Chosen One' the Formula of a New Equinox. A new epoch of sexual liberation had dawned, whose sacrament was orgiastic promiscuity (*"The word of Sin is Restriction"* - **Liber L. vel Legis**, I, 41). That Crowley synchronised his ecstatic revelation with the Spring Equinox, was a nice touch.

Crowley left Egypt armed only with a philosophers' stone, Sex Magick, with which he will vanquish Mathers - An assertion explicitly confirmed in notes subsequently expunged from all published accounts. Moreover, the garbled entries in his personal diary may be illegible, but not their corresponding dates, which chart a clear timeline of events between 16 and 25 March. Similarly, his **Book of Results** (almost certainly written at Boleskine prior to the spring of 1906) also focuses on the same period (16 – 23 March). One journal terminates on 23 March, the other on 06 April. Neither records any reference whatsoever to the 'cross-examination,' Boulak visit, Rose's discovery of the stele, Crowley's request for or receipt of a French translation, or the three-day reception event. For my money, the only serious contender accounting for these inexplicable gaps in Crowley's record is an inescapable conclusion that the occurrences described never actually happened. At this time, Crowley's scheme required only a means of kicking Mathers in the halo. Aiwass and **Liber L.** are just a distant twinkle in his wand. That Crowley returned from Cairo not as the 'prophet of a New Aeon,' but merely a man intent on destroying Mathers, and usurping his position as head of the Golden Dawn, is evident from his activities in the summer of 1904.

> "*July 1904 is however the date of an essay 'The initiated interpretation of ceremonial magick' which I prefaced to my edition of The Goetia. I had employed Mathers to translate the text of The Lesser Key of Solomon the King of which The Goetia is the first section. He got no further; after the events of 1900, he had simply collapsed morally. I added a translation of the conjurations into the Enochian or Angelic language; edited and annotated the text, prefixed a 'Preliminary Invocation', added a prefatory note, a Magical Square (intended to prevent improper use of the book) and ultimately an Invocation of Typhon when the First Magical War of the Aeon of Horus was declared.*" (**Confessions**, page 362)

Though not mentioned in **Confessions**, Crowley fronted this work with a macabre note:

"*TRANSLATED INTO THE ENGLISH TONGUE BY A DEAD HAND*"

The term 'dead hand' usually alludes to the work of a seasoned expert. However, Crowley intended it as a reference to Mathers' impending destruction, at his hand! In short, Crowley steamrollered over Mathers, abstructed his translation and grafted this into a book relating to Crowley's post-Cairo work evoking Beelzabub and his forty-nine servitors. In publishing the **Goetia**, Crowley symbolically hauled Mathers from his mount and grabbed its reins. As if wanting to commemorate his glorious coup, Crowley immortalised the moment with an instantly recognisable photograph – A curious image that has evoked decades of speculation in consequence of the book carefully positioned on his coffee table. The publication in question appears to be a copy of Crowley's three-in-one **Holy Books**, as published in 1910. Incidentally, one 'expert' suggested that the recently rediscovered Windram (*"Flashing Colours"*) copy is the very same item as featured in Crowley's photograph. If so, this nudges the date forward by two years, to 1912 (as inscribed in that particular volume). Whether 1910 or 1912, this book equates to an image supposedly portraying Crowley in his mid-thirties. To highlight this discrepancy, simply arrange the three heads (below) in 'age order.'

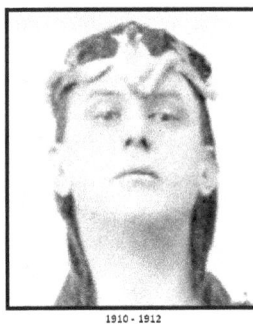

1910 | 1910-1912 | 1914

Between the 10 January 1910 *"Divorce"* photograph and 1914 *"Englishman in New York"* specimen, Crowley's appearance undergoes a radical transformation. He first loses ten years then gains fifteen. Clearly, 'something' is not quite right about the accepted dating of this photograph.

Dark | Composite | Light

The image in question depicts a transitional moment between Crowley's pre-Horus, Golden Dawn Enochian period and his post-Horus, Thelemic Aiwass phase. Actually, there are at least two extant versions of this pose, taken seconds apart and distinguished by a slight difference in the angle of Crowley's head. The variants also possess distinct tonal qualities. One is noticeably lighter, with less contrast. When superimposed, the result indicates that Crowley probably inhaled between first and second 'snaps.'

Crowley first published the photograph in **Book 4** (1911), which also includes a short description of Magickal implements positioned strategically on the altar. (With respect to the phial of *"Holy Oil,"* this description is especially apt as its placement conceals a transcription error in Crowley's replica of the stele). A chapter in **Book 4** titled *"The Book,"* describes this volume as *"The Book of Spells or Conjurations..."* which the **Holy Books** are not, but the **Goetia** is. Curiously, in his 1951 typescript catalogue of *"Crowleyana,"* the usually reliable Gerald Yorke suggests *"Photo of A. C. as 5°=6☐ in the A∴ A∴ 1907."* Following this is a photograph of Crowley as *"Prince Chioa Khan"* – An image intimately acquainted with the Cairo Revelation. Incidentally, the scenery visible behind Crowley's enthusiastic halo is, to my mind, not reminiscent of an arid Egyptian desert and more akin to a lush Scottish country panorama, perhaps the estate at Boleskine.

The contentious 'Magus' photograph is staged carefully and the result of a professional studio. Clad in a robe akin to that worn by a Neophyte of the Golden Dawn, Crowley poses formally behind a meticulously positioned collection of occult paraphernalia. He clearly invested time and money into capturing this particular imagery. So, what event does it celebrate? What message was he trying to convey? The 'obvious' answer is **Holy Books**, were it not for Crowley's impossibly youthful features. The next-best contender is perhaps a suggestion that Crowley intended the photograph as a companion to the version of **Liber L. vel Legis** scheduled for **Collected Works Vol. III.** This scenario fails in consequence of him not yet having scribed the *"inspired"* works comprising **THELEMA** – A title clearly legible on the book's front cover, as is Fuller's 'pillars' design, and this graphic brings into play yet another complication. In *"Notes on Conversations...,"* Crowley states that he first met Fuller in *"1904-1905,"* yet his 1924 diary suggests *"1906-07."* The September 1907 '**Appendix**' theory also falls down in consequence of Crowley not yet having made the *"intelligent study"* yielding *"interesting and helpful"* results. Since he's not yet 'realised' the wonders of **Liber L.**, Crowley can hardly erect an altar around them.
At the other end of this scale, we have a seemingly absurd notion of a photo taken in the summer of 1904, originally with a copy of the Goetia – as was (by some feat of airbrushing) subsequently replaced with a **Holy Books**.

On consideration of this fiendishly complex paradox, I began to wonder if the 'baby-faced Magus' picture offered a tantalising clue, marking the transition between one form of **Liber L. vel Legis** and another. Crowley returned to Boleskine with only the idea of a 'New Equinox' scheme featuring sexual Magick (first to destroy Mathers, then to form a Magickal Link with the Secret Chiefs). At this stage, there's no cross-examination of Rose, no visit to the Boulak, no translation or versification, no Aiwass and no **Book of the Law**. The only reliable contemporary source, his diary, confirms this by sketching a sequence of events culminating in a declaration, "*Equinox of Gods*" on 20 March. Even the dubious **Book of Results** follows this basic template. Of his fragmentary personal diary entries, two in particular stand out:

March 22	X.P.B.
	(May this and the entry March 24, refer to the brother of the A∴ A∴ who found him?)
	E.P.D. in 84 m.
	(Unintelligible to us; probably a blind.)
March 24	Met اجيحبا again.

Crowley later backtracked and assured readers that these encounters never happened. However, the "*silly no-reason un-connected with Magick*" rationale he employed to whitewash these "*intentional blinds*" crumbles in consequence of a blot on the record that Crowley had good reason to forget. The Arabic characters of the mysterious Egyptian Adept equate to a rough transliteration of the name **Big Beast**. Crowley appears to be suggesting that 'he *didn't* meet himself, twice' – Even by Cairo standards, that's a difficult concept to swallow! However, take Crowley's cover sheet notes and diary entries at face value, and the discrepancies vanish. These clearly suggest a timeline in which Crowley meets with a mysterious "*brother of the A∴ A∴*" - An Egyptian adept named **Big Beast** who supposedly adapted a stele translation into a ritual (presumably **The Great Invocation**) by which Aiwass was evoked to dictate **Liber L.** (to **The Beast**, who certainly wasn't Crowley). Remember that back in April 1904, Crowley's connection with '666' was but a "*mocking reference*." Remember also, that the original material written to preface **Liber L. vel Legis** states "*Given from the mouth of Aiwass to the ear of* **The Beast**."

As if to emphatically absolve himself from any suspicion of authorship, Crowley dated the document (08, 09 & 10 April 1904) to several days after his departure from Cairo. On second thought, he realised that the clue was too subtle for most. To eradicate the slightest doubt, he appended a rather clumsy "*which came into my possession in July 1906*" note – Presumably at this time his Egyptian adept chum mailed Crowley the original manuscript?

Rather surprisingly, Crowley spent the summer of 1904 hurling Magickal mud at Mathers then quickly tired of the affair and amused himself with mundane pastimes – Aiwass was devastated, apparently! **Liber L. vel Legis** vanished from sight until the spring of 1906, when Crowley's occult partner, Jones, began to express an interest in reformulating the A∴ A∴. At this point, the 'Chosen One' spotted a fabulous opportunity to upgrade his pending Equinox scheme.

Incidentally, Crowley's original intention of employing **Liber Legis** to stage a re-run of the Golden Dawn myth (via a mysterious Egyptian rather than a German contact) does raise an interesting question with regard to the infamous 'number riddle.' If someone else wrote **Liber Legis** (as Crowley explicitly states) then on making an *"intelligent study"* he becomes the one who follows, and the one destined to solve the puzzle. Remember that, in **Magical and Philosophical Commentaries on the Book of the Law**, Crowley wrote - *"Be ye well assured all that the solution, when it is found, will be unquestionable. It will be marked by the most sublime simplicity, and carry immediate conviction."* How did he know this?

Rather than slip the borrowed document discretely into **Collected Works Vol. III** and subsequently self-discover its wonders, Crowley now intends to delegate the job to Jones. This revision offers Crowley's revelation more gravitas, but is not without complications. Jones' familiarity with the stele versification (but not **Liber L. vel Legis** itself) compels Crowley's second cover sheet note (i.e. *"except the translations of the Stele inscriptions,"* which he also revised in the typeset Appendix, to *"…the **verse** translations…"*) Jones' occult seniority also presents

Crowley with a significant problem. The new Magickal Link is not yet live, and Jones outranks Crowley. When ET arrives, they'll want to chat with Jones, not Crowley. As such, Crowley can't introduce **Liber Legis** to Jones, until after he's found a way of outranking him.

Throughout 1907, Crowley plays a double hand. He's putting together the A∴ A∴ (Astrum Argenteum, or Silver Star) with Jones, whilst keeping his gestating Egyptian revelation under wraps. In the autumn of 1907, these two strands converge. By this time, he's channelled half-a-dozen 'Libers' for inclusion in **Holy Books**. This material includes a stripped-down **Liber Legis**, which Crowley is now presenting merely as one of his inspired works. Consequently, the earlier (contradictory) version he discretely expunges from **Collected Works Vol. III**.

Rather bizarrely, **Holy Books** fails to note **Liber L. vel Legis**' especial significance. Inexplicably, the introductory section, titled **Liber LXI vel Causæ,** omits any mention of **The Book of the Law**, Thelema, and all components we recognise today as the Cairo myth. Indeed, this short piece is essentially an apology for the order's previous, flawed incarnation, with a promise to 'do better' this time. It is interesting to note that Crowley has not yet out-flanked Jones, as is evident by Line 25 of a section entitled **The History Lection**, which reads:

*"Now when P. had thus with bitter toil prepared all things **under the guidance of D.D.S.**"*

Unquestionably, the most perplexing statement made in **Liber Causæ** relates to the thorny issue of *"Authority:"*

*"**Without Authority they could not do this**, exalted as their rank was among adepts. They resolved to prepare all things, great and small, against that day when such Authority should be received by them, since they knew not where to seek for higher adepts than themselves, but knew that the true way to attract the notice of such was to equilibrate the symbols. The temple must be builded before the God can indwell it."*

Why was Crowley so reluctant to reveal **Liber Legis** and its divine mandate? Incredible as it may seem, **Liber Legis** can only appear in the form it does (in **Holy Books**) if Crowley has not yet pitched the reception story to Jones. Moreover, the cover sheet note dated *"Oct. 09"* hints that Crowley intended to use the prefacing material until very close to the 1910 publication of **Holy Books**. Again, this seems absurd, yet indicates a scenario in which even at this very late stage Crowley is still playing **Liber Legis** as the work of a mysterious adept resident in Cairo – Why?

One further anomaly haunts the **Holy Books**. In the 47th verse of **Liber Legis**' third chapter, Aiwass dictates a clear instruction to Crowley, insisting:

> "***III, 47. This book shall be translated into all tongues: but always with the original in the writing of the Beast****; for in the chance shape of the letters and their position to one another: in these are mysteries that no Beast shall divine.*"

Why does Crowley ignore a direct command from the gods and publish **Holy Books** without a facsimile of the manuscript? This, he allegedly rediscovered in June 1909, so why not employ it, as instructed? In fact, the manuscript's debut appearance, reproduced at minute scale, does not happen until March 1912, almost three years later, and anyone wanting a good look has a further 24 years to wait – Why?

Crowley's reticence to share his New Covenant may well have a solution of such excruciatingly sublime irony as to command an irrational notion of genuine divine intervention. Unbeknown to the **Great Beast**, his creation of the **Liber L. vel Legis** manuscript evoked a malevolent and unseen demon that lurked patiently in the thick darkness for five years. In late 1909, Crowley inadvertently manifested this *"Dweller on the Threshold"* to visible appearance with nothing more than a candle. What he saw must have sickened his soul to its very core. Crowley can only have interpreted this catastrophic vision as an unexpurgated act of vengeance direct from the terrible and wrathful God Almighty of his boyhood in Hell.

Whilst editing material scheduled for inclusion in **Holy Books**, Crowley chanced to hold a manuscript page against a source of light. It only took a moment for him to notice a small and, for all practical purposes, imperceptible detail. Unfortunately, with reference to the reception story, this inherent property was fatal. Indelibly branded on each leaf of his Foundation Document is a seal acknowledging Crowley's completion of a lifelong ambition – That of committing the unforgivable sin.

In consequence of an almost unbelievably cruel twist of fate, Crowley wrote **Liber L.** on *"Standard Typewriting"* paper, as manufactured by Scottish papermaker Alex Pirie & Sons, especially for the booming London market – As is testified by a watermark embossed into each sheet. Anyone struggling to understand why this is devastating to

Crowley's case need only consider a hypothetical, though entirely likely conversation between the two protagonists.

Whilst finally holding the handwritten validation of their new Order reverently in his trembling hands, G. C. Jones whispers:

> "*So, this is the legendary manuscript, lost for five long years?*"
>
> "*It sure is!*" Crowley replies.
>
> "*So, this is the Founding Document of a New Aeon, as dictated by a herald of the gods and scribed by your elusive adept mate in Cairo?*"
>
> "*It sure is!*" Crowley assures.
>
> "*So, where did 'Big Beast' get his hands on a ream of paper only available in London?*"
>
> "*Beam me up, Aiwass.*" Crowley pleads.

Apologists of Crowley, Aiwass, **Liber Legis** and Thelema will automatically conjure numerous hypothetical solutions to this rather vexing conundrum – All of which are specimens of the 'clutching at straws' mentality underpinning ludicrously improbable explanations of, for example… Aiwass forgetting 'Verse Two,' Rose's scribbled grocery list on the manuscript, the nonsensical cover sheet material, etc.. Not surprisingly, even the most outrageously inventive visualisation fails to come within 666 miles of the most likely, elegant and obvious scenario.

To compound his woes, the watermark also casts a long shadow across Crowley's revised plan. The cover sheet material is scribbled on paper from the Cairo Hotel, why not the rest of **Liber Legis**? Why did Crowley haul a bulky ream of cheap paper halfway across the globe and use this to scribe a hugely important communication? If the groom did intend to spend his honeymoon bent over a typewriter, there's no wonder Rose took to the bottle!

The 'London' watermark issue was not in itself insurmountable, especially for someone already 'up to his neck in it,' with little to lose. Alas, and as Crowley was acutely aware, his manuscript and accompanying mythology were cobbled together with misinformation and fabrications. This 'final straw' surely weighed on his conscience like a corpse under the patio. The sheer magnitude of Crowley's guilty reaction is demonstrated by his otherwise inexplicable disinclination to obey Aiwass' explicit command and accompany all printed editions with a manuscript facsimile. This material is absent from both 1907 **Collected Works** Appendix and 1910 **Holy Books**. The absurd and miniscule reproduction in 1912 **Equinox I, 7** is rationalised with a distinctly questionable explanation (*"The reproduction of Liber Legis has been done thus minutely in order to prevent the casual reader from wasting his valuable time over it"*). **Equinox I, 10** includes a revised typescript, but no manuscript facsimile. A decade later, in 1924, and having made no progress towards world domination with his current *"Prophet of a New Aeon"* scheme, Crowley considers yet another major upgrade. On 04 April 1924, he writes:

> *"There comes into my mind to write a 'popular' explanation of **Liber Legis**, in the form of a non-contentious and 'noble' book, written with the idea of bringing Heaven into the hearts of the Common People."*

It is almost amusing to imagine the feedback from individuals who purchased a copy on reading the advert, in anticipation of a work along the Prentice Mulford School of Spirituality, and received Crowley's bile drenched, god stamping war engine. Thankfully, Crowley elected to flog his dead horse one last time. After brooding on the watermark dilemma for over a decade, he settles on an inventive, if not entirely effective solution. In a despairing attempt to obliterate the tell-tale evidence, Crowley *"rebacked"* each of the sixty-five manuscript leaves with a sheet of linen, probably whilst in residence at Cefalu. In 1926, he tentatively trials his doctored facsimile in a deluxe edition distributed only to eight key individuals. Not until 1936 (**Equinox of the Gods**), an aptly Thelemic thirty-one years after his alleged reception of **Liber L. vel Legis**, does Crowley finally release a full account, accompanied by a typescript and decent sized facsimile of the rebacked manuscript. By this time, Jones, Jones and Fuller have vanished into the mist, Rose has passed away (she died in 1932) and Crowley is finally confident enough to open his literary closet. Nevertheless, he still feels compelled to address *"very serious questions"* raised by those closest to him, and enclose a facsimile of the manuscript in a separate folder – As though still attempting to distance it from the corresponding typeset version.

Although he probably never realised, the 'London' watermark was but one of two vicious practical jokes visited on Crowley by gods presumably irked at his hijacking of their good name and repute. According to its archives, the 'London' brand of Pirie & Sons' "*Standard Typewriting*" paper was not commercially available until late in 1905 – An issue discussed at length in **Part 2(B), Appendix I - *Pirie says 'No!'***

"The first rule of life is to tell a good lie & stick to it"

Aleister Crowley - Memoranda to 1938 diary

Aleister Crowley
(aka *Vi Veri Vniversum Vivus Vici, Magister Templi, The Great Beast 666* and, in certain quarters, *Ol' Fakey*)

Posing with the Magickal paraphernalia of his War Engine in a photograph, taken in late 1907 or early 1908, in celebration of his reformulation of the $A\therefore A\therefore$ and imminent publication of **Holy Books**. A mock-up of which (not the Windram copy, which won't be printed for several years) is also included, along with a reproduction of the stele as pasted to a sheet of hardboard. Note the ribbon carefully positioned to conceal a rough edge and phial of Holy Oil obscuring a transcription error in the stele hieroglyphs. The 'crystal' is probably a convex lens balanced on the rim of a brandy glass.

A general misconception regarding the date of this image originates from Grant and Symonds' assumption (in the 1969 edition of **Confessions**) that a photograph first published in 1911 (**Book 4**) was also taken in that year. Crowley's 1929 edition of **Confessions** does not specify a date.

XVI. The Grate Beast

Liber L. vel Legis' inclusion in **Holy Books Vol. III** marked a pivotal change in Crowley's thinking. His much-debated 'baby-faced Magus with Stele' image captured the moment at which Edward Alexander Crowley fulfilled his mother's prophesy and became **The Great Beast 666**. It is also the fulcrum about which, "*a highly interesting example of genuine automatic writing*" as penned by a reclusive Egyptian adept named '*Big Beast.*' transformed into a divine proclamation of Crowley's advancement to Messiah. The transition was neither smooth, nor seamless.

Ultimately, it may prove impossible to chart with certainty the various twists and turns of fate responsible for **Liber L. vel Legis'** miraculous transformation between November 1902 and March 1912. However, this work demonstrates that even a superficial perusal of the extant record raises a multiplicity of baffling contradictions. All of which resolve into an overwhelming likelihood that the events Crowley narrated in published accounts did not occur as described, and probably never happened at all.

To digress, slightly - Folklore suggests that 'once upon a time' a wandering minstrel fell asleep beneath a tree and experienced a dream in which a Leprechaun strummed a melody that, on waking, he remembered, and which we know today as **Londonderry Air**. Perhaps Crowley would have described this surreal occurrence as "*a highly interesting example of genuine automatic song writing?*" Much as the sceptic in me balks at a suggestion of supernatural shenanigans, in this particular instance I accept the fable at face value and genuinely believe that the fairy-dust sprinkled onto this tune enhances, not detracts from an appreciation of it. Why, because of all the music I have heard down the years, **Londonderry Air**, perhaps uniquely, evokes sensations of such exquisite poignancy as to evoke an unmistakable quality of otherworldliness.

At some point in the future, a historian of traditional Irish music may discover that its composer actually penned the tune in a grotty railway station, whilst waiting for an overdue train. This scenario would not dampen my admiration for a singularly haunting melody, nor would a subsequent expose revealing the composer as a drug-addled, mass-murderer. The quality of compartmentalisation is possible in consequence of two uniquely human traits. Firstly, we can separate the creation, from its creator. In other words, we don't automatically 'shoot the messenger.' In this respect, Crowley makes life extremely difficult. The sentiments of Karl Germer's third wife, Cora, aptly summarise the modus operandi of a man who, throughout his life, habitually rode roughshod over the emotional, physical and financial wellbeing of all who associated with him, and seemingly with absolutely no sense of remorse or contrition. In a letter penned in 1930, Cora hissed:

> "*My dear Mr Crowley. The $15,000* [In 1930, this sum approximated to around £10,000, or a staggering half-a-million Pounds by today's standards] *I have given to you were spent not in real constructive work but in expensive cigars, cognac, cocktails, taxis, dinners, wives, sweethearts, or anything you desired at the moment. I never expect to see one cent of this money, for I know if you make any you will spend it on yourself. I consider you a supremely selfish man... You spend as much in a week on cigars and cognac as I do in two months on myself personally.*
>
> *By the time I have paid the household expenses and given the rest to you and Miss Jaeger, there is no more. I am not trying to insult you, But I think you have a Me and God complex.*
>
> *God Almighty Himself would not be as arrogant as you have been, and that is one of the causes of all your troubles.*"

In more recent times, when asked 'what was Crowley really like?' A former friend and associate of the **Great Beast** replied:

> "*Just be thankful that you did not know him personally!*"

A chilling, understated silhouette teasing the imagination with sinister themes too terrible for words. This, along with Mrs Germer's condemnation, sketches the outline of a loathsome, unrepentant and reprehensible character wholly irreconcilable with Crowley's claim to be, essentially, the successor to Jesus.

Secondly, and as my grandmother often said, "*The proof of the pudding is in the eating.*" Irrespective of many discrepancies raised in this work, it is my personal opinion that Crowley's reception story fails most injuriously on this abstract and subjective point. Somewhat paradoxically, Aiwass certainly grasped the import of this old adage. He reminded Crowley twice:

> "*III, 42. Success is thy proof*
>
> *III, 46. Success is your proof*"

If Thelema 'worked,' if it did what is claimed on the label, then all other trivialities rescind to dots on a distant horizon… but it doesn't! In **Equinox of the Gods** (page 104), Crowley wrote:

> "*I, Aleister Crowley, declare upon my honour as a gentleman that I hold this revelation a million times more important than the discovery of the Wheel, or even of the Laws of Physics or Mathematics.*"

In the century following Crowley's revelation of Thelema, countless inventions have transformed our world. A handful of these modern wonders are, arguably, comparable with the wheel (jet engine, Internet, antibiotics, television, etc.) most are not - They are just great ideas that work, and which make life easier. Conversely, the miraculous, universal and unprecedented benefits Crowley claimed on behalf of his New World Religion have utterly failed to realise any of their alleged potential. In his lifetime, Crowley accomplished nothing of his divinely-sanctioned calling as vanguard of a New Aeon. The children who bore his post-mortem dream (Germer, Jones, Reuss, Neuburg, etc.) made no ground towards a realisation of their Master's Thelemic vision of humanity. The flags of Crowley's Magickal grandchildren still droop limply in a stagnant, ill breeze. Today, an idea can traverse the globe in seconds, gathering millions of fans in the process. Yet, Crowley's supposed 'genius,' and New World Religion still loiter on the periphery of history, in a file marked "*Like, whatever.*"

Thelema failed because all three of the signatures underwriting **Liber L. vel Legis** are bogus. The **Book of the Law** is not a new rulebook and contemporary Bible for Mankind. It is an encrypted occult code-book unintelligible to all but its author. It is the circuit diagram of a theoretical hotline to the "*Secret Chiefs,*" the construction of which can only be attempted by individuals with a deep knowledge of Golden Dawn mysticism. Aleister Crowley finished **Liber L. vel Legis** in early 1906. It was an attempt to provide his pedantic A∴ A∴ buddy, Jones, with the Founding Document his old school sensibilities demanded, before launching a new, improved Golden Dawn founded on Enochian material cherry-picked from the deceased Order's corpse. In connection with this overhaul, it is pertinent to mention that the Enochian word for one is 'L', or 'EL,' and Crowley initially titled his Cairo Revelation **Liber L**. - The implication being that he originally conceived **Liber L.** as the first book of his improved and revised Enochian vision of the reformulated (post-

Osiris) Golden Dawn. The aborted 1907 Appendix, scheduled as **Liber Legis**' debut appearance, included two Enochian Calls. Incidentally, 'AL' is also an abbreviation of "*Anhalonium Lewinii*" – A psychoactive compound Crowley repeatedly referred to in his 1906 private diary.

At its heart, **Liber L. vel Legis** is a clumsy attempt to emulate the Golden Dawn's own creation myth, in which 'manuscripts found on a bookstall led to a mysterious German high adept who authorised the finders to work occult rituals encoded within.' Crowley substituted '**Collected Works Vol. III**' for 'bookstall,' 'Egyptian' for 'German' and… TADA! Crowley may have been aware of the Golden Dawn's less than praeterhuman pedigree. He was intimately familiar with the shortcomings of his forged certificate of authenticity, but signed the job off, regardless. In this respect, Crowley's short-term, egocentric obsession with self-gratification is most acutely exposed. Had he genuinely believed himself to be "*the Chosen One*" through which flowed the Word of God, he would not and could not have lied! If Crowley truly believed that he transmitted the message of a New Aeon, then he surely realised that even an incidental kink in the circuit terminated the current. If revealed, any deception fatally injured the illusion, and betrayed the faith of all who invested in his great pyramid scheme. A New Aeon is for life, not just Crowleymas!

If Crowley intended to cultivate an improved brand of the Golden Dawn, then history has certainly obliged his wishes. Somewhat ironically, it is almost inevitable that Thelema will follow its predecessor into the unforgiving abyss of yesterday. Today there is little to distinguish between the elitist clique pedantically preserving the fossilised remains of a Victorian relic, and those acting likewise on behalf of Edward Alexander Crowley and his splintered personality.

666 I simply went over to Satan's side; and to this hour I cannot tell why. There was a good deal of morbid curiosity among the saints about "the sin against the Holy Ghost" which "could never be forgiven." I must find out what that sin was and do it very thoroughly. No matter how much I disbelieved in Jesus, no matter how many crimes I piled up, He might get me in spite of myself. The only possibility of outwitting Him was to bring him up against His own pledge that this particular sin should never be forgiven, with a certificate from the recording angel that I had duly done it. In my search for a suitable sin which might earn me the diabolical V.C..
Aleister Crowley 666

Part Three (prelude)

Of Thelema and True Will

07.08 Where do we go from here?

The issues aired in this publication are of immense significance to all with an interest in Edward Alexander Crowley, be this Magickal, mundane or monetary. If correct, they fall into the category of proper '*shit hits the fan' stuff!* To my mind, it appears almost certain that there was no 'cross-examination' of Rose, no Boulak visit, no reception, no Aiwass, no **Book of the Law**, no lost manuscript and no Thelema. All were fantasies conjured from the mind of an obsessive psychopath, in furtherance of his grand delusion of '*I, Crowley, the Chosen One.*'

Liber L. vel Bogus – The Real Confession of Aleister Crowley merely scratches the surface of a very deep mystery of which many facets remain concealed. With respect to uncovering the true genesis and evolution of **Liber L. vel Legis**, this work is but a preliminary exploration. I have uncovered only the head of a sphinx still mostly buried in the sand. It is now the responsibility of the Thelemic community as a whole to apply their own trowels, and assist in the excavation.

Before shuffling away to winter in the relative sanctuary of a Swiss fallout bunker, I close my suitcase with a personal observation that, given the content of this work, may well sound like an absurd contradiction -

Rather paradoxically, maybe even perversely, my investigation into the mysteries of **Liber L. vel Legis** strengthened a belief that Aleister Crowley was the single most important individual Mankind has produced in the last ten-thousand years. I remain convinced that he alone noticed a small yet monumentally significant development in the core operating system of our species. This he equated with the imminent birth of a new epoch and predicted global changes that, since September 2007, have rocked our world to its foundations. Crowley was not merely the prophet of a new epoch, but actually precipitated the onset of a 'Magickal Current' that will shape our world for the next two thousand years.

The third part of this work discusses a mechanism by which Crowley can rightly claim a unique place in the annals of human history by simultaneously fulfilling the dual roles of '*Wickedest Man in the World*' and '*Instigator of the New Aeon of Horus.*' Aleister Crowley invented the angst-ridden, hormonal teenager and provided a template for every idealist, anti-hero and rebel without a cause. He is the father of the counter-culture and grandfather of the Facebook generation. His impact on today's society is immeasurable.

With hindsight, Crowley could have saved himself considerable time and trouble had he simply left matters at "*Do what thou wilt shall be the whole of the Law,*" then watched-on in horror as the children of Horus mutated his Holy Wafer into a microwavable pizza slice. As events transpired, nobody paid much attention to the obeahs and wangas, the mantras and spells, or the rituals and New World Religion. For that matter, the mountaineering, chess, poetry, art, travelogues, fiction, social commentary and even the floppy bow-ties inflamed the imagination of only a lamentably small clique of aficionados... but "*Do what thou wilt...*" Now, that is a different story. That is a glitzy soundbite and indispensible fashion accessory for an emerging generation who believe it their absolute right to 'do as they want, when they want, and with no regard for others.' Crowley's mantra speaks volumes to a desensitised, supersaturated generation that demands everything, now, without effort, cost or consequence. We cannot blame Crowley for a culture that transliterated "*Do what thou wilt*" into "*Do what I want,*" **Liber OZ** into **Liber OMG** and **Liber L** into **Liber LOL**. We live in hope that, having gorged itself to bloatation on an orgy of liberties unimaginable in

Crowley's day, the bastard offspring of his New Aeon will come to understand (by Magickal or other means) the 'responsibilities' inherent in 'rights' so familiar as to breed contempt.

A careful study of unpublished source material reveals enough hints as to deduce the faint outline of a brief moment when once-in-an-epoch circumstances conspired to jemmy open a 'window' closed for ten millennia. One particular facet of a ritual Crowley enacted between 10PM and midnight on the night of Sunday 20 March 1904 forged a genuine, though fleeting Magickal Link with something entirely beyond his comprehension. Not an intellectualised visualisation of symbolic god-forms originating in his mind, but a flash-bulb glimpse of the chaotic, fractal blueprint on which Mankind's third stage of evolution is already evolving. Alas, his focus on fabricating a petty scheme to wrest control of the Golden Dawn from Mathers was so intense that Crowley paid scant attention when Horus stepped out from the shadows to offer him a light.

Crowley smashed the ultimate taboo of a society from which he demanded unconditional acceptance and adulation. The effect on his psyche was so dramatic as to punch down to the deepest level of human consciousness. From the silt of these unfathomable depths, Crowley dredged a priceless insight.

> "*I am alone: there is no God where I am.*" (**Liber L. vel Legis II, 23**)

Edward Alexander Crowley held a golden evolutionary key in his hand. Yet, was so entrenched in Old Aeon mentality, so beset by insecurities and so ill-at-ease with its origin, as to bury his magnificent insight beneath a pantheon of gods and myriad layers of cloying intellectualised dogma. In surrendering to his raging ego, Crowley misdirected himself (and everyone else) into a cul-de-sac of deception. He took a sublime minimalist concept and transformed it into a clunky Victorian automaton that sharpened pencils with its arse.

To be continued…

New Dawn Fades

The world is changing. I feel it in the water, smell it in the air, taste it in food and hear it in my thoughts. It is the night terror first glimpsed darkly in the dreams of our grandparents. It is the formless horror that gnawed just beneath the awareness of our parents. It is the disturbing undercurrent evoking in us tangible, yet nebulous, sensations of foreboding. It is the slow, silent tide of futility lapping ominously at the thighs of our children.

It is here.

A seed of change sown by machinery powering the Industrial Revolution, its first, fragile tendrils forced their way towards the light through the accumulated debris of two world wars. Its roots, engorged with the blood of one-hundred million spent lives, burrow deep into the soft white underbelly of a world in chaos. Its petals manufactured from the glossy pages of newspapers and magazines. Its alluring scent is borne upon electronic waves radiating from slick advertising campaigns offering impossible dreams to an increasingly disillusioned generation. Its heady pollen stimulates our deepest pleasure centres into orgiastic frenzies of instantaneous self-gratification. Toxic juice dribbling from the first fruit of its bitter harvest stifles our lives within a cloying miasma of fear, impotence and despair.

It is here.

Our government holds up its hands in defeat. The police, judicial system, educational apparatus, media, science, religion and every other edifice of civilisation has proved equally ineffectual in even defining, let alone decapitating, the writhing hydra whose tentacles ensnare and enslave all. Nor have any provided an antidote to the deadly infection, fast approaching pandemic proportions, threatening to tear apart the very fabric of our society.

It is here.

Supplemental Material

Additional Information — Page 221
The Definitive R. T. Cole — Page 222
Bibliography of works referenced — Page 228
Table 01 — Page 229
Table 02 — Page 230
Table 03 — Page 232
My Top 10 favourite AL-nomalies — Page 235
AL cetera — Page 240

When asked to comment on **Liber L. vel Bogus**, Aleister Crowley replied with an enigmatic mystical gesture thought to represent an occult sign pertaining to a secret (11°) ritual of Sex Magick titled the "*Self-Hoor Invocation Technique.*"

Additional information

• The numbering of chapters in this publication conforms to correlations of the twenty-two Tarot Trumps with respect to their arrangement on the Tree of Life. Retained throughout is Crowley's spelling of the words 'Boulak' and 'Brugsch.' The word 'Magick' and its derivatives I employ in preference to 'magic.'

• In analysing, cross-referencing and illustrating the concepts outlined in this publication, a significant proportion of its text is, by necessity, devoted to an extensive reproduction of directly quoted material. This is a labour-intensive, time-consuming and tedious process. Despite all efforts to ensure the contrary, errors will inevitably creep in. I earnestly request that readers consult the original publication or source document in all dubious instances. Please report any errors to the author, for correction in subsequent editions.

• Anyone with information that may clarify, expand or refute any issue raised in this publication should contact the author, with a view to inclusion in subsequent editions. I am indebted to numerous individuals for their diligence in noting several 'gremlins' lurking in the first edition. All known issues have now been addressed.

• The final six sections of **Liber L. vel Bogus – The Real Confession of Aleister Crowley**, comprising Part **II(B)** of **The Governing Dynamics of Thelema**, are scheduled for release as an Appendix in a volume of the same name, along with an expanded and revised republication of parts **I** and **II(A)**. An index of section titles is included below.

I	Pirie says 'No!'
II	**ShadowZone** presents the final, post mortem cut
III	Interview with the Vamp's Ire
IV	Blaggers of the Lost Bullshit
V	Four out of five ain't bad
VI	Convinced, now…

With the exception of '**V**,' these segments focus on 'third-party' documentation pertinent to Crowley's reception myth. It is ironic that this intriguing material will only be of interest to those whose resolve to believe Crowley, at any price, it will merely strengthen.

• For the benefit of any who feel obliged to redress a sense of outrage at my expose of Crowley's myth by picking apart this work line by line, I suggest that you first apply the same level of meticulous scrutiny to Crowley's reception fable. In so doing, you will save considerable time and trouble.

The Definitive R. T. Cole – An interview published in the April 2015 edition of **The New Aeon** magazine, shortly before the publication of this work.

The Definitive R. T. Cole

This year sees the release of **Richard T. Cole's** long-awaited, much anticipated and hugely contentious *"Liber L. vel Bogus – The Real Confession of Aleister Crowley."* As a way of getting the New Year off to a sizzling start **The New Aeon** braved the frozen wastelands of South Yorkshire to Vape a pipe of pieces with the man who's got Crowleyites on the edge of their seats.

Is **The Great Beast 666's** legacy now divided into 'pre' and 'post' **Bogus**?

[*This Interview (which came into my possession on 01ˢᵗ April 2017) is a highly interesting example of genuine automatic writing. Though I am in no way responsible for any part of the document, except this note, I publish it amongst The New Aeon, because I believe that its intelligent study may be interesting & helpful. The reproduction of this article has been done thus minutely in order to prevent the casual reader from wasting valuable time over it. - R. T. C.*]

TNE - Richard, I'd like to offer my thanks for you taking time out to speak with us. I hope you are well?

RTC - Considering recent events, I'll say only that I'm hugely relieved that I included the 'Styx Recovery Option' on my insurance policy (chuckles…) and discovered the joys of Vaping! It's all the benefits of smoking, but with none of that unsavoury death stuff. Wonderful!

TNE – Hey! You're preaching to the converted. I switched last year. *"Arctic blast"* is my flavour of the month. What's steaming out of your tank?

[We omit the record of a long and futile Vaping divination]

Let's start with a word about the new book. It's been a long time coming. Is there any particular reason for the delay?

RTC - With tongue only slightly in cheek, I could say that *'the Magickal essence of Aleister Crowley guided the progress of Bogus, every step of the way.'* I could equally suggest that an overabundance of evidence bogged matters down, considerably. Oh, yes, plus the cumulative weight of Black Magick, Voodoo and god knows what other occult shenanigans being hurled in my direction (laughs...)

TNE – Black Magick to wreck your publication schedule! Are you serious?

RTC - (laughs...) No comment... (looks to the heavens...) *'Give me a break, chaps. Just work the legs!'* (laughs...)

TNE – There's been a lot of speculation and controversy surrounding the book. Did you expect this?

RTC - Oh, good grief, yes! I certainly anticipated some species of backlash... It kicked-off from the moment I mentioned an intention to unleash the accursed thing and I soon grew weary and frustrated at constantly defending a work that nobody had actually read, yet which everybody seemed eager to trash. I totally 'get' that it's going to be quite a blow to, well... To people like myself, but it needed saying. The whole AL discrepancy issue has cast a shadow over the Crowley scene for decades. To a greater extent the stock response is usually one of *'fingers in ears, I'm not listening, I'm not Listening, I'm not listening.'* That, or a cobbling together of impossibly unlikely circumstances rather than accept an infinitely more probable scenario that just happens to contradict Crowley's official story. Repeatedly hearing why the *'best route from Leeds to Manchester passed through Boleskine'* really eroded my will to live.

TNE – The promo-blurb has received criticism for being too 'aggressive.' For example, your **Facebook** page makes more than a few inflammatory statements. I quote: *"There is no cross-examination of Rose. No visit to the Boulak. No praeterhuman entity. No Aiwass. No Book of the Law. No Thelema. All were fantasies conjured from the mind of an obsessive psychopath, in furtherance of his grand delusion of 'I, Crowley, the Chosen One...' and the deception does not end with Crowley!"* Did you intentionally set out to... outrage?

RTC - (Chuckles) Well... It served its purpose! Like a catchy melody that gets stuck in your head, even if you don't like the song... Advertising, by nature, seeks to promote. As such, I can't fault my new Social Media and general cyber-reality consultant. As was recently noted on the Facebook jobbie, traffic to just three threads, on one website, is closing in on 100,000 hits. In some ways, I still think it's quite surreal that a book exploring just three hours in Crowley's life has evoked so much curiosity...

TNE – But these three hours are central to Crowley's... what, legend... legacy... historical record... If the Cairo Revelation is bogus – great title, by the way - the whole house of cards collapses.

RTC - Thanks! Look at it this way - Anyone who genuinely believes Crowley's story and swaps a Bible for AL isn't going to recant in consequence of anything I print. The great corporate Thelumpic machine will grind on, regardless. In fact, I'm not saying that an angel didn't whisper AL in Crowley's ear. I'm not saying that AL has no divine, mystical, occult or even inspirational qualities. I'm just saying that, whatever it is, and wherever it came from, Crowley did not receive the text on 08, 09 and 10 April 1904.

TNE – So, there is a Thelema?

RTC - Not in the sense, literal and metaphysical, touted by Crowley. In this respect, for my money the most fascinating aspect of **Bogus** related to the emergence of a hitherto unexplored and hugely significant segment of Crowley's life. Alas, until there's a general acceptance of '*something being very wrong in the state of Thelema*' and until this develops momentum enough to precipitate a thorough investigation, well… until these criteria are met a great chunk of Crowley's life remains concealed beneath a flimsy blind that convinces nobody. **Bob Freeman**, the **Occult Detective**, perfectly encapsulated the situation on his [1]blog: "*Anyone who hasn't questioned at least some of Old Crow's account haven't really been paying attention.*"

TNE – It's certainly a difficult book to ignore, or remain on the fence about. What was the deal with the Christmas "*Stocking Filler*?"

RTC - That was my way of jump-starting a flat battery. I'd not done a jot on the thing for over a year, and a fairly eventful year at that what with the 'f-k' kerfuffle and appearance of the 1907 Appendix. The Christmas PDF was never intended to contain any great revelations. It was just a catch-up and an introduction to what follows.

TNE – The incredible dancing notebook trick was quite a revelation…

RTC - (laughs…) Yes, good ol' **OS23**. What a ferkukkle, eh. It's unfortunate that the group selling Crowley 'the man,' also runs 'the Messiah' franchise. A bloke flogging DVDs of his alien abduction won't feature an advert for his brother's creative filmmaking business amongst the trailers. OTO has sidestepped the discrepancies for decades and withheld source documents enabling people to make up their own minds. When key notebooks start vanishing from the record, with such athleticism, you've got to start wondering what's going on. **Bogus** makes a big point of saying '*Don't believe a word I or anyone else says. Check everything, for yourself, from source documents, and make up your own mind.*' Of course, that isn't going to happen until OTO unlocks its skeleton closet.

TNE – Is this likely?

RTC - Ahhh, so many promises, over so many years, but so little output…

TNE – Did writing this book change your opinion of Crowley? It's very different in flavour to "*Thelema Revisited*" or "*Un-Magickal Record.*"

RTC - No, not really… "*T.R.*" was a postcard from Cefalu, "**Un-Magickal Rec.**" was a postcard from history and "*A postcard from Hell*" was… just that. **Bogus** is another postcard, this time from Cairo, in fact it's two. The first section comprises a lengthy psychological profile that really helps to put AL in context. This was written by a fairly eminent consultant who agreed to participate only on guarantee of anonymity. That alone is an intensely frustrating indicator of Crowley's enduring toxicity.

TNE – Frustrating, why?

RTC - Well, Crowley claimed that Thelema was… '*A million times more important than the wheel, physics and mathematics.*' Yet, a century later the inventor still rates only one of two news stories. It's either '***Troubled sprog of Celebrity X joins sinister Satanic cult***,' or '*Deranged murderer obsessed with the books of infamous Satanist Aleister Crowley.*' Despite all efforts to paint Crowley's poltergeist white, he's still **The Wickedest Man in the World.**

TNE – Do you think history has treated Crowley unjustly?

RTC - That's a tricky one. Fair enough, the title dumped on him by the media is a bit 'pantomime.' Then again, Crowley did his best to live up to it. On the other hand, I'm convinced that he remains the only person to spot the onset of an entirely new phase of human evolution, a third epoch if you like. Look at the world today, 'something' appears to be ripping it apart at the seams. Maybe Crowley was right. Perhaps Horus is currently sweeping away the old aeon debris… but that's an entirely different kettle of ectoplasm.

TNE – Is Thelema the antidote?

RTC - (Chuckles…) It didn't cure Crowley's disease.

TNE – Which was?

RTC - Acute nomenclature. Terrible thing. It killed one of his kids, allegedly.

TNE – You are saying that Crowley gilded his lily?

RTC - Just a bit, yes. He had a fabulous insight, "*I am alone. There is no God where I am,*" then buried it beneath a pantheon of gods, deities and archaic rituals. Same with Thelema. He took a sublime minimalist concept and turned it into a clunky Victorian automaton that sharpened pencils with its arse. He should have left it at "*Do what thou wilt...*" then watched-on in horror as the proles turned it into '*Do what we want.*' C'est AL vie!

TNE – **Bogus** is definitely a book that is generating a lot of heat. Are you going to end the suspense and reveal a release date?

RTC - Absolutely… not! It's caught me out three times already. I'll just hint that this year is the 111th anniversary. An apt date would be April 01st or 08th, but we'll just have to wait and see how events pan out. There's also another book covering similar material due out this year. It could be a fun idea to unleash **Bogus** on the same date.

TNE – Another book? Do tell.

RTC - Yes, [2]**Paul Feazey** from www.lashtal.com is promising to release something along the lines of "*Cairo, the Definitive Guide.*" I'm fairly ravenous to get my hands on a copy of that.

TNE – Does **Mr Feazey** share your views on Crowley's reception of **Liber AL**?

RTC - (chuckles…) Secretly, yes… Everybody does, secretly. Seriously, though… Until I read it, I'll not know for sure what his take on the reception myth is.

TNE – When did you first notice something was not quite right with Crowley's story?

RTC - Probably back in the 80s. I saw a photocopy of the infamous 'cover sheet' and wondered why Crowley couldn't decide what he meant, or when he meant it. After that, I started collecting any discrepancies I stumbled over. By 2012, I decided to shape this material around a timeline by comparing published stuff against Crowley's original source notes. At this point, I thought I'd already amassed a fairly damning case, but even a cursory inspection of the extant record opened up an entirely unanticipated level of intrigue.

This will rumble on for years, decades. **Bogus** doesn't even scratch the surface of a very deep mystery. The first part concerns itself exclusively with Crowley's own words and works. The second spotlights various oddities arising from third-party sources and will appear as an Appendix to the four part **Governing Dynamics of Thelema**. I'm not saying too much about this right now. After that, it's down to everyone else to continue the excavation, or not, as the case may be.

TNE – I'm taking it that you don't have a signed confession from Crowley…

RTC - (laughs…) Believe me, there's a good few who wouldn't accept an admission direct from the mouth of Crowley's ghost! But, no, it is all relative. You can argue about the reality of existence until you're blue in the chakras, but the trick is to make it personal. Take it all down to point-blank, black or white. Read the book and then ask yourself a simple question – *"If I was on trial for a serious crime, would I hang the next twenty or so years of my life on a defence equivalent to Crowley's reception story?"*

TNE – I'll read it and let you know. Would you?

RTC - Crowley was a singularly remarkable man, maybe even unique… but the only angel whispering to **The Great Beast 666** in April 1904 was his missus, Rose and she was probably asking why the waiter was dressed-up as Horus.

TNE – Richard, it's been lovely chatting with you. I'm hoping we can get together again once the book is out. Is there anything you'd like to say by way of wrapping this up?

RTC - Yes, thanks, it's been… emotional. I'd just like to remind anyone who wants to get involved in the great debate that the interactive **Bogus** [3]**Facebook** page, not surprisingly titled *"Liber L. vel Bogus – The Real Confession of Aleister Crowley,"* is a good place to start.

---

[1] https://authorbobfreeman.wordpress.com/2015/01/

[2] On April 19, 2015, Mr. Feazey posted two notices on www.lashtal.com announcing "*My plans for publication are in any case cancelled,*" and "*… publication plans for the related book have been aborted.*" Two days later, Mr. Feazey suggested "*… it seems that my own research is less significant (and would be less impactive) than I previously thought*" as a reason for withdrawing his book.

[3] https://www.facebook.com/pages/Liber-L-vel-Bogus-The-Real-Confession-of-Aleister-Crowley/1687315198161452?fref=ts

Bibliography of works referenced

Confessions (Crowley): *Cape, London* 1969
Equinox I, 7 (Various): *Weiland & Company, London* 1912
Equinox I, 8 (Various): *Weiland & Company, London* 1912
Equinox I, 10 (Various): *Weiland & Company, London* 1913
Equinox III, 1 (Blue Equinox) (Various): *Samuel Weiser & Co., NY* 1972
Equinox of the Gods (Crowley): *Level Press, NY, CA* 1972
777 & Other Qabalistic Writings (Crowley): *Samuel Weiser, NY* 1982
The Sword of Song (Crowley): *S. P. R. T., Paris* 1904
Why Jesus Wept (Crowley): *S. P. R. T., Paris* 1904
The Book of Thoth (Crowley): *Samuel Weiser Inc., NY* 1978
The Book of Lies (Crowley): *Samuel Weiser Inc, NY* 1970
Collected Works (Crowley): *S. P. R. T., Foyers* 1905, 1906, 1907
THELEMA – The Holy Books (Crowley): *Privately printed* 1910
Magick, 2nd revised edition (Crowley): *Samuel Weiser Inc., Maine* 1997
Book 4 (Crowley): Samuel Weiser Inc, NY, 1992
Magical Record of the Great Beast 666 (Crowley): *Duckworth & Co., London* 1972
Perdurabo (Kaczynski): *New Falcon Publications, US* 2003
Red Flame, Issue No. 8 (Cornelius'): *Berkeley, CA* 2000
The Magical and Mystical System of the A∴ A∴ (Eshelman): C.O.T., 2000
Aleister Crowley Desk Reference (2nd rev.) (Cornelius): *Teitan Press,* 2013
King of the Shadow Realm (Symonds): *Duckworth & Co., London* 1989
Do What Thou Wilt (Sutin): *St. Martin's Press, NY* 2000
The Beast Demystified (Hutchinson): *Mainstream, Edinburgh & London* 1998
Legacy of the Beast (Suster): *W. H. Allen, London & Edinburgh* 1988
Star in the West (J.F.C. Fuller): Walter Scott Publishing Company 1907
Un-Magickal Record of the Great Beast 666 (Cole): *OrangeBox,* 2011
The Invocation of Hoor (Katz): *Forge Press, England* 2010
Genesis of the Book of the Law Pts I, II & III (Hulse): *Holmes publishing,* 2001
ShadowZone – Volume I, Number 1 – Beast Goes To Hell: *King Features Synd., 1949*
The Zohar Code (Bethsheba & Steven Ashe): Privately published, 2014
Real Action for Men - Volume I, Number 3 - The Beast With Two Backs (Feature by Jackson Burke)**:** *Four Star Publications, NY* 1957

OS27, OS23 & other unpublished correspondence, documentation and material from various sources

Table 01

Comparison of content as reproduced in **Equinox I, 7** (1912), **Equinox of the Gods** (1936) and Crowley's vellum notebook OS27 (1904). The corresponding page numbers, as printed in Marcus Katz's (2010) book (**The Invocation of Hoor**), shown in square brackets.

OS27	Equinox I, 7	Equinox of the Gods
Front cover The Invocation of Hoor		Reproductions of stele with paraphrased versification
Note by Gerald Yorke [09]		The Summons
The Invocation of Horus Description [10]		Liber AL vel Legis typeset
Preliminary Banishing [11]	Genesis Libri AL	Genesis Libri AL
The Invocation of Horus [14]	Diary 01 January to 06 April	Diary 01 January to 06 April
The dance [32] The Supreme Ritual [32] Stele ritual sketch [32] ABRAHADABRA [33] To Invoke [33] To obtain LVX [34]	Book of Results 16 – 18 March	Book of Results 16 – 18 March
Revised ritual B2 To have any knowledge [27]	Cross-examination	Cross-examination
Talismans of XXII against Golden Dawn [35] (At Boleskine, in the summer of 1904)	In the museum at Cairo Stele translations Reproductions of stele with paraphrased versification	In the museum at Cairo Stele translations
Five missing pages [36]	Book of Results 19 – 23 March	Book of Results 19 – 23 March
Ballasti Ompehda Sekhet [37]	Festival of the Equinox	Invocation of Horus Divine vision of Ouarda
Tarot correspondences 2 – 10, four suits [39]	Invocation of Horus Divine vision of Ouarda	Qabalah name coincidences
*The Book of Results [43]	Comment	Liber L. vel Legis Festival of the Equinox
*In the museum at Cairo 49]	Liber Legis Manuscript facsimile	Very serious questions Written 1920-23 at Cefalu
*Golden Dawn to be destroyed [52]		Liber Legis Manuscript facsimile

*The three sections in grey appear at the back of OS27. For whatever reasons, Crowley finished his Tarot correspondences then inverted the notebook and started again with the *Book of Results*.

▶◉◀

Table 02

Comparison of entries as recorded in Crowley's personal diary and occult **Book of Results** entries between 09 February and 08 April 1904.

Date	Diary	Book of Results
Feb. 9	To Cairo	
Feb. 11	Saw b.f.g. b.f.b. (This entry is quite unintelligible to us.)	
Feb. 19	To Helwan as Oriental Despot. (Apparently P. had assumed some disguise…)	
Feb. 20	Began golf.	
March 16	Began INV. [Invocation] IAO [See Liber Samekh]	Die Mercury. I invoke IAO Intuition to continue ritual day and night for a week. [Ouarda] says "*they*" are "*waiting for me.*"
March 17	Thoth appeared.	It's 'all about the child,' also 'all Osiris.' Thoth, invoked with great success, indwells us.
March 18	Told to INV. [invoke] Horus as the Sun by new way.	Revealed that the waiter was Horus, whom I had offended and aught to invoke. The ritual revealed in skeleton. Promise of success [Saturn] or [sun] and of Samadhi.
March 19	Did this badly at noon 30.	The ritual written out and the invocation done – little success.
March 20	At 10 p.m. did well – Equinox of Gods – Nov – (? New) C.R.C. (Christian Rosy Cross, we conjecture.) Hoori now Hpnt (obviously "*Heirophant*").	Revealed that the Equinox of the Gods is come, Horus taking the Throne of the East and all rituals &c are being abrogated. Great success in midway of invocation. I am to formulate a new link of an order with the Solar Force. 7=4 [Note on opposite page]
March 21	in IAM (? One o' clock) [Sun enters Aries]	Moon Sun enters Aries [Vernal Equinox]
March 22	X.P.B. (May this and the entry March 24, refer to the brother of the A∴ A∴ who found him?) E.P.D. in 84 m. (Unintelligible to us; probably a blind.)	The day of rest, in which nothing whatever of magic is ever to be done at all. Mercury is to be the great day of invocation.
March 23	Y.K. done (? His work on the Yi King)	The Secret of W, the seer. 1. Mercury of Ank-f-n-honsu = [Ou Mh] 2. Mars in Libra = the ritual is of sex; Mars in the house of Venus exciting the jealousy of Saturn or Vulcan

March 23 cont…		**3.** Moon in Cancer the 4 of cups means purity in the path. These produce **1** K of W = Force **2** P of C = Initiation **3** Mercury = Wisdom in work He that abideth in the midst is Mars in Pisces giving as the symbol of Horus as Kephra. But 666 explains all this and more.
March 24	Met اجيب again.	
March 25	823 Thus 461 " " = pfly2bz 218	
(Blot)	wch trouble with ds.	
(Blot)	P.B. (All unintelligible; possibly a blind.)	
April 06	Go off again to H, taking A's p.	[To Helwan, then Port Said, then Paris and Boleskine.]
April 08	[Lease on Cairo apartment expires.]	[The apartment is deserted when Aiwass calls.]

Table 03

A brief chronology of modifications Crowley incorporated into his New Equinox scheme between November 1902 and September 1936.

Nov. 1902	Crowley does not visit Boulak Museum on his first vacation to Cairo, though records stele hieroglyphics (from unknown source) in a notebook – Subsequently re-dated from '1902' to '1904.'
Nov. 1903	Initial attempt to forge New Magickal Link with the Secret Chiefs evokes an astral glow and much frustration.
Mar. 1904	Returns to Egypt with an idea of Sex Magick based on stele imagery. Tri-sexual ceremony with Rose and Hamid convinces Crowley that he can usurp Mathers and initiate a New Equinox of sexual liberation, with sex as its ultimate sacrament and Crowley at the reins.
06 Apr. 1904	Departs Egypt for Boleskine. Dined in Paris with Arnold Bennett on 26 April.
Summer 1904	Utilises his new brand of occultism to wage Magickal War on Mathers, and publishes **Goetia**.
Spring 1906	Starts talking about the formulation of a new Order, with G. C. Jones and intends to drop a typescript of **Liber L. vel Legis** into the third volume of **Collected Works**, as the creation of a mysterious adept named '*Big Beast.*' i.e. Crowley's Egyptian equivalent of the Golden Dawn's German authority, Anna Sprengel.
July 1906	Crowley came into possession of the manuscript.
27 July 1906	Samadhi attained, with promotion to Magister Templi, and declined.
Mk. 1(A) Sept. 1907	**Collected Works Vol. III** aborted Appendix
	Crowley is so twitchy about removing any suspicion of involvement as to amplify a subtle reference to a dictation starting on 08 April (two days after his departure) into a declaration that his receipt of the manuscript post-dated its creation by two years. G. C. Jones' familiarity with the stele versification compels a further adjustment to the prefacing material. He's also dropped the (public) sexual aspects from his revelation. Crowley's original notion was nothing more elaborate than a reworking of the Golden Dawn myth in which certain documents (as found on a bookstall) are subsequently revealed as a skeleton occult system facilitating a Magickal Link with Secret Chiefs governing human evolution, plus the address of a mysterious German adept to rubber-stamp the façade before vanishing into the ectoplasm. Substitute 'bookstall' for '**Collected Works Vol. III**' and 'Egyptian' for 'German' and you're not far from Crowley's initial start point. At this prototype stage, Crowley has only a nebulous concept of a stele, whose discovery and translation led to a ritual (presumably **The Great Invocation**) by which Aiwass was invoked (and presumably dictated **Liber L.** to the mysterious Egyptian adept – A manuscript Crowley only came into possession of some two years later. Given the inclusion of two Enochian calls, he is also of a mind to incorporate aspects of this system into **Liber L. vel Legis** – Itself titled with the initial letter of the Enochian alphabet.
1907	Fuller's prize winning essay, the **Star in the West,** published. Crowley

1907 cont…	states this is a *"very complete and just exposition of my views,"* but feels compelled to mention an oddity that everybody is already wondering about…*"and it is especially to be noticed that within the one hundred and thirty-three pages there is no reference to **The Book of the Law**.*"
Nov. 1907	Appendix dropped from **Collected Works Vol. III** coincides with Crowley and Jones' (as senior officer) reformulation of the A∴A∴, citing Aiwass, but no mention of the **Book of the Law**. All of the *"inspired"* works used in **Holy Books** are now written, including the opening statement **Liber LXI vel Causæ** - Which also neglects mention of Thelema, the **Book of the Law**, Crowley's role of Prophet of the New Aeon, Aiwass, the reception, and all other goodies now associated with the Cairo myth.
1907/1908	'Baby-faced Magus with stele' photo session.
October 1908	Magickal Retirement published as **John St. John** – No mention of **Liber L**, or its supporting cast.
21 Mar. 1909	**Equinox I, 1** published, with no mention of **Liber L**, or its supporting cast.
28 June 1909	Manuscript found in Crowley's attic at Boleskine House, but nobody mentioned it was missing and Neuburg's Magickal Record (perhaps written by Crowley) fails to mention the momentous event.
Oct. 1909	*"I meant I could be…"* cover sheet amendment made, perhaps for inclusion in **Holy Books**. At this time, Crowley is still touting **Liber Legis** as the work of a mysterious Egyptian adept. Fuller sent a typescript and the cover-sheet. Incidentally, *"Sticky Fingers"* Fuller's reluctance to hand back Crowley's works is probably the only reason the cover sheet and Appendix survive. Destroying these toxic documents, he would have saved Crowley innumerable problems down the line.
24 Nov 1909	Crowley and Rose divorce.
Dec. 1909	Accepts the promotion offered in July 1906.
1910	**Bagh-I-Muattar**, or **Scented Garden**, published. Of this, Crowley observes - *"It is especially to be noted that, although I have packed every kind of magical and mystical lore into the volume, there is nowhere any reference to **The Book of the Law**."*
Mk. 1(B) Spring 1910	**Holy Books Vol. III**
	Bare-bones version stripped to just the three chapters, reproduced without preface, introduction or explanation, as one of Crowley's *"inspired"* writings. This marks the crossover from a document written by another, to one penned by Crowley himself - Though it is apportioned no especial significance. Explicit instruction to include a manuscript facsimile ignored.
Apr. 1911	The *"Looking Glass"* Trial blows apart any plans Crowley then had in place. With Jones and Fuller gone, he can rewrite the story to taste, though working within the boundaries of documentation retained by Fuller.
Autumn 1911	Rose institutionalised on grounds of alcoholic dementia.
Mk. 2(A) Spring 1912	**Equinox I, 7**
	No typeset version of **Libel L.** included, though this publication introduced the now-familiar reception components and expanded on the stele's discovery and significance. The role of Aiwass and the manuscript fundamentally revised. *"New Aeon"* supersedes Crowley's original title *"New Equinox."* Crowley becomes the Prophet of this new

Spring 1912 cont…	epoch and sole mouthpiece of the incoming pantheon of gods. Manuscript reproduced at miniscule size, accompanied by Crowley's baffling explanation of this.
Mk. 2(B) 21 Sept. 1913	**Equinox I, 10**
	Crowley reverts to **Mk. 1(B)** version, albeit using a corrected typescript, stripped to the bare three verses with brief prefacing note ("*as delivered by LXXVIII to DCLXVI.*") Again, a stipulation regarding the inclusion of a manuscript facsimile he ignores.
09 April 1926	"*Tunis*" edition deluxe boxed set privately issued in a 'mates only' edition of eleven copies.
11 Feb. 1932	Rose Dies.
Mk. (3) Sept. 1936	**Equinox of the Gods**
	The same as **Mk. 2(A)**, though Crowley grafted-on further embellishments to garnish the central myth, and responds to certain "*serious questions*" arising in connection with his alleged reception. The first (published) edition incorporating a reasonably sized facsimile of the manuscript. The last person who could contradict him died four years previously.
01 April 2015	**Liber L. vel Bogus** **The Real Confession of Aleister Crowley**

MY TOP 10 FAVOURITE AL-NOMALIES

Toxicity Rating: 31/100

Mush - My countdown starts with an old favourite, and a great place to bury a multitude of sins. The **Great Beat 666** can bang-on for pages about a boulder in the middle of nowhere, but get him talking about any part of the Cairo myth and his mind turns to mush. Crowley admits it. We all know it, and it doesn't bode well… (See pages 1 – 248)

Toxicity Rating: 33/100

Our Ada - Praeterhuman envoy of the gods finds time to slip the names of two of Crowley's mistresses into the **Holy Books** – That's an inspired, class (A) act. Sheer impudence inserts this unlikely brace of acrostics into the chart. (See page 131)

Toxicity Rating: 35/100

There is no AL in the West - Fuller's sickly eulogy extols Crowley as the best thing since loaves and fishes, but his **Star in the West** doesn't mention **Liber L. vel Legis**. *"Nice try, but no £100 prize for your essay"* says Aiwass. Console yourself with eighteenth place in the table. (See page 183)

Toxicity Rating: 37/100

Am I Isis or Nuit? - Crowley initially describes stele imagery as the heavenly Isis, then changes his mind, to Nuit, then reverts to Isis in print. Crowley's triple-whammy of confusion, correction and concealment demands a place in this countdown. Right, that's 17th place. No, I meant, 19th… Actually, I did mean 17th. (See page 160)

Toxicity Rating: 39/100

Rose fills-in the gaps - She wasn't in the room. She can't hear Crowley's HGA, anyway, and despite Aiwass' explicit instructions to the contrary, Crowley lets a woman scribble her grocery list all over his Liber. (See page 191)

Toxicity Rating: 41/100

Wears the B2? - It certainly erodes credibility that the revelation was first a sex-bomb with which to kick Mathers in the baubles. Then it wasn't. Look again and it has miraculously transformed into a nonsensical ritual that somehow worked second time around. *"Ritual this… Ritual that. Oh, can't we just have one night in with the TV"* sighs Ouarda. (See various pages)

Crowley goes 'Catholic' and Pulls Out at the first minute - Alys' determination to come mincing out of the temple-closet all guns blazing lasts about ten minutes. By the time his feet droop over a stag's head by the Boleskine fireside, his Middle-Eastern fervour to spearhead a campaign of omni-sexual liberation has wilted into the Haggis supper. By monster-spawning season, both his "*revelation*" and "*ritual*" have disentangled themselves from any sexual position, and notion to destroy Mathers. The B2 material is not so much 'censored' as castrated from the record and Crowley discretely slides his blazing Gay Rights torch in the direction of Quentin Crisp. From now, it's all good, wholesome, married sex, "*strongly male to female; free from any similar impulse towards my own sex.*" Is Crowley trying to convince us, or him? (See various sections)

Doesn't anyone care that I've found the flaming manuscript? - Manuscript found after five years *in absentia*, but Neuburg doesn't even notice. Not to worry, nobody noticed it was missing in the first place and Crowley carried on regardless, anyway. (See page 187)

'9 − 7 = 4' - Is this from the '*0=2*' branch of mathematics? - Crowley's been wrestling with **AL** for seven years, in Virgo 1909, really! Someone remind him that it's actually five years, and get the old faker to change the date of that page of stele hieroglyphs from 1902 to 1904. (See page 173)

That's Gonna McHurt - Five pages of something 'too hot to handle' poetically ripped from a vellum notebook, to conceal its belatedly Scottish heritage. The less said about this act of literary desecration, the better. (See various pages)

A long and futile excuse - The Tarot reading that was two Tarot readings that were an I Ching divination. That was actually a contemporary **Book of Thoth**, which Crowley wrote at Boleskine and then forgot all about, except to note its omission. (See page 142)

Now, when did we do that ritual? - Date confusion between first and second performance of Rose's nonsensical (and miraculously successful on repetition) ritual as a crude cloak of invisibility over 'X' rated sexual shenanigans. Seems that the "*waiter*" really was Horus - "*Squeeze my lemon dry, Hamid, and for Aiwass' sake slide a jellied-Thoth down her throat to keep the drunken bitch quiet,*" instructs Crowley. The honeymoon clearly exhausted Crowley. It took three-and-a-half years for him to muster enough energised enthusiasm as to record the pivotal 'cross-examination' of Rose – *Like, whatever.* (See page 120)

A Book of Mixed Results - Absurd sequence of events recorded in a **Book of Results** which itself is absurdly placed within a velum notebook. Pull the other one – That has unspoiled and authoritative bells on it. (See page 146)

Why we are still weeping - Title of "*Best Prophesy Ever*" goes to **Why Jesus Wept**, accompanied by a best mocking reference award to **Ascension Day**. With predictive capabilities of this calibre, Crowley should have spent more time at the racetrack. (See page 126)

Change not so much as the style of a letter - **Liber L. vel Legis** undergoes six distinct phases of' evolution then vanishes, only to resurface as something entirely different. Wait a decade and, yes… There's definitely a praeterhuman entity materialised in the hat. Now, that's Magick! (See page 192)

Just say, "*I made it AL up*" and we'll AL move on - By his own admission, Crowley incorporates garbled entries, misinformation, glaring omissions, U-turns and outright fabrications into his journals and other material relating to the Cairo myth for "*some silly no-reason un-connected with Magick.*" What will the Secret Chiefs make of this farce? (See various sections)

Will someone please cover up that cover sheet - The cover sheet that could get someone committed. Crowley can't make his mind up what he wrote, when he wrote it, when he obtained it, or what he meant, then finally scrapped it. Add his cerebral meltdown to the equally baffling version of **Liber L. vel Legis** lobotomised from the 1907 **Collected Works** Appendix, and *we're not in KansAL anymore, TOTO.* (See page 68)

Now you've seen it. Now you don't - Crowley's paints his Magick with all the colours of a stele he hasn't yet seen whilst repeatedly visiting the wrong museum and describing a building that closed years before his fictitious visit with Rose. (See page 169)

Harpocrates Rules KO - Mortified by Aiwass' spectacular cock-up, Crowley brushes the fiasco under his carpet and plays the 'Harpocrates' card. His contemporary mundane and Magickal journals fail to mention, in any capacity, the 'cross-examination,' Boulak visit, three-day reception and a shed-load of other events Crowley later relies on in Cairo – Almost as if the whole thing never happened, at all. (See multiple sections)

A praeterhuman entity with short-term memory loss – The supreme champion of discrepancies dwells in an entirely different palace to all other contenders. In the white-heat of dictation, Aiwas passes the stele versification to the 'Chosen One,' who fumbles and forgets all about 'Verse Two.' Crowley later kicks the ball into an empty net with a liberal own-goal, but the crowd is already streaming away. Last one out turn off the lights (See page 71)

Alys Through the Looking Glass

"Mr Crowley, you are a man of notoriously evil character. That has been established. It is not even questioned. Your literature shows it, the admissions of Jones himself shows it, and what was said to Jones's own solicitor shows it. Carry on like this, sir, and a decade from now you will be THE WICKEDEST MAN IN THE WORLD!"

Justice Scrutton, 27 April 1911

The Re-trial

"Well, if I were on trial for a serious crime I certainly wouldn't hang the next twenty or so years of my life on a defence equivalent to Crowley's reception story!"

Whilst browsing my 'Top Ten' countdown, I ask again if you would sit easy in the dock with your liberty reliant upon an account so riddled with omissions, deletions, U-turns, contradictions and outright lies as to destroy any semblance of credibility? Conversely, imagine yourself as a jury member. Do you believe Crowley's alibi?

"Not a cat in Hell's chance!"

Liber L. vel Bogus
Aleister Crowley
Richard T. Cole
L. vel Bogus
Cole

AL cetera

Information reproduced herein manifested in response to a small edition of promotion & review copies dispatched shortly prior to publication. In presenting this material, I am indebted to the wisdom and fortitude of an elusive Adept known colloquially as Ahmed Dillo. Time constraints precluded its incorporation into relevant chapters. As a compromise, and in preference to omission, I include it as an additional section of Supplemental Material.

1 – Cat Scratch Fever

The following quotes are extracted from **Dear Yeats, Dear Pound, Dear Ford: Jeanne Robert Foster and Her Circle of Friends (Writing American Women)** by **R. & J. Londraville** (Syracuse University Press (Hardcover), September 01, 2001). Unlike the questionable account provided by Jackson Burke (see page 40), this material constitutes solid examples of atrocious 'psychopathic' behaviour exhibited by Crowley, including a further instance of threats made at knife-point - As precipitated by the breakdown of his relationship with American poet Jeanne Robert Foster (aka 'Hilarion' and 'the Cat').

"In the United States, Crowley used his personal magnetism and devious charm to arouse interest in those he met. [...] Quinn wrote to WBY [William Butler Yeats] on 24 April 1915: *"He is a perfect misfit here of course... His writings have no popular appeal. One hears awful things about him but beyond a big capacity for strong drink I have seen nothing crooked about him."* (Pages 90 & 91)

Crowley was an enigma to some, a devil to others, and the latest flavour to sophisticated New Yorkers. Traveling in the circles she did, Jeanne was bound to meet him. Her studies in the occult and theosophy made her naturally curious about this strange and intriguing man. Her dear and devoted friend, J. B. Yeats [father of WBY], was to *"watch in horrified fascination as his son's old enemy proceeded to captivate the sensitive and vulnerable 'loveliest of women.'"* (Page 91)

Crowley asked her [Jeanne] to quit her job with the **Review** and go to work for him as a ghostwriter. [...] She told Crowley that she would consider it.

240

William M. Murphy writes: "*For a time he succeeded in duping Jeanne Foster, who was betrayed by his ugly good looks, his charisma, his position as leader of a magical cult, and his reputation as a poet. She was disturbed and fascinated by him, alternately attracted and repelled.*" In early summer 1915, when Jeanne finally asked her friend John Butler Yeats for his opinion about Crowley, he replied judiciously on 04 July, "*Learn magic by all means, but be careful of the magician. They that sup with the devil must have a long spoon.*"

But she didn't heed her friend's advice. By September 1915, Jeanne's relationship with Crowley had become more complicated. William M. Murphy describes one version of events: "*His innate cruelty soon destroyed her illusions. He was vicious of tongue, constantly berating people he considered his inferiors, and the pressure became too great for Mrs. Foster, a kindly and idealistic person, to bear. To Crowley's fury, she left him...*" (Pages 91 & 92)

Crowley returned to his rented studio at Carnegie Hall, where he made plans for Jeanne to do writing "*far more meaningful than any writing you might do for a magazine.*" She was not interested when she found that most of the help he wanted was clerical; he particularly wanted her to clean up his grammar and diction. Her refusal made Crowley incensed at her impertinence. Finally, he shouted, "*If you refuse my orders, I will kill your mother. She is with you now, and I will kill her before your eyes.*"

This outburst startled Jeanne, both for its vehemence and irrationality. She was used to managing ill-tempered men with her charm, but Crowley's anger frightened her. At the time her mother was visiting at Jeanne's apartment in New York. [...] They were awakened about midnight by the appearance of a hideous apparition perched at the foot of the bed. Jeanne did not panic, but recited a white-magic spell that, she said, caused the demon to disappear. She then explained the circumstances to her shaken mother, who chastised her daughter for her involvement with such a depraved magician.

Jeanne had trouble getting rid of Crowley. She said that he bothered her incessantly. William M. Murphy writes that when Jeanne returned to New York after the western trip, she was "*badly shaken.*" Several events tested her mettle.

He [Crowley] wrote letters to Matt Foster – anonymously – warning him that Jeanne was plotting to poison him and that she was "*living with a wealthy lawyer.*" (Pages 96 & 97)

Once Crowley threatened her with a "*curious looking knife*" after she emerged from work one day in midtown Manhattan. John Butler Yeats wrote to Quinn on 14 March 1916: "*He* [Crowley] *boasts that he is not afraid because John Quinn will always find bail for him and protect him. She* [JRF] *thinks he is a cocaine fiend. At the very start I warned her, so*

> *that she has never let him get so much as a letter from her. He has some girl with him, and he sent this girl to her with a message to say that she [JRF] must help him or he would destroy her. The girl wept all the time while giving the message. Mrs. Foster told her politely to go to the devil. The Government here and the English government are both busy watching him with detectives. The English authorities say he is a spy and that he has been to Canada.""* (Page 97)

At the time, Canada was of vital strategic importance to Germany, as was Mexico. Sabotage plots to blow-up canals used for transporting war goods to Britain (via America) abounded - Hence the unsavoury connotation. Today, a desire to 'enter Canada' is not particularly questionable, though consent is required and knives frowned upon.

In connection with Burke's questionable article, it is useful to consider Crowley's own account of the incident. In **Confessions** (page 78), he writes:

> "*I arranged to meet her on her evening out at a safe distance from Streatham and we drove in a cab over to Herne Hill, indulging in a mild flirtation on the way. On Sunday morning, however,* **I brought things to a point**. *I made an excuse for staying away from the morning meeting, got the girl into my mother's bedroom and made my magical affirmation.*"

Of all the phrases he could have chosen, "*...to a point*" is unfortunate as (to my mind) it tacitly suggests a knife (or knitting needle). Burke 'may' have read Mandrake's 1929 **Spirit of Solitude**, seen 'point' and got all creative. If not, his allegation (if fabricated) is an odd coincidence.

US occultist Paul Foster Case provides a further description of Crowley's unsavoury repute. In a letter to Israel Regardie, dated 10 August 1933, he writes:

> "*And these investigations I have just mentioned came to pass just before I had completed preparations for the actual use of the formula available to the $5°=6^\square$ Grade. Perhaps the most conspicuous example of the unfortunate consequences of the use of these formulas is A.C. himself; but there are plenty of others that I know personally whose personal shipwreck has been just as complete, even though their small tonnage, so to say, makes the loss seem less deplorable than the disintegration of that great genius who I admire and love as much as you do, though my personal contact with him has been slight. [...] The whole Enochian procedure is indubitably potent. So are some of the practices of the Obeah, to which I have given long study, ever since I spent my childhood winters in the West Indies.*
>
> *So, too, are mescal buttons, and hashish, and even Scotch whiskey, but even the Chinese in Lamb's essay had to learn sooner or later that it is not necessary to burn down a house to roast a pig, so, I fear, will those who rely on G.D. formulas for magic learn to their cost, perhaps too late...*"

2 - Bollocks dropped at the Boulaks!

Since around 1835, French scholar, archaeologist, Egyptologist and founder of the Egyptian Department of Antiquities (later the Supreme Council of Antiquities), Auguste Mariette (seated left, in picture), petitioned the Khedive (viceroy) for a museum. In 1858, his determination paid dividends in the form of a small shop in Boulaq (north of Cairo).

"At first it was installed in four or five small rooms built along the Nile, which we see depicted in the photographic Album published by Mariette but it was soon moved a few meters away to a new building constructed squarely on the bank of the same river. Restored between 1878 and 1880 after a great flood had destroyed it and protected against the return of the water by a large masonry platform it was expanded and almost doubled in scope in 1882. It possessed considerable land used for temporary storage where it was hoped that new rooms might be added later and it seemed as if it might stay forever in the place where Mariette had first established it. [...] The Boulaq Museum closed in May 1889 and, to the astonishment of the Egyptians who had hardly dared hope for such speed, the Giza Museum opened its doors in December of the same year." Gaston Maspero (from French magazine **La Nature**, 1890).

The *"Giza Museum"* mentioned above is the **Khedival Palace Museum** at Giza (now within the grounds of Cairo Zoo). Not where the pyramids are, but another location called Giza (or Ghizeh) a mile or so upstream (south) and on the other bank. Prior to this relocation, the Stele's item number resided in the 400s. Incidentally, item '666' then referred to a clay tile bearing the image of a bull. At **Khedival Palace**, the stele became item number '666,' and was incorrectly labelled as deriving from Gumah. It was actually Deir al Bahri – The error a consequence of correct information being lost, along with most of Mariette's sketches and notes, in the flood of 1878.

The **Khedival Palace Museum** was also relatively short-lived, as described in the preface to the first guide to the new Cairo Museum, written by Maspero and translated by a couple called Quibell. The museum referred to is the present **Egyptian Museum**, on Tahrir Square:

> *"The Gizeh Museum, like that of Bulak before it, is now but a thing of the past. The moving of the monuments, begun on March 9th 1902, was finished four months later, on the 13th of July. The setting up in the new rooms had, from the beginning, proceeded so as to keep pace with the moving, so that in the early days of August the new Cairo Museum could already, if necessary, have admitted the public: nothing remained to be done but to cover over the bases and pedestals, and to give to the walls and pillars the trifling repairs always needed after thousands of heavy objects have been moved into place.*
>
> *The inauguration took place on the 15th of November* [1902]*, and since then the rooms have remained open to visitors."*

Auguste Mariette died in 1881 (replaced by Gaston Maspero). His ashes and commemorative statue eventually found a good home in the **Cairo Museum**, in Tahrir Square:

> *"The statue arrived in Cairo on the 14th of February 1904, was put in place by Monsieur Alexandre Barsanti, Conservateur du Service, and the day of the inauguration was finally set for Thursday the 17th of March."* 1905 **Annales de Service of the Egyptian Museum**, p.54.

This fascinating history is relevant to Crowley's reception story in the following ways:

1) He first visited Egypt between 14 October and 05 November 1902. At this time, the **Khedival Palace Museum** had closed and its successor, the **Cairo Museum**, was not yet open to the public. As such, Crowley's awareness of the stele (as recorded in a notebook originally dated "*1902*" and subsequently amended to "*1904*") cannot derive from a first-hand viewing of the artefact. Other possible sources I discuss on page 138.

2) As of May 1889, the actual "*Boulak Museum*" ceased to exist. Given this, Crowley could not have visited it in March 1904. The **Khedival Palace Museum** closed its doors prior to Crowley's 1902 visit to Cairo, not the **Boulaq Museum**.

3) One argument in particular employed to defend Crowley's apparent revelation in a building that closed fifteen years prior to his honeymoon, is a notion that "*Boulak*" was a general 'one-size-fits-all' colloquial name apportioned to numerous museums in Egypt, over a fifty year time span. To my mind, an analogous scenario is that of Highbury Stadium, former home of Arsenal Football Club. In 2006, the club vacated its old arena and relocated to new premises, the Emirates Stadium. At its inauguration ceremony, everyone spoke with great reverence for the old stadium. Highbury was, unquestionably much-loved, fondly remembered and lamented. Moreover, the event was big news and widely reported in the media. My point is this – From its opening, to date, staff, fans and anyone with a passing interest may compare the Emirates Stadium with Highbury, but nobody would mistake one for the other. For the benefit of anyone in doubt, the Cairo Museum obligingly provided a sign over its entrance. Though engraved in Latin, not Egyptian, Crowley's education included tuition in this language.

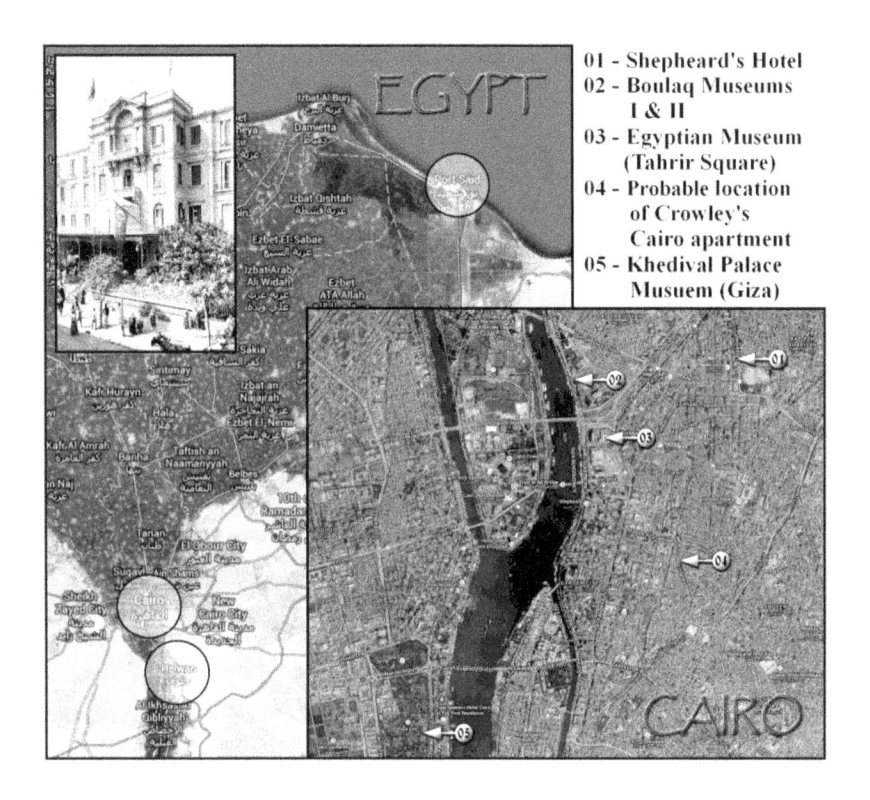

01 - Shepheard's Hotel
02 - Boulaq Museums I & II
03 - Egyptian Museum (Tahrir Square)
04 - Probable location of Crowley's Cairo apartment
05 - Khedival Palace Musuem (Giza)

3 – Pagicles

Page 108 – An investigation into the specifics of Crowley's return to Boleskine, from Cairo, evokes a number of curious discrepancies. Though complex to follow, various inventive solutions posited revolve around shipping records relating to the S.S. Osiris. Stated briefly - If Crowley left Egypt approximately a fortnight after his reception of **Liber Legis**, he cannot meet Annie Bessant, nor can he dine in Paris with Arnold Bennett, on 26 April.

This anomaly, as with the majority discussed in this work, arose in consequence of Crowley changing his story, but leaving a trace of the old version. All oddities are seamlessly resolved if we accept that Crowley departed Cairo on 06 April and set-sail five days later. This notion, though a heresy to some, dovetails with the accounts of Bessant, Crowley (he wrote to her, about their meeting on the Osiris, in 1925), Bennett and extant shipping records. It is also pertinent to remember that, whilst in Paris, Crowley collected stock of **Why Jesus Wept** – A poem triumphantly declaring *"the young warrior of a new* *religion is upon thee; and his number is the number of a man*" three months before Aiwass mentioned the promotion.

In this context, it is interesting to note that the 1936 edition of **Equinox of the Gods** suggests reception dates starting on 01 April (as does the record of Leila Waddell). This curio, I suspect, represents Crowley's initial, though subsequently aborted attempt to address the 'time crisis.' By winding back the reception by a week, he can accommodate reliable accounts from Bennett and Bessant. Unfortunately, in plugging one hole he opens a bigger fissure - A situation in which he receives the last Chapter of **Liber Legis** on 10 April, with a suitcase under his arm, and produces the typescript at some point along the 150km dash to catch a ship embarking the following morning (no wonder errors crept in!) Oh, yes, and he somehow remembered this frantic scramble as occurring 'about a fortnight after...' Incidentally, symbolism printed on the spine of **Equinox of the Gods** shows an Eye of Horus above a Vesica Piscis, so represents the rear of a woman, face down.

Page 129 - Bey is not the family name of Mr. Brugsch, it is an Ottoman title similar to O.B.E.. 'Pasha' is an also honorific title, like an M.B.E. There are many 'Beys' though none are necessarily related. Two who are, Emil and Emile Brugsch (brothers), worked at the Egyptian Museum and both held the rank of 'Bey.'

666 Saw b.f.b.
b.f.g. Aleister Crowley

It's lowercase so not names; the b.f. must be the same in each case so that leaves b. and g. Has to be a complementary pair of things - blackberries and grapefruit? Nah, I reckon it's boy and girl and have thought this since I first saw it in 1972. Actually, I'm amazed anyone could think otherwise. Saw big fat boy and big fat girl!
Anonymous - Attributed to Ahmed Dillo

The Governing Dynamics of Thelema

Richard T. Cole

Published one-hundred and eleven years after Aleister Crowley's alleged reception of **Liber L. vel Legis**, Richard T. Cole presents an in-depth exploration of the man, the Magickian, the myth and the legacy – **The Governing Dynamics of Thelema** comprises:

Part **I**
Of Aleister Crowley

Part **II**
Of **Liber L. vel Legis** (Sections A & B) Revised & Enlarged

Part **III**
Of Thelema

Part **IV**
Of the New Aeon of Horus

AVAILABLE SOON

LIBER L. + VEL BOGUS
The Real Confession of Aleister Crowley

SUB FIGURA LXXX

Being Parts I & II(A) of
THE GOVERNING DYNAMICS OF THELEMA

Catalogue Number – LLVB03-1/02LULU
Second, corrected edition

Privately Published, Printed & Distributed
© 1983 - 2014 – All Rights Reserved

ISBN 978-1-900962-86-5

Lightning Source UK Ltd.
Milton Keynes UK
UKHW010628080121
376670UK00001B/168